The Representation
of the Self in the
American Renaissance

The Representation of the

SELF

in the American Renaissance

JEFFREY STEELE

The University of North Carolina Press

Chapel Hill / London

© 1987 The University of North Carolina Press
All rights reserved
Manufactured in the United States of America

Library of Congress Cataloging-in-Publication Data

Steele, Jeffrey, 1947–
  The representation of the self in the American
Renaissance.

  Includes index.
  1. American literature—19th century—History and
criticism. 2. Self in literature. 3. Psychology in
literature. 4. Emerson, Ralph Waldo, 1803–1882—
Knowledge—Psychology. I. Title.
PS217.S44S74   1988   810'.9'003   87-4050
ISBN 0-8078-1750-3

To Jocelyn, Doran, and Brendan

Myth does not start from a finished
representation of the I and the soul
but is the vehicle which leads to
such a representation; it is a spiritual
medium through which subjective reality
is first discovered and apprehended
in its distinctiveness.

—Ernst Cassirer, *The Philosophy of Symbolic Forms*

Contents

Preface

This book began as a study of Emerson and Jung. Struck by the uncanny resemblances between Emerson's vision of self-reliance and Jung's model of individuation, I imagined a point-by-point analogy between their two psychologies. But as I continued this project, I eventually confronted an impasse—the approach I was using necessitated uncritical faith in the very materials I was examining: both Emerson's and Jung's vision of the unconscious had taken on for me a quasi-theological value. As I came to realize that this problem of critical faith was my true subject, I saw that both Emerson and Jung demanded of their readers complete acceptance of their psychological paradigms. In order to comprehend their texts, one had to become the self that they imagined. Failure to do so left one outside of the hermeneutic circle they established. This process, which I call "psychological mythmaking," forms the focus of the present study.

I should emphasize that this is neither a Jungian nor a Freudian study of American writers. Similarly, it is not a book that explores in detail the textual deformations that result from the play of unconscious forces. Although such close reading has a part to play in the argument that follows, it is subordinated to a general examination of the difficulties—for any period—of using unconditioned terms such as the *unconscious*. The unconscious that each writer articulates implicates the reading subject as one of its predicates. Thus, before one can analyze the linguistic results of unconscious forces, the manifold play of signifiers, one must distinguish the model of the unconscious that one is using. Jung and Freud, Emerson and Melville, all promulgate different myths of the mind and its dynamics. Although Freudian semiotics has become a powerful tool, the current interest in Freud has led to psychological paradigms that are accepted in many quarters as uncritically as nineteenth-century America embraced Emerson. It is precisely the expense of such acts of faith that I propose to examine.

I am grateful to Joel Porte, who first suggested to me that Emerson and the unconscious was a topic worth exploring. I am indebted to Merton M. Sealts, Jr., Walter Rideout, and Sargent Bush for their support and encouragement throughout this project. For their thoughtful criticism of the introduction, I thank my colleagues in the Draft Group: Jay Clayton, Betsy Draine, Patty Fumerton, Phillip Herring, Michael Hinden, Leah Marcus, Carol Pasternack, Cyrena Pondrom, Tilottama Rajan, and Eric Rothstein. I am grateful to Susan Friedman for her expert readings of three chapters, and to Kevin Van Anglen, who kindly shared with me his extensive knowledge of Thoreau. I am indebted to John Carlos Rowe, whose incisive reading of an earlier version of the manuscript helped me greatly in the process of revision. I would like to thank especially two colleagues, William Andrews and Gordon Hutner, whose critical judgment and sage advice have been a source of support from the beginning.

I would like to express my gratitude to my editor, Sandra Eisdorfer, for her guidance. I should also like to thank Kathy Dauck, Mary Ann Ford, and Saragale Tucker for their patience as they typed what must have seemed like endless revisions into the word processor.

I am deeply indebted to the Graduate School of the University of Wisconsin—Madison for salary support during four summers of research and writing. I would also like to express my gratitude to the Institute for Research in the Humanities at the University of Wisconsin—Madison for the one-semester fellowship that gave me the time to write a large portion of this book.

Part of chapter 2 was published in an earlier version as "Interpreting the Self: Emerson and the Unconscious," in Joel Porte, ed., *Emerson: Prospect and Retrospect* (Harvard English Studies 10, 1982: pp. 85–104).

Finally, I would like to express my deep gratitude to my parents, who taught me to love books and learning, and to my wife, Jocelyn, whose good humor and wisdom have been a constant source of strength.

Abbreviations

CE   Nathaniel Hawthorne. *The Centenary Edition of the Works of Nathaniel Hawthorne.* Edited by William Charvat, Roy Harvey Pearce, Claude M. Simpson et al. 16 vols. to date. Columbus, Ohio: Ohio State University Press, 1962–. Vol. 1, *The Scarlet Letter.* Vol. 2, *The House of the Seven Gables.* Vol. 3, *The Blithedale Romance.* Vol. 9, *Twice-Told Tales.* Vol. 10, *Mosses from an Old Manse.*

CMR Henry David Thoreau. *A Week on the Concord and Merrimack Rivers.* Edited by Carl F. Hovde, William L. Howarth, and Elizabeth Hall Witherell. Princeton, N.J.: Princeton University Press, 1983.

CW   Ralph Waldo Emerson. *The Collected Works of Ralph Waldo Emerson.* Edited by Robert E. Spiller, Alfred R. Ferguson, Jean Ferguson Carr et al. 3 vols. to date. Cambridge, Mass.: Harvard University Press, 1971–. Vol. 1, *Nature, Addresses, and Lectures.* Vol. 2, *Essays: First Series.* Vol. 3, *Essays: Second Series.*

D   *The Dial: A Magazine for Literature, Philosophy, and Religion.* 4 vols. 1840–44. Rpt. New York: Russell & Russell, 1961.

Dall   Caroline Healey Dall. *Margaret and Her Friends, or Ten Conversations with Margaret Fuller upon the Mythology of the Greeks and its Expression in Art.* 1895. Rpt. New York: Arno Press, 1972.

EL   Ralph Waldo Emerson. *The Early Lectures of Ralph Waldo Emerson.* Edited by Stephen E. Whicher, Robert E. Spiller, and Wallace E. Williams. 3 vols. Cambridge, Mass.: Harvard University Press, 1959–72.

ER   Edgar Allan Poe. *Essays and Reviews.* Edited by G. R. Thompson. New York: The Library of America, 1984.

J   Henry David Thoreau. *Journals.* Edited by Elizabeth Hall Witherell, William L. Howarth, Robert Sattelmeyer, Thomas Blanding. Princeton, N.J.: Princeton University Press, 1981–. Vol. 1, *Journal: 1837–1844.* Vol. 2, *Journal: 1842–1848.*

JMN   Ralph Waldo Emerson. *The Journals and Miscellaneous Notebooks of Ralph Waldo Emerson*. Edited by William H. Gilman, Alfred R. Ferguson, George P. Clark et al. 16 vols. Cambridge, Mass.: Harvard University Press, 1960–82.

L   Ralph Waldo Emerson. *The Letters of Ralph Waldo Emerson*. Edited by Ralph L. Rusk. 6 vols. New York: Columbia University Press, 1939.

LG   Walt Whitman. *Walt Whitman's Leaves of Grass: The First (1855) Edition*. Edited and introduced by Malcolm Cowley. 1959. Rpt. New York: Penguin Books, 1976.

LMF   Margaret Fuller. *The Letters of Margaret Fuller*. Edited by Robert N. Hudspeth. 4 vols. to date. Ithaca, N.Y.: Cornell University Press, 1983–.

M   Margaret Fuller. *Memoirs of Margaret Fuller Ossoli*. Edited by Ralph Waldo Emerson, James Freeman Clarke, and William Henry Channing. 2 vols. Boston: Phillips, Sampson & Co., 1852.

MD   Herman Melville. *Moby-Dick: An Authoritative Text*. Edited by Harrison Hayford and Hershel Parker. New York: W. W. Norton & Co., 1967.

NF   Walt Whitman. *Notes and Fragments: Left by Walt Whitman*. Edited by Richard Maurice Bucke. London, Ontario: A. Talbot & Co., 1899.

P   Herman Melville. *Pierre, or The Ambiguities*. Vol. 7 of *The Writings of Herman Melville*, ed. Harrison Hayford, Hershel Parker, and G. Thomas Tanselle. Evanston and Chicago: Northwestern University Press and The Newberry Library, 1971.

PT   Henry David Thoreau. *The Portable Thoreau*. Edited by Carl Bode. New York: Viking Press, 1964.

RP   Henry David Thoreau. *Reform Papers*. Edited by Wendell Glick. Princeton, N.J.: Princeton University Press, 1973.

T   Edgar Allan Poe. *Tales and Sketches*. Vols. 2 and 3 of *The Collected Works of Edgar Allan Poe*, ed. Thomas Ollive Mabbott. Cambridge, Mass.: Harvard University Press, 1978. These two volumes are numbered with consecutive pagination.

W   Ralph Waldo Emerson. *The Complete Works of Ralph Waldo Emerson*. Edited by Edward Waldo Emerson. 12 vols. Boston: Houghton Mifflin Co., 1903–4.

Wa   Henry David Thoreau. *Walden*. Edited by J. Lyndon Shanley. Princeton, N.J.: Princeton University Press, 1971.

WNC Margaret Fuller. *Woman in the Nineteenth Century: A Facsimile of the 1845 Edition*. Edited by Joel Myerson and introduced by Madeline B. Stern. Columbia, S.C.: University of South Carolina Press, 1980.

YES Ralph Waldo Emerson. *Young Emerson Speaks: Unpublished Discourses on Many Subjects*. Edited by Arthur C. McGiffert. Boston: Houghton Mifflin Co., 1938.

The Representation
of the Self in the
American Renaissance

ONE

Psychological Mythmaking

The key to the period appeared to be that the mind had become aware of itself. Men grew
reflective and intellectual. There was a new consciousness.
—Ralph Waldo Emerson, "Historic Notes of Life and Letters in New England"

Looking back in 1880 upon that American cultural phenomenon known
as Transcendentalism, Emerson selected self-consciousness—the mind's
awareness of itself—as the "key to the period." A deceptively simple
statement, Emerson's assertion points us toward a set of problems that
contemporary philosophers and literary theorists are beginning to unfold. What constitutes self-consciousness? What are the literary strategies
that allow the rarest of glances—the mind's fascinated gaze at itself?
Emerson's statement challenges us to explore the labyrinth of reflection—a house of mirrors that has led some to inspiration; others, like
Melville's Pierre, to despair.
   The focus of this study will be psychological mythmaking. At issue
will be those privileged figures and rhetorical strategies through which
writers during the American Renaissance attempted to disseminate their
sense of the mind. From this perspective, psychology is seen as a self-
constituting myth—mental traits becoming visible once they are named.
Without the appropriate terminology, phenomena such as subjectivity,
the imagination, the unconscious remain invisible. F. O. Matthiessen
draws our attention to the constituting power of terminology when he
reminds us that Samuel Taylor Coleridge contributed to psychological
discourse in English terms such as *subjective, psychological, intuitive, idealize, organic,* and *self-conscious.*[1] Much of the fascination of the nineteenth
century resides in the apparent ease with which its writers mapped new
psychic territories, laying down a grid of terms and attitudes that helped
to establish subjectivity as we know it.
   One such term is the *unconscious.* We can understand the nineteenth-
century obsession with the unconscious as part of a larger problematic of
selfhood. Compelled to validate the individual as a self-motivating entity,

writers focused their attention upon the dynamics of a psychological growth arising from the depths of the mind. Defining one pole of this examination of the self in America, Emerson interprets the individual as the function of an inner essence that exfoliates itself in an organic process: "All our progress is an unfolding, like the vegetable. You have first an instinct, then an opinion, then a knowledge, as the plant has root, bud, and fruit" (*CW*, 2:195–96).[2] From this perspective, the secret of being is to efface oneself before inner power, becoming a transparent medium formed by the "God within." But if Emerson sees through personality to a transcendent source beneath, other writers—notably, Poe, Hawthorne, and Melville—view the self as an opaque mask that reflects social demands and refracts unconscious impulses. Personality is not effaced in their fiction; rather, the human face is imagined as a disguise. In opposition to images of personal transfiguration, we find instead a more secular concern with impersonation and masquerade.

Instead of attending to the disguises and self-deceptions of consciousness, Emerson articulates from the beginning of his career the accessibility of the divine "voice" within. Emerson's model for spiritual revelation is "eloquence"—in Harold Bloom's terms, "Influx" as "a mode of divination, in the Vichian or double sense of god-making and of prophecy."[3] Emerson aims to communicate the power of this internal voice to auditors whom he will teach to recognize and assimilate its rhythms. "There is this supreme universal reason in your mind," he preaches in 1832, a reason that "is the Spirit of God in us all" (*YES*, 186). The facts of Emerson's literary career (which begins with preaching and lecturing), as well as his habitual use of metaphors of voice to express his sense of spiritual intuition, suggest that his early works are best approached through critical methods that attend to the dynamics of "spoken" presentations. "During the nineteenth century," Lawrence Buell reminds us, "the idea of the sermon as a means of expounding and enforcing doctrine tended to give way to the idea of the sermon as an inspirational oration."[4]

In his discussion of Emerson's vision of "eloquence," F. O. Matthiessen stresses the centrality of speech to Emerson's presentation of his myth of the mind: "A man speaking to men first unlocked their primitive awareness of themselves—in such a conception of consciousness Emerson broke through the mere intellectualizing with which he was often charged, to at least a glimpse of the deep subconscious forces that remain buried in men unless quickened to life."[5] The connection that Matthiessen makes for us is the link between Emerson's figure of the orator and his myth of the unconscious. The orator, more than most men, has the power to reveal the hidden depths of the psyche. How does he do this? To answer such a question, we must amplify Matthiessen's discussion with a body of theoretical knowledge developed since his time—contemporary theories of reader-response and reception aesthetics. In the process, we shall consider the relationship between Emerson's psychological mythmaking and his presentation of a transfigured "voice" that his audience is motivated to internalize. Just as a psychoanalyst's "patient introjects . . . certain idealized aspects of the analyst, which become a living presence within the patient, an internal voice," Emerson's auditors learn to model themselves on the ego ideal that he presents to them.[6]

Rather than viewing Emerson as a writer who happened to deliver several inspiring addresses such as "The American Scholar" and "The Divinity School Address," let us recall that he was an adept public speaker who adapted rhetorical strategies refined on the pulpit and lecture platform to the demands of later publication. Most of Emerson's important doctrines are presented in his early lectures, yet most critics continue to begin with *Nature* and the essays, ignoring the performative aspect of his compositions. "Emerson's tendency from the first," one scholar writes, "is to efface himself, to leave the reader no clues as to how his text is to be privately performed."[7] But this eliminates from critical awareness the original circumstances of Emerson's work—its performance before a specific audience. That such performances *are* directed is a point that many students of reader-response and reception aesthetics adamantly maintain. Hans Robert Jauss, for example, compares the literary work to "an orchestration that strikes ever new resonances among its readers."[8] At the same time, he asserts that the work "predisposes its audience to a very special kind of reception by announcements, overt and covert signals, familiar characteristics, or implicit allusions."[9] As Emerson quickly discovered, not every member of his audience was prepared to assimilate his ideas. Yet, from the first, his works provided clues as to "how his text is to be privately performed." This is especially evident if we begin with Emerson's spoken presentations as a model indicating the kind of literary response at which he aimed.

Reflecting upon the difficulties of oral presentation, Emerson in 1835 relates the "convertibility" of a speaker's audience to the rhetorical persona which that speaker projects: "Every ear is yours to gain. Every heart will be glad & proud & thankful for a master. There where you are, serve them & they must serve you. They care nothing for you but be to them a Plato be to them a Christ & they shall all be Platos & all be Christs" (*JMN*, 5:37). Here, as throughout his career, Emerson focuses upon the "power" of eloquence. "A lecture . . . is an organ of sublime power," he observes in 1839 (*JMN*, 7:224). In 1847 he notes that the masterful orator "should bring [his audience] at will into that key which he desired" (*JMN*, 10:24–25). Such statements conflate the classical view of rhetoric with Romantic conceptions of genius. Both the great rhetorician and the genius were viewed by Emerson's age as vehicles of an audience-shaping power. Considering the rhetorical impact of Milton's writings, William Ellery Channing observes: "The great and decisive test of genius is, that it calls forth *power* in the souls of others. It not merely gives knowledge, but breathes energy."[10] Thomas DeQuincey's well-known distinction between the "literature of knowledge" and the "literature of power" enforces a similar point; the latter, he argues, results in the "exercise and expansion" of "your own latent capacity of sympathy with the infinite."[11]

Emerson's advance upon the popular conception of genius is his close attention to the dependence of audience response upon the orator's self-construction. An orator's mastery, his comments suggest, depends upon the face that he wears, upon the voice he assumes. One's audience cares little for the speaker's private personality, but rather for the dramatized role ("a Plato," "a Christ") they are offered. If members of the audience assume this mask, and become Platos and Christs themselves, then they are converted. What is at issue is the audience's identification with and participation in a dramatized model of being, a shared persona that will alter their "horizon of expectations."[12]

Among the most important effects of discourse, Emerson's remarks imply, is the construction of a role that is offered to the auditor as the key to the orator's position. The secret of eloquence, he notes, is to "have a great superseding personality" (*JMN*, 9:361). But this personality—we must remember—is a fictive construct, a contrived persona. Henry Nash Smith describes this aspect of Emerson's self-presentation when he analyzes his use of "hero types" such as "the Scholar, . . . the Man of Genius, the Seer, the Contemplative Man, the Student, the Transcendentalist"—roles that function as "ethical ideal(s)."[13] Similarly, Lawrence Buell observes that "Emerson persuades us that his first person is universal," constructing in the process what Buell terms an "exemplary voice."[14] Although both Smith and Buell focus primarily upon issues of voice and persona in Emerson's writing, their observations can be expanded to implicate a conception of Emerson's audience. Literary comprehension, from this perspective, involves a special kind of role-playing—an audience's identification with the dramatized persona that it is offered.

Emerson's early works attempt to convert his audience by means of dramatized personae offered as role-models. Serving as ethical ideals, such figures project paradigms of being that authorize individual existence in terms of powers intuited within. They display "self-reliance" by demonstrating the assimilation of "unconscious reason." Emerson's auditor learns how to respond to powers "hidden" within the mind by provisionally identifying with Emerson's persona as an explanatory model that can orient one's being—a process analogous to the way a psychoanalyst's "patient re-forms his or her self by internalizing certain valued or idealized qualities of the analyst."[15] Adopting the psychological orientation of this mask, Emerson's auditor utilizes a new model for interpreting the self, a new set of interpretive strategies for construing the psyche. Indeed, each auditor must internalize this model in order to understand the sermon, lecture, or address to which he or she is listening. In so doing, the auditor assumes the mantle of Emerson's "transparent self."

Without an acceptance of the role cast for them and of its distinctive psychological dynamics, the spiritual effects predicated upon that role will strike auditors as so much "nonsense." Such was the effect upon Andrews Norton, the bastion of the Unitarian establishment, who refused to assume the model of self-interpretation upheld by Emerson in "The Divinity School Address." "A bad book," Walker Gibson argues, ". . . is a book in whose mock reader we discover a person we refuse to become, a mask we refuse to put on, a role we will not play."[16] Refusing to wear the Transcendentalist persona, Norton found that Emerson's appeal to intuited centers of spiritual authority invoked an unacceptable role. "There can be no intuition, no direct perception, of the truth of Christianity, no metaphysical certainty," Norton exhorted, defending a model of selfhood confirmed by historical and institutional norms.[17] Norton was understandably threatened by a version of reading, of self-reading, that shifted meaning from scripture to audience, from objectified biblical text to the text inscribed by divine Reason within individual psyches. To the extent that they rejected faith in the unconscious as a source of light (rather than darkness), readers of Thoreau, Whitman, and Fuller equally rejected the view that a spiritual power could be found within the mind.

What Norton refuses to lend Emerson is hermeneutic faith in his fiction of the self. But in order for that fiction to function, a provisional acceptance of its contours is necessary. Rudolf Bultmann clarifies this hermeneutic aspect of psychological mythmaking when he argues that "a valid meaning for the mythical picture of the world" depends upon an interpretive stance that makes such mythical meaning available.[18] Any interpretation, he continues, "*is governed by a prior understanding of the subject*, in accordance with which it investigates the text."[19] "Without such a *prior understanding* and the questions initiated by it, the texts are mute."[20] In other words, literary comprehension necessitates an act of involvement, a "living relationship" between text and interpreter, that allows meaning to unfold.[21]

If one is interpreting the psyche, openness toward its potential meaning is also necessary. Freud, for example, touches upon this hermeneutic problem of psychological belief when he observes that the psychoanalyst aims to produce in the analysand "an assured conviction of the truth of [the analyst's] construction" of his or her case history.[22] The readers of Emerson, Thoreau, Whitman, and Fuller occupy a position similar to that of Freud's patients; their self-recognition becomes a function of the psychological frame of reference with which they are presented.[23] Just as a successful cure in psychoanalysis involves the negotiation between analyst and analysand of a shared interpretation, these writers transform their readers by fusing the reader's horizon of self-expectation with an expanded horizon embodied in their respective literary personae. Emerson, Thoreau, Whitman, and Fuller all cultivate in their readers "openness to offers of identity"—an openness that is the first step toward a shift in the reader's sense of the self and its relation to inner and outer reality.[24]

If psychoanalysis involves a process of providing the analysand with a new language with which to construe his or her being, a similar point can be made about the language of religious conversion. The act of being "saved" or "born again" necessitates the assimilation of a new spiritual terminology, frequently presented through dramatized models of self-perception and behavior. Ernest Bormann, for example, analyzes the process of religious conversion in terms of "the sharing of fantasies" presented by means of self-dramatization. In the "evangelical style," he observes, a "new rhetorical community" was molded by "the practice of telling one's conversion experience" in a form that "impelled the adherents to adopt a life style consonant with the scenarios of how a newly born Christian lived."[25] As we shall see, Emerson combines the practices of both psychoanalytic and religious rhetoricians; his writing attempts to enact a process of conversion through self-presentations that awaken hermeneutic faith in divine power located in the unconscious.

Because of this theological concern with the process of conversion, Emerson—like Bultmann—maintains a model of self-interpretation that takes into account "prior understanding." His literary practice is predicated upon the assumption that he can change the reader's very being by giving him or her a new way of interpreting the self. With Thoreau, he realizes that the "universe constantly and obediently answers to our conceptions" (*Wa*, 97). "That which we do not adequately believe," Emerson accordingly observes, "we cannot adequately say" (*EL*, 2:300); "what you have within that only can you see without" (149). "If you look without awe or wonder into the attributes of the soul," he asserts elsewhere, "it is all idle to discourse of history. It can teach you nothing, until you feel your interest in it, your right over it" (11). In many of his early works Emerson addresses the possible disbelief of his audience by using rhetorical models that compel interest and then belief in his myth of self-reliance. As we shall see in chapter 6, such a construction of the self contrasts with the skeptical viewpoints of Poe, Hawthorne, and Melville, who undermine the very self-faith Emerson promotes.

Recent studies of reader-response and the aesthetics of reception confirm the dramatistic conception of the reading process underlying our interpretation of Emerson above. Walker Gibson, for instance, analyzes the "fictitious reader" as the "mask and costume the individual takes on" in order to comprehend a work of literature.[26] Similarly, Georges Poulet describes reading as a process in which one puts on another's personality: "Because of the strange invasion of my person by the thoughts of another, I am a self who is granted the experience of thinking thoughts foreign to him. I am the subject of thoughts other than my own. My consciousness behaves as though it were the consciousness of another."[27] Using this passage to compare the reading process to psychoanalysis, Marshall Alcorn and Mark Bracher explain that the "alien subject is . . . introjected—much as the analyst is by the patient—becoming a living presence in the reader's consciousness."[28]

Clarifying this introjection, Wolfgang Iser argues that the reading self takes on two roles—one modeled upon the voice or persona of the text, the second involving "the real 'me'" who observes this process of identification:

> As we read, there occurs an artificial division of our personality, because we take as a theme for ourselves something that we are not. Consequently when reading we operate on different levels. For although we may be thinking the thoughts of someone else, what we are will not disappear completely—it will remain a more or less powerful virtual force. Thus, in reading there are these two levels—the alien "me" and the real, virtual "me"—which are never completely cut off from each other. Indeed, we can only make someone else's thoughts into an absorbing theme for ourselves, provided the virtual background of our own personality can adapt to it. Every text we read draws a different boundary within our personality, so that the virtual background (the real "me") will take on a different form, according to the theme of the text concerned.[29]

Literary comprehension, in other words, involves both identification with a dramatized persona and a sense of critical distance.

Iser's comments suggest two complementary approaches to the text, depending upon whether one examines "the alien 'me'" (the persona with whom one identifies) or "the real 'me'" (the sense of self distinct from that dramatization). The first approach is represented by those phenomenologies of reading that focus upon the reader's "participation in" or "identification with" a literary voice that is taken as being "present." What is at issue is the way that voice functions, creating a mode of being that the reader is motivated to assimilate. From this perspective, the persona's voice unfolds a dramatized worldview that articulates a specific stance toward existence. According to Paul Ricoeur, the literary work presents the reading "I" with a *proposed world* which I could inhabit and wherein I could project . . . my ownmost possibilities."[30] By entertaining this "proposed world" and the dramatized persona who inhabits it, the reading "I" undergoes "imaginative variations of the ego"—a process of transformation initiated as the reader tries on a new persona.[31] According to Ricoeur, it is thus necessary to "explicate the type of being-in-the-world *in front of* the text," a model of reading that underlies my interpretations of Emerson, Thoreau, Whitman, and Fuller.[32] Each of them, I argue, establishes a "field of potential being" that dramatizes for the reader a regenerated self.[33]

But Iser's second reading role suggests that critical awareness of the rhetorical demands of a text depends upon a reciprocal movement of demystification. The "literary text," Iser observes, "involves the reader in the formation of illusion and the simultaneous formation of the means whereby the illusion is punctured."[34] The reader "oscillates between involvement in and observation of those illusions."[35] By "illusion," Iser means the imagined pattern of consistency, the gestalt, that a reader imposes upon the experience of a literary text. Our sense of a consistent voice or persona presented as a model of being typifies such an illusion; it is a critical fiction necessary for understanding, but one that oversimplifies the text: "The moment we try to impose a consistent pattern on the text, discrepancies are bound to arise. These are, as it were, the reverse side of the interpretive coin, an involuntary product of the process that creates discrepancies by trying to avoid them. And it is their very presence that draws us into the text, compelling us to conduct a creative examination not only of the text but also of ourselves."[36] Opposed to the "hermeneutics of faith" devoted to the discovery of textual consistency through the construction of critical or psychological fictions, there stands what Paul Ricoeur has called the "hermeneutics of suspicion." From this viewpoint, one looks upon dramatized patterns of consciousness as "'false' consciousness" that must be unmasked and demystified.[37]

This demystification attends to what slips out of the "consistent pattern" imposed by identification with an author's voice. It stresses, instead, the necessary incompleteness of any model of a text or the self, which must cancel from awareness terms and values inconsistent with the order that it constructs. In chapter 6 I shall utilize such a skeptical model of reading in order to highlight the hermeneutic suspicion that enables Poe, Hawthorne, and Melville to dismantle the "transcendent persona" perfected by Emerson and his circle. All three writers challenge unified conceptions of the self by shifting their attention to what Transcendentalist models of the self conceal, demonstrating in the process that idealized personae conveniently repress the recognition of the individual's social constitution. On the social stage, a person's role—they show us—is shaped in response to the demands, frequently the ideological demands, of others.

Ultimately, both hermeneutic faith and hermeneutic suspicion are necessary for an understanding of psychological mythmaking. Without the critical distance of suspicion, we would not be aware of the fictionality of dramatized selves, for only a vantage point outside such personae can prevent the uncritical acceptance of their assumptions and emotional rhythms. As a result, we shall cultivate in this study a critical distance that uncovers the rhetoric of regeneration at the same time that we attempt to maintain contact with its demand for critical faith. Such a perspective allows us to see Emersonian self-reliance as one of the most compelling psychological myths invented in the nineteenth century. Appreciation of the power of that myth needs the hermeneutic faith that reveals how it functions as a potential "variation" of our own ego, but it also demands the critical distance that uncovers the extent of the existential claim that Emerson is making upon his audience. Or, as Hans Robert Jauss explains, "aesthetic experience" involves a dynamic process of participation and distancing.[38]

Chapters 2 to 5 of this study emphasize participation by focusing upon the rhetorical power of the Transcendentalist self. Reading literature as "an 'act' or 'experience,'" we shall view the literary text as "a living, conscious reality, a thought that thinks to itself and which, in thinking, becomes thinkable to us—a voice that speaks to itself and which, in so speaking, speaks to us from within."[39] Our criticism will thus involve the imaginative reconstruction of the existential orientation articulated by each author, an orientation that becomes apparent as we subordinate our "subjective personality to a new subjective identity which is gradually created and revealed in the course of the book."[40]

But this act of sympathetic identification constitutes only one-half of the interpretive process—positing what Wolfgang Iser has called the "alien 'me'" involved in "thinking the thoughts of someone else."[41] In order for our identification or absorption in the voice of a text to appear within the field of critical reflection, a reciprocal act of distancing is necessary. At the same time that we try on and speak through the Transcendentalist mask, achieving a liberating sense of freedom, we must maintain the awareness that we are acting. Only by becoming aware of the stage on which we have been placed, only by seeing the role we mime as an ontological paradigm, can we measure its rhetorical and existential power. Our sense of a persona's being staged initiates attention to the self enacted by American Romantic texts as an act of psychological mythmaking. At that point, the stage that we have been occupying turns into a phenomenological field of reflection in which images and scenes of being can be interpreted as provisional roles that are used to orient an audience spiritually and existentially. Regeneration, in these terms, entails the reader's identification with a dramatized orientation.

Through the empathetic reconstruction of the text's consciousness, we attempt to unfold the demands or claims that each writer makes upon his or her audience. If, as Paul Ricoeur suggests, the text unfolds "a *proposed world*," then the mode of being dramatized through the persona's relation to that world can be seen as an existential model offered to the reader as a role to be worn or rejected. However, this self-construction becomes apparent only if we complete the critical act by a second maneuver. This step necessitates viewing the self proposed by the text as a persuasive fiction. At this point, the reader—in Iser's terms—forms "the means whereby the illusion is punctured."[42] As we shall see in chapter 6, the skepticism of Poe, Hawthorne, and Melville helps us to puncture the imperialistic claims of Transcendentalist rhetoric and thereby to see how their psychological mythmaking functions.

Their critique of Emerson reminds us that the positing of mythological figures depends upon a sense of lack, a spiritual vacuum that such figures are intended to fill. For example, Emerson's "Orphic poet" in *Nature* exists as an inspiring figure because of the gap between his message and the quotidian existence of Emerson's audience. His role reminds us of the rift between spiritual aspiration and its fulfillment: "Man is the dwarf of himself. . . . his waters have retired; he no longer fills the veins and veinlets: he is shrunk to a drop" (*CW*, 1:42). In such terms, Emerson emphasizes that his discourse arises as a response to a perceived spiritual crisis. A sense of alienation sets the stage for his mythmaking. By defining our distance from transcendence, Emerson gives his myths of transparence and presence a motivational power as images of transfigured being that are meaningless outside of the context of spiritual desire. In such terms, we can understand Jacques Derrida's observation that "it is a non-origin which is originary."[43] Rather than focusing upon the power of Emerson's psychological myths, we attend here to the conditions that make such myths possible.

At this point, we switch from imaginative participation in the energies of Emerson's self-reliant personae to a consideration of the conditions that allow such personae to appear. We move back from the "illusion" formed by the reader of Emerson's text (as Iser would put it) to the backdrop of desire which that illusion conceals. Identification with Emerson's literary voice is supplemented by analysis of that voice as a strategic fiction covering certain anxieties, weaving over them its myth of transcendent power. This act of repression is revealed by a reading that develops (in a photographic sense) the shadowside or "negative" of Emerson's presentation of the self—his sense of the friction impeding perfect self-articulation, of the absence constituting his original desire for transcendence.

By illustrating the interdependence of affirmative and skeptical strands in Emerson's rhetoric of regeneration, we shall try to glimpse the hidden strategies and assumptions that make that vision possible. Such an enterprise will succeed to the extent that we can momentarily entertain and yet ultimately distance ourselves from Emerson's representation of the "transparent persona." We will need to balance the two sides of Iser's "implied reader"—the engaged "I" and the observing self. The difficulty in reading Emerson (or Thoreau or Whitman or Fuller) is to understand his idealism without necessarily buying his metaphysic, without accepting uncritically the transcendent terms that anchor his thought. Instead, we shall "lend" them credence (rather than "buying" them) and then examine the implications of that act of lending. The unconscious or the Oversoul are both myths—fictions designed to orient individual being as the expression of a transcendent source. Similarly, Emerson's conception of the individual, self-reliantly intuiting and assimilating creative energy, is equally a fiction—but a fiction that numerous readers have found both explanatory and compelling. The challenge is to analyze the literary strategies that enable Emerson to promulgate a vision of the self that resonates to the present day.

As we stand finally outside of Emerson's staging of the self, we become aware of the theatricality of self-representation. Emerson, Thoreau, Whitman, and Fuller all stage rhetorics of regeneration that dramatize for their readers roles they are motivated to inhabit. The reader's being, in other words, becomes the function—the predicate—of Tran-

scendentalist ideology. To the extent that the reader accepts and participates in this staging of the self, the proffered role becomes invisible, for
it is accepted as natural—the way things are. From this perspective, the
self scripted by the American Transcendentalists is a *myth* in Roland
Barthes's sense of the term. It both establishes and then mystifies a set of
power-relationships that constitute the understanding of their audiences.
Inside the stage the reader is able "to consume myth innocently" because
"he does not see it as a semiological system but as an inductive one";
"the myth-consumer takes the signification for a system of facts: myth is
read as a factual system, whereas it is but a semiological system."[44]

In an effort to understand the meaning of the grandest regenerative
claims of Transcendentalism, we shall find it necessary to stand for a
while on the stages erected by Emerson, Thoreau, Whitman, and Fuller.
Only by provisionally donning the roles that they have imagined for us
can we test their attempts to constitute a new kind of self-reliant individual. As a means to that end, chapter 2 develops the general outlines
of Emerson's mythologizing of the unconscious as a quasi-theological
source. My strategy is to examine the psychological rhetoric of Emerson's early enthusiasm—the stage of "freedom," as Stephen Whicher calls
it. Beginning with Emerson's sermons, I examine the development of his
rhetoric of regeneration in "The Philosophy of History" (a major lecture
series), in *Nature*, in "The American Scholar" and "The Divinity School
Address." The preponderance of spoken works on this list reflects the
conviction that Emerson's vision of the self assumes the presence of an
audience that is to be converted. Dramatizing humankind's ontological
alienation in his early works, Emerson then offers his audience a myth of
the unconscious as a substitute for more traditional conceptions of godhead. Emerson persuades his audience to adopt his model of the unconscious by means of dramatized personae that they are offered as models
of regenerated being.

In the next three chapters I analyze the psychological mythmaking
engaged in by three contemporaries whom Emerson strongly influenced—Thoreau, Whitman, and Fuller. By reading *Walden*, "Song of
Myself," and *Woman in the Nineteenth Century* in relation to specific
essays selected from Emerson's *Essays: First Series*, I can further illuminate how Transcendentalist "rhetorics of regeneration" redefine the stage
upon which the reader exists. Each work defines a renewed being predicated upon the recovery and expression of divine powers found within
the self. Instead of focusing upon each writer's theory of the mind, I
attend to how that vision of psychology functions rhetorically. Motivating their readers to identify with the personae posited in their texts,

Thoreau, Whitman, and Fuller provide ontological paradigms that attempt to reconstitute their readers' existence. If Emerson reconstitutes the self by promoting faith in the unconscious, Thoreau and Whitman elaborate that model of self-reliance by attending to the ways in which the release of unconscious power refashions the individual's sensuous involvement with the world. Margaret Fuller, on the other hand, reveals the ways in which Emerson's model of the self depends upon a masculine conception of spirit. Her contribution to psychological mythmaking during the American Renaissance is a feminized model of psychic energy and its expression.

TWO

Emerson's Myth of the Unconscious

THE "GOD WITHIN"

Emerson taught a generation of Americans how to read themselves. In his early sermons, lectures, and addresses he articulated a new model for interpreting the self—one that located ultimate meaning in the depths of the psyche rather than in institutionalized norms. More than a social vision, as both a theory of the mind and a quasi-theological doctrine, "self-reliance" changed his audience's self-conception by formulating a different set of rules for construing the psyche. According to Octavius Frothingham, "Transcendentalism . . . was an assertion of the immanence of divinity in instinct, the transference of supernatural attributes to the natural constitution of mankind."[1] This internalization of godhead depended upon the acceptance of a new psychological language that reset the horizon of human potential.

The key term in this new psychological language is what Emerson calls "the Unconscious," as in the following passage written in 1837: "& so the great word Comparative Anatomy has now leaped out of the womb of the Unconscious. I feel a cabinet in my mind unlocked by each of these new interests. Wherever I go, the related objects crowd on my Sense & I explore backward & wonder how the same things looked to me before my attention had been aroused" (*JMN*, 5:427). Earlier that year, on January 5, Emerson had used his lecture "Literature" as an opportunity to discuss that "portion of ourselves" that "lies within the limits of the unconscious" (*EL*, 2:56). That same month Francis Bowen complained in the *Christian Examiner* of Germanic distortions of the English language represented by words like the *Unconscious*: "Among other innovations in speech made by writers of the Transcendental school, we may instance the formation of a large class of abstract nouns from adjectives,—a peculiarity as consonant with the genius of the German language, as it is foreign to the nature of our own. Thus we now speak of the *Infinite*, the *Beautiful*, the *Unconscious*."[2] Emerson needed a new terminology to express his perception of the mind. Without words like the *unconscious* (decidedly outside the empiricist epistemology prevailing in Unitarian circles), his presentation of spiritual and psychological regeneration would have lacked a transcendent ground.

Linking Emerson's conception of the unconscious to similar ideas in works by Johann Wolfgang von Goethe, Jakob Boehme, Ralph Cudworth, Immanuel Kant, and others, Gay Wilson Allen concludes that "Emerson was familiar with the theory that an 'unconscious' mind somehow influenced or even blindly directed consciousness."[3] A number of later critics have expanded Allen's argument by focusing upon points of similarity between Emerson's ideas and the theories of the Swiss psychoanalyst Carl Jung. Martin Bickman, for example, argues that Emerson and Jung share a common conception of symbolism. "However different their approaches may be," he writes, "the symbol for both Emerson and Jung is the cutting edge of consciousness, the primary means of transposing the unknown into at least the suspected, the intuited, the embodied."[4]

Rather than elaborating further the extensive similarities between Emerson's and Jung's ideas, I will take a different tack. I will consider how their conceptions of the unconscious function within what I shall term the "rhetoric of regeneration." Given Emerson's and Jung's common Romantic inheritance, the similarities between their visions of the mind are not at all surprising. Indeed, one could document that Goethe, Friedrich Schelling, Coleridge, Thomas Carlyle, and numerous others viewed the mind in roughly analogous terms. Such is the import of M. H. Abrams's discussion in *The Mirror and the Lamp* of "The Psychology of Literary Invention: Unconscious Genius and Organic Growth."[5] A more interesting question moves from the history of ideas to consider the rhetorical functioning of this Romantic psychology of the unconscious. Why does it arise at this time? How does it work? What is its appeal to a nineteenth-century audience? To answer such questions, we need to focus upon the religious ramifications of Emerson's myth of the mind, a myth that aimed at solidifying piety in an age of crumbling faith. As Stephen Whicher argues, Emerson "wants . . . what Edwards, what New Englanders, had always wanted, an *assured salvation*, not simply moral capacity. . . . This salvation is what was given him by the revelation of the God within."[6] For Emerson, faith in the unconscious secures an ontological ground equivalent to that promised to earlier generations by divine grace. By locating the locus of God's power within the self, Emerson's vision of the mind satisfied a theological hunger; it provided the foundation for belief.

Like the psychological theories of Carl Jung, Emerson's early works

create "figures of the mind" that serve as interpretive conventions allowing his audience to read their own lives in terms of divine powers intuited within. Both Emerson and Jung see participation in the power of
the unconscious as leading to an increase of being. In their psychological
models, authenticity and inauthenticity are defined along an ontological scale graduated according to one's reception of divine forces found
within the psyche. At the extreme of inauthenticity, life takes on an
"unreal" quality such as that attributed by Emerson to the "spectral"
preacher characterized in "The Divinity School Address" (*CW*, 1:85). In
contrast, authentic being is realized by those who open themselves to
what Emerson calls "the eternal revelation in the heart" (81).

As one reads through Jung's essay "The Spiritual Problem of Modern
Man," one cannot avoid being struck by the way Jung repeats many
of the same images used earlier by Emerson. "The ancients were self-
united," Emerson had observed. "We have found out the difference of
outer and inner" (*EL*, 2:168). Jung comments in similar terms on the
"unprecedented tension . . . between outside and inside, between objective and subjective reality"—a tension that leads to the reevaluation of
the inner, the subjective.[7] Emerson evoked a myth of "One Man" reunit-
ing the isolated members of his audience. Jung recurs to the same myth,
indeed to Emerson's very sources: "in one of its aspects the psyche is not
individual, but is derived from the nation, from the collectivity, from
humanity even. In some way or other we are part of a single, all-embracing psyche, a single 'greatest man,' the *homo maximus* to quote Swedenborg." The resemblances between Emerson's thought and Jung's can be
multiplied—so much so that one accedes quickly to Martin Bickman's
observation that "one of the problems in juxtaposing Emerson and Jung
is not that they have so little in common but that they have so much."[8]

Responding in similar ways to their respective senses of cultural crisis,
of decaying religious sensibility, both Emerson and Jung develop psychologies aimed at restoring faith. The goal of each is to inspire, to
transform his audience by moving them from complacency to crisis and
finally to a new awareness of individual spiritual potential. Emerson
patterns his lectures and addresses upon models adapted from the pulpit;
Jung also orients his rhetoric in terms of religious intentions. "Jungian
psychotherapy," in the words of Dieter Wyss, "is not an analytical proce-
dure in the usual sense of the term, although it adheres strictly to the
relevant findings of science and medicine. It is a *Heilsweg* in the two-fold
sense of the German word: a way of healing and a way of salvation."[9]
The experience of the unconscious, Jung himself affirms, is "a genuine
and incontestable experience of the Divine."[10] Like Jung, Emerson nour-

ishes the vision of divinity buried in the heart of the psyche. He engages in psychological mythmaking, founded upon the development of depth psychology as a substitute religion.

Emerson thus sees the act of becoming conscious as a process that displaces attention from the demands of the ego toward symbols of transcendent spiritual authority. Consciousness, he asserts, must be de-centered from self-absorption to a position halfway between the ego and the divine psychic depths that are intuited as the source of future unfold-ing. Emerson describes this decentering in the following terms: "The constant warfare in each heart is betwixt Reason and Commodity. The victory is won as soon as any Soul has learned always to take sides with Reason against himself; to transfer his Me from his person, his name, his interest, back upon Truth & Justice" (*JMN*, 5:391). The goal, Emerson continues in this same entry, is to "break off your association with your personality & identify yourself with the Universe." Elsewhere, Emerson describes this decentering as a "self-surrender" that lifts one beyond "friction" or "wilfulness" (*EL*, 2:49, 69). In order to release our creative potential, he asserts in his early lecture "Art," we must "hinder our indi-viduality from acting": "So much as we can shove aside our egotism, our prejudice, and will, and bring the omniscience of reason upon the sub-ject before us, so perfect is the work" (49). The result of such a shift from personal interest is an attitude of faith toward an unseen transcen-dent power residing within the unconscious.

It is important to stress that Emerson's unconscious is collective, not personal. This is perhaps the most difficult aspect of his thought for a modern reader. Accustomed as we are to the Freudian vision of a per-sonal unconscious, it takes an effort of imagination to appreciate psycho-logical theories based upon an unconscious that transcends the self. But it is precisely Emerson's conviction that the unconscious extends beyond the individual that gives it theological authority. The challenge facing the modern reader, trained to see a much different kind of unconscious, is to bracket the assumption that psychological dynamics must be defined in personal, largely Freudian, terms long enough to see the rhetorical and theological value of Emerson's position. If we can succeed in suspending the myth that the unconscious must be personal, then we shall recognize that much of Emerson's importance comes from his popularizing of a depth psychology that involved him like Jung in "a genuine and incon-testable experience of the Divine."[11]

Each person, Emerson argues, occupies a potentially unique relation-ship to this universal center of power. "In him, under him, is the same world as another beholds; but it is the world seen from a new point of view; the more deeply he drinks of the common soul, the more decided does his individuality become" (*EL*, 2:100). By standing squarely "upon the basis of the world" and allowing one's will to become the "effluence of Reason" (152), the individual incarnates a spiritual authority that gives weight to being. The individual avoids the inauthenticity of the "spectral" preacher in "The Divinity School Address"; instead, he is "wholly his own man" (175). Paradoxically, the "peculiar reception of the Common Reason" (147), of universal unconscious forces, enhances individual characteristics. The centered person has "the common faculties under a bias" and thus exhibits a "character altogether new and original" (100).

In very similar terms Carl Jung argues that the displacement of consciousness toward the unconscious promotes the true "idiosyncrasy" of the individual, "a unique combination, or general differentiation, of functions and faculties which in themselves are universal."[12] Jung calls this process "self-realization" and, more frequently, "individuation"—a conception that parallels Emerson's ideal of self-reliance.[13] He defines individuation as the process through which the self "becomes conscious of his invisible system of relations to the unconscious," and goes on to describe it as a process of self-interpretation that involves both the projection of archetypal images (for example, in dreams) and the conscious assimilation of their power. Instead of focusing solely upon the dream-image or the archetype, Jung teaches his patients to uncover the relationship between dreaming and self-analysis.

By necessity, both individuation and self-reliance promote a faith in the hidden self, nourished by the suspension of disbelief in the impulses and images rising from the unconscious. "A man conversing in earnest," Emerson observes in *Nature*, "if he watch his intellectual processes, will find that always a material image, more or less luminous, arises in his mind, cotemporaneous with every thought, which furnishes the vestment of the thought" (*CW*, 1:20). The growth of self-awareness depends upon an interpretive process in which such images are framed by interpretive strategies that give them meaning. Emerson's psychological mythmaking thus interiorizes the classic hermeneutic circle: "'Every scripture is to be interpreted by the same spirit which gave it forth,'—is the fundamental law of criticism. A life in harmony with Nature, the love of truth and of virtue, will purge the eyes to understand her text" (23). In order to understand a text, Emerson asserts elsewhere, we must connect its "images to some reality in our secret experience" (*EL*, 2:15). When the text involved is the psyche itself, then the hermeneutic frame not only constitutes the object of knowledge (Emerson's myth of the unconscious), it becomes part of our awareness of the self and its motives. The interpreting "I" merges into the interpreted being who uses the process of self-interpretation as the founding act of its own selfhood. This process threatens to lapse into a vertiginous spiral of self-reflection unless some stable, transcendent ground can be found within the psyche. This finally is the dilemma of Melville's Pierre, but it is also the problem confronted at the beginning of Emerson's "Experience": "Where do we find ourselves? In a series of which we do not know the extremes, and believe that it has none. We wake and find ourselves on a stair; there are stairs below us, which we seem to have ascended; there are stairs above us, many a one, which go upward and out of sight" (W, 3:45). The way Emerson stops such ontological insecurity is by finding an unchanging "First Cause" within the psyche (72).

The result of this faith in the unconscious is an unfolding of the self. In everyone, Emerson writes, there is "some faculty never yet unfolded" (EL, 2:9). "As the mind unfolds," he later asserts, it begins "to publish in the colors of the pleasant light the secrets which preexisted in the closet of the mind" (176). Such unfolding is necessary for psychic and spiritual maturity, for the "fruit" of a person's "Nature . . . must grow out of him as long as he exists" (95). Carl Jung shares Emerson's faith in the divine potential of the self. In *Psychology and Alchemy*, for example, he equates the Eastern mandala, often imagined as an unfolding lotus blossom, with the alchemical vessel. In both instances an unfolding center (the calyx of the lotus and the inside of the vessel) becomes a field of projection for images reflecting the unseen center that moves "once more into the field of consciousness."[14] This reception is facilitated by a "willing suspension of disbelief" that brackets and suspends ordinary standards of judgment, creating a phenomenological field revealing the "presence" of intuited powers. Both the analytic session and the Emersonian essay posit a circle of faith that embeds images of divine power within interpretive contexts. Acceptance of these "symbols of transformation" (as Jung calls them) uncovers the transcendent ground they incarnate.

Ultimately, Emerson attempts to resist modern processes of secularization by mythologizing the unconscious. Giving his writing a distinctive theological character, his prospective viewpoint defines human development in terms of a transcendent limit toward which the individual aspires. It presents a figure of "spirit or mind" that "mediate[s] self-consciousness" by positing "a telos to . . . 'becoming conscious.'"[15] In a manner similar to Jung's collective archetypes, these psychological myths such as the "One Mind" function as ideals energizing spiritual desire. In the process, they facilitate resistance to what Paul Ricoeur describes as "the *extension of rationality* to all areas and levels of reality."[16] Opposing "the expulsion, out of consideration and out of language, of the cosmic sacred, of the psychic sacred," Emerson's myth of the unconscious establishes a region where the mysterious can be nourished. It locates the sacred within, clearing a space for its appearance. Rather than allowing his audience to see themselves as isolated units, Emerson motivates them to interpret themselves through psychic models that promulgate collective participation in divine power. Each listener is made "a subject that is spoken to," who is taught to hear within the mind the promptings of spirit.[17] In an increasingly materialized age Emerson's "rhetoric of regeneration" holds forth the promise of personal salvation.

INTERPRETING THE SELF

In his early works Emerson began promulgating his psychological myth by teaching a new terminology to his audience. His task was to show them how to apprehend powers hidden within their own minds, at the same time that he persuaded them to accept this new reading of the self. By modeling themselves upon Emerson's idealized paradigm of the psyche, his auditors might gain access to a new landscape of being. The foundation of this reinterpretation of existence was faith in the unconscious as a divine source. Staking an existential claim upon the very lives of his listeners, Emerson articulated that demand through literary methods learned in the pulpit. "Many of the Transcendentalist writings," Lawrence Buell reminds us, ". . . are either sermons or at one remove from sermons. . . . Emerson's essays were, in large part, originally delivered as lectures in the lyceum, the conventions of which were in turn strongly indebted to the pulpit."[18] Viewing the sermon as "an inspirational oration," Emerson began his public literary career by teaching his congregation to recognize the dimensions of a divine power within.[19]

In the introduction to his collection of Emerson's sermons, *Young Emerson Speaks*, Arthur Cushman McGiffert draws our attention to the ways these sermons anticipate the mature psychological theories: "The second way of religious knowledge he calls the 'heart,' the 'moral faculty,' the 'moral sense,' the 'oracle within.' . . . The validity of this intuitional method of knowing God arises from the structure of the mind itself. . . . The young preacher has not yet invented the term 'Over-soul' for this theory of the immanence of God in human personality. Biblical words like the Holy Spirit, or Emmanuel, or God within us still satisfy him. But the idea is there."[20] Equally significant is Emerson's use of rhetorical forms that engage his audience in a mutual process of psychological discovery. For example, he "frequently introduces brief bits of fabricated dialogue or interrogation into his sermons—thus dramatizing his hearers to themselves."²¹ Similarly, Emerson holds up his own meditations as a model for his congregation to follow: "he seems to be thinking out loud in the pulpit . . . endeavoring to share with his congregation the process by which he has reached his conclusions."²² Thus, from the beginning, Emerson uses dramatizations of the self—either of himself as exemplary persona or of his implied auditor—as vehicles for his reinterpretation of psychology.

Any reader of Emerson's early sermons has to be struck with the variety of terms used to describe the spiritual energies buried within the self. In his first sermon he advises his audience to listen to "the monitor" within who teaches us that "thoughts and passions . . . are so many integral parts of the imperishable universe of morals" (*YES*, 11, 2–3). Shortly thereafter he is telling them to heed "the man within the breast" (65), "the great secrets of my own nature" (96), and the "spiritual force" (105) that reveals "God in me" (132). He teaches his auditor to attend to the "intimations of Divine Wisdom in his own mind" (167)—intimations that reveal "the eternal reason which shines within him, the immortal life that dwells at the bottom of his heart" (183). We are to hear the "inward voice" (188) that manifests "supreme universal reason in your mind"—"the Spirit of God in us all" (186). By overcoming egotism and partiality, we regain "union" with the "source" (201) and attend again to "the voice of the whole creation" (202). Such phrases promise the immanence of divine energies that are made present without hindrance. The mere recognition of God within seems sufficient to eliminate all temporal and spatial barriers that might inhibit regeneration.

"There is a revolution of religious opinion taking effect around us," Emerson confidently asserts; for the first time, man "contemplates . . . his own proper nature" (*YES*, 199). This revolution is whispered by "the voice" of "the Father" within (200), a voice that Emerson dramatizes as arising within the mind of his implied auditor: "I know I have a witness in every one of your hearts which hath affirmed the same thing many times and put it beyond a doubt. Let me exhort you to lend an ear to all the good and sacred promptings that hitherto you have withstood" (162). Such passages exemplify what Jacques Derrida characterizes as "the privilege of the *phone*"—an assumption of the "absolute proximity of voice and being, of voice and the meaning of being, of voice and the ideality of meaning."²³ Eliminating the gap between signifier and signified, Emerson's conception of "voice" at this stage in his career announces a divine Truth immediately apparent. All sense of mediation, of contingency, vanishes when this voice is heard. As Emerson later observes in *Nature*, "outlines and surfaces become transparent, and are no longer seen; causes and spirits are seen through them" (*CW*, 1:30). Commenting upon such a privileging of meaning, Derrida writes, "the signifier seems to erase itself or to become transparent, in order to allow the concept to present itself as what it is, referring to nothing other than its presence."[24] *Voice*, *transparency*, and *presence* are all key terms in Emerson's rhetoric of regeneration. Together, they establish the accessibility of innate spiritual energies, as psychological wholeness is given in a flash of immediately assimilable insight.

We can thus read Emerson's psychological mythmaking as an attempt to overcome what Jacques Derrida calls *différance*, for it asserts the possibility of having direct access to ideas without the temporal and spatial detour of passing through unreliable signifiers. "He that purges out of his thought every vestige of personal limitation and respires the air of pure truth," Emerson later asserts, "will speak or write or do what is durable, what is intelligible to all times and countries" (*EL*, 2:12). Emerson's assumption that the personal can be eliminated leads him to define literature as "the record of human thought in written language" (56). Although the greatest works "exhibit the inwardest parts of human nature" (59), this inner realm is not the personal unconscious of Freud— but rather, a world of "truth" that is "impersonal and immortal" (58). Even though Emerson recognizes the intertextuality of literature—"what is already writ is a foundation of the new superstructure" (64)—he is not led by such insights toward a Derridean model of deferral. Instead, the ontological priority of the spiritual truth within leads him to a model of expression in which literary form, the signifier, becomes invisible.

Given this view, it becomes inevitable that he would select the "orator" (*EL*, 2:57) as the exemplar of creative expression. Giving voice to the spirit that we carry within, the great speaker "separates for us a truth from our unconscious reason" (57)—the sheer power of his eloquence becoming a vehicle for the divine breath, the *pneuma*, that we all contain. Confronted by powers that "press upon the soul with the force of a personal address" (*YES*, 199), Emerson teaches his listeners the value of eloquence, which is the human perfection of "voice" and hence the action that brings one closest to divinity. The great speaker becomes the organ of a universal power that he both releases in the minds of his auditors and exemplifies in his own person:

> The mightiest engine which God has put into the hands of men to move men is eloquence. . . . When great sentiments call it out from a great mind and especially when it rises to topics of eternal interest, it is glorious to see how it masters the mind, how it bows the independence of a thousand to the reason

of one; how it goes on with electrical swiftness from unobserved beginnings, lifting him that speaks and them that hear, above the dust and smoke of life, searching out every noble purpose, every sublime hope that lurks in the soul. Then is that sympathy lofty and pure; then the speaker and the hearer become *the pipes on which a higher power speaketh. It is like the breath of the Almighty moving on the deep.* [*YES*, 26; italics mine]

Properly executing his role, the great preacher or orator exhibits to his auditors the contours of a divine power that they can then discover within.

Emerson's account of the decay of Christianity in "The Divinity School Address" illustrates the priority he gives to the transcendental signified, the divine voice found in the unconscious, over any individual act of signification. As it has moved from the original intuition of Jesus, who "saw with open eye the mystery of the soul" (*CW*, 1:81), the church has allowed vision to be obscured by form, the divine idea by the play of signifiers, "tropes" (81) and "official titles" (82). Attention to universal spiritual truth, Emerson complains in similar fashion, has been displaced by the "exaggeration of the personal . . . the *person* of Jesus" (82). By asserting that the "soul knows no persons" (82), Emerson subordinates theories of personality or of a personal unconscious to his vision of a collective unconscious. In place of the individual gesture or the specific unreliable word, he offers direct access to a divine ground of being, discovered in imagined moments where all signifiers become "transparent."

Like Edmund Husserl (as Derrida characterizes his thought in *Speech and Phenomena*), Emerson excludes from meaning "everything that escapes the pure spiritual intention, the pure animation by *Geist*."[25] Such unmediated access to spiritual truth is located by Emerson in "me myself" where I find "God in Me" (*CW*, 1:82). Ostensibly bypassing the dilemma of signification, the unavoidable erosion and misdirection of meaning, Emerson interiorizes the process of expression—thus giving each individual the means to apprehend spiritual truth directly without passing through the annoyance of unreliable signs. The model of signification that follows from such a position is allegorical. The word or gesture becomes a transparent emblem that turns invisible as inner meaning shines through.

For fifteen years (from 1826 to 1841) Emerson's public writings enthusiastically celebrate the power of "the Unconscious" that "is ever the act of God himself" (*JMN*, 4:309–10). Seeing the soul as "God's image" (*YES*, 182), Emerson utilizes a Neoplatonic paradigm of representation. "To exist," R. A. Yoder observes of this model, "is to have emanated, and to emanate is to descend or fall from the One."[26] Emerson's sense of the disparity between transcendent power and daily being measures the individual's distance from a lost unity, envisioned as a transcendental signified found in the unconscious. If the mind is put into the right frame, Emerson suggests, the self will be transfigured.

But the act of regeneration, Emerson discovered, involves more than listening to the divine voice within; it necessitates a process of spiritual development, an unfolding in time. In *Natural Supernaturalism* M. H. Abrams describes the basic outline of this process as a "circular or spiral quest" for a lost "primal unity."[27] Beginning with a recognition of "self-division," the Romantic writer moves from alienation toward a vision "of the awesome depths and height of the human mind." Ultimately, Abrams dates this quest-pattern back to "the tendency, grounded in texts of the New Testament itself, to internalize apocalypse by transferring the theater of events from the outer earth and heaven to the spirit of the single believer." Reflecting such an internalization, Emerson's writing portrays both images of transcendence and the quest toward this "apocalypse." Not only does it present timeless moments of vision (such as the "transparent eye-ball" epiphany in *Nature*, an image of "primal unity"), it also depicts moments of unfolding being in time ("I expand and live in the warm day like corn and melons"). The challenge for Emerson is to connect vision and being, to convince his audience that the unconscious is both a collective ground and a personal source, both the end of the quest and the means of getting there.

The Swedenborgian dream of "correspondence," which Emerson found in the writings of Sampson Reed, epitomizes his dual concern with the self's development and its ultimate transfiguration. Imagining "the whole of Nature" as "a metaphor or image of the human Mind" (*EL*, 1:24), Emerson is lured by the psychological myth of a completely readable and accessible psychic text that would unlock its secrets for the individual who has learned the right key. This theme is evident as early as Emerson's lecture series on "Science" (1833–34). Moved by "strange sympathies," the sense of an "occult relation" between the mind and nature, Emerson begins to analyze the dependence of psychological reflection upon images derived from the material world (10). He is struck by the "correspondence of the outward world to the inward world of thoughts and emotions, by which it is suited to represent what we think" (24). "The very existence of thought and speech," he observes a paragraph later, "supposes and is a new nature totally distinct from the material world; yet we find it impossible to speak of it and its laws in any other language than that borrowed from our experience in the material world"

(24). Given the potential correspondence of mind and nature, the challenge confronting Emerson is to find the right natural images to symbolize the power buried within. By properly conjoining inner power with natural analogues, he might link vision and existence, his sense of a divine unconscious with being-in-the-world.

Emerson's solution to this problem is to develop a model of psychology based upon the activity of interpretation. The vision of divine energies within continues as the touchstone of transfigured being, but this vision operates as an emblem defining the endpoint of spiritual aspiration. Aiming toward an illumination that has not yet been fully achieved, the individual must learn to interpret signs that reveal one's assimilation of spiritual power. As a consequence, self-understanding becomes a hermeneutic process in which one is committed to interpreting the self. Since Emerson sees the same force motivating insight and constructive activity, both moments of vision and of being-in-the-world become the focus of interpretation. If epiphanies are read as emblems of momentarily achieved power, one's relationship to the world also reveals spiritual energies whose effects can be read in the materials that have been manipulated. Emerson's auditor must learn to recognize both the "gleams of a better light," "examples of Reason's momentary grasp of the sceptre" (*CW*, 1:43), and the existential "lesson of power" that "is taught in every event" (25). Emerson's visionary faith in the "God within" thus combines with the perception of psychic growth measured in terms of one's progressive mastery of one's world.

Emerson's concern with interpreting the self is typical of the Romantic period. Searching for the origin of each entity in "a profound, interior, and essential space," Romantic writers confronted a world in which generative principles had become internalized. Things, Michel Foucault argues, had started to "turn in upon themselves, posit their own volumes, and define for themselves an internal space." As a result, the search for transcendent principles necessitated the imaginative reconstruction of hidden "depths"—the site of "great hidden forces developed on the basis of their primitive and inaccessible nucleus, origin, causality, and history."[28] Similarly, the interpretation of human activity, exemplified by the literary criticism of Friedrich Schleiermacher, involved the imaginative reconstruction of another person's subjectivity. "What is to be understood," Hans-Georg Gadamer explains, "is now not only the exact words and their objective meaning, but also the individuality of the speaker, that is, the author." At the center of such "psychological interpretation" is "a divinatory process, a placing of oneself within the mind of the author, an apprehension of the 'inner origin' of the composition

of a work."[29] But the danger faced by Schleiermacher and other Romantic interpreters was that the individual threatened to become "a mystery
that could never be quite grasped."[30] Motivation later takes on such a
quality of mystery and ambiguity in the writings of Hawthorne and
Melville, but Emerson attempts to forestall this darkening of the self by
viewing human will as the function of a collective energy that the individual embodies. The value of the hero, the genius, or the great orator, is
that the life of each becomes a symbol of a divine unconscious realizing
itself through active involvement in the world.

Emerson's lecture series "The Philosophy of History" (delivered the
winter following *Nature*) is largely devoted to interpreting the self's
relationship to this transcendent center of power. In his attempt to communicate the divine impulses that he intuits within the depths of the
mind, Emerson maps onto his audience a set of interpretive procedures
by which they might define and assimilate unconscious energy. He attempts to startle "the soul awake" (*EL*, 2:84) by means of a discourse
upon the unconscious and the relation of consciousness to that hidden center of "power." Unconsciousness, the lost innocence of culture's
childhood, is no longer a real possibility. But through self-conscious
openness to the power within, faith might remain viable. Defining the
"horizon" of thought, Emerson helps his audience to intuit the spiritual
energy waiting to "dawn" beyond it. Signs of such power become guide-
posts to the energy that might be released from the unconscious of each
auditor.

This attempt to "lift the veil of the Unconscious" constitutes what
Emerson calls a "science of the mind" (*EL*, 2:167). Analyzing the functioning of "deeper causes" within human behavior (172), he defines what
we recognize as a depth psychology—a model of interpretation oriented
toward the recovery of unconscious powers. Our "manners," he asserts,
"evermore publish" the "hidden man"; they "proceed directly from the
character of which they are the involuntary signs." Each one of us, he
continues, "has his proper forms of living, speaking, motion, address,
which are independent of his will but wholly dependent on his character
and condition, and therefore are the same index of his genius or turn of
mind. That circumstance constitutes their value to the historian and
philosopher, that they are the unconscious account which [the] party
gives of himself" (130–31). This account, Emerson notes later in his
lecture "Manners," leads us toward a vision of the "Unconscious" that "is
ever the act of God himself" (135). Although children and primitives
maintain an "engaging unconsciousness" (135), the challenge confronting
the mature adult is to recover this power, now found in the "centre
within" (142).

Emerson's interpretation of "the secrets which preexisted in the closet of the mind" (*EL*, 2:176) depends upon his analysis of "relation." For unconscious creative energies can emerge only when they have material to work through, forms that exist as a field for their projection: "Put Napoleon into an island prison and let the great faculties of that man find no men to act upon, no Alps to climb, no stakes to play for, and he would beat the air and appear stupid. Then transfer him to large countries, dense population, complex interests, and antagonist power and you shall see him unfold his masterful energies" (17). Emerson never ceases to marvel over the fact that we are not imprisoned, that "out of the human soul go as it were highways to the heart of every object in nature, and so subject them to the dominion of man" (17). By becoming an "active soul," one realizes the power latent within. The "scholar," Emerson later observes, "loses no hour which the man lives"; through action, "he unfolds the sacred germ of his instinct" (*CW*, 1:61).

By relating to the world through the projection of unconscious forces, the psyche promotes its own self-analysis: "each object unlocks the faculty which is exercised upon it and makes it for the first time known to us" (*EL*, 2:18). This faculty is "known" because projected unconscious forces, once they have shaped objective facts, become accessible to interpretation. Like a geologist, one can determine the dimensions of power by analyzing its effects. Emerson exhorts his audience to practice such self-interpretation in order to recognize the unconscious "Ideas" that rule their lives: "We must always be prisoners of Ideas we are just beginning to apprehend; when by and by we understand them and see how we were guided and led we are already following another clue, or tyrannised over by another Ruling Thought, which we can no more see around" (170). In a manner similar to Carl Jung's insistence that his patients interpret the unconscious archetypes controlling them, Emerson advocates the "act of reflection" that places life "in perspective" (144–45). One gains control over the energy within through a process that "separates for us a truth from our unconscious reason, and makes it an object of consciousness" (57).

When such "truth" is "separated by the intellect," when "any sentiment or principle" is "disentangled from the web of our unconsciousness," we "acquire" ourselves (*EL*, 2:57–58). Unseen principles of behavior become part of our conscious repertoire of motives. Or, as Emerson had phrased this process in *Nature*, "That which was unconscious truth, becomes, when *interpreted* and defined in an object, a part of the domain of knowledge,—a new weapon in the magazine of power" (*CW*, 1:23; italics mine). By learning the "laws of the mind" (*EL*, 2:147), the individual recovers the previously inaccessible energies of the buried self.

The process of self-recovery begins with the perception of a distance from unconscious spontaneity. Until self-consciousness sees itself as alienated, there is no need for a myth of the unconscious as an ontological ground. But once reflection realizes its "poverty," it is challenged to regain the security of a period when *God* and *man*, *Unconscious* and *consciousness* were not disparate terms.

This was the position Thomas Carlyle had held in "Characteristics" when he characterized self-consciousness as a "disease" because it indicated the loss of unconscious vitality. The "sign of health," Carlyle asserted, "is Unconsciousness."[31] Thoreau made a similar point in "Life without Principle" when he observed: "Those things which now most engage the attention of men, as politics and the daily routine, are, it is true, vital functions of human society, but should be unconsciously performed, like the corresponding functions of the physical body. They are *infra*-human, a kind of vegetation. . . . Thus our life is not altogether a forgetting, but also, alas! to a great extent, a remembering of that which we should never have been conscious of, certainly not in our waking hours" (*RP*, 178–79). Self-consciousness, for both writers, measures the distance of one's "fall" from psychic health. Consequently, the aim of Carlyle, Thoreau, and Emerson—according to Geoffrey Hartman—is to escape "the corrosive power of analysis" and regain "anti-self-consciousness."[32] Their Romantic quests aspire toward visions of unified being, but the very existence of psychological awareness measures the distance from that goal.

Yet if a self-conscious sense of alienation is a sign of disease, it is also the first step toward recovery, for the recognition of alienation inaugurates the journey back toward psychological and spiritual wholeness. In such terms, the Jungian therapist Edward Edinger argues that "the experience of alienation is a necessary prelude to awareness of the Self."[33] To extend this to a theological frame of reference, we might say that Emerson prepares for the discovery of the unconscious through the humiliation of self-consciousness in a process roughly similar to the Puritan "preparation for grace." Acceptance of a higher spiritual authority follows the discrediting of ordinary patterns of cognition. We see this humiliation of consciousness in Emerson's lecture "The Present Age," where he explicitly challenges his auditors to overcome their self-conscious alienation. Complaining that his listeners have fallen away from the "One Mind," whose currents circulate only when they sleep, Emerson measures the distance they must cover. He sees a "common law" beneath the surface of their lives, but few have the "negligent self-forgetting greatness" (*EL*, 2:162) necessary to embody it.

By defining his auditors' distance from unconscious energy, Emerson establishes the precondition for its articulation. Human beings, he complains, have become too critical: "The trait which philosophers agree to designate our age withal is its Reflective character. It is alleged that the habit of the cultivated intellect of the present day is reflection, not instinct. Ours is distinguished from the Greek and Roman and Gothic ages and all the periods of childhood and youth by being the age of the second thought. The golden age is gone and the silver is gone—the blessed eras of unconscious life, of intuition, of genius" (*EL*, 2:168). Instead of self-surrender, Emerson finds a plethora of "intention"; instead of imagination, an overabundance of "critical judgment" (169).

Worst of all, he sees around him a general loss of faith in anything larger than the individual: "Always over the man impended something greater than he, to command his reverence and to call out his faculties. But we are of age. We have lost all reverence for the state. It is merely our boardinghouse. We have lost all reverence for the Church; it is also republican. We call a spade, a spade. We have great contempt for the superstitions and nonsense which blinded the eyes of all foregoing generations" (*EL*, 2:169). By dramatizing this loss of reverence for external institutions, Emerson prepares his audience for a reorientation of their faith upon psychological grounds. His account of the evils of the present age clears the ground for an evocation of the "good fruits" that "will appear" from within (170). "This despondency, this want of object in life, this nakedness," he asserts, "are the temporary symptoms of the transition state, whilst the man sees the hollowness of traditions and does not yet know the resources of the soul" (170). Those "resources," he emphasizes, are to be found in the unconscious.

In this way, Emerson's "rhetoric of regeneration" commits his audience to the rhythm of spiritual crisis and recuperation. Characterizing his auditors' "fall" from psychic wholeness, Emerson defines the unconscious as the repository of a unifying power. Evoking the decay of religious institutions, he develops a myth of internalized spiritual authority to compensate for the erosion of authority without. The menace of disinheritance is thus exchanged for promised access to "areas of human experience" (in Martin Bickman's terms) that have "more ontological validity than any other."[34] According to Michel Foucault, such a presentation of the unconscious is a necessary consequence of self-reflection; it is "the shadow cast by man as he emerged in the field of knowledge."[35] In his early works Emerson attempts to illuminate that shadow, to rejoin individual awareness and transcendent being, by imagining the unconscious—not merely as the "unthought"—but as the divine origin of thought itself. By lifting "the veil of the Unconscious," he hopes to end "man's alienation by reconciling him with his own essence."[36]

One's sense of the validity of this psychological mythmaking varies according to the critical perspective from which it is observed. For a deconstructive critic, Emerson's movement from the dramatization of alienated self-consciousness to a myth of the unconscious betrays nostalgia for lost origins—a nostalgia that culminates in a compensating sublimation. Utilizing a critical paradigm based upon the Freudian myth of a personal unconscious, Harold Bloom thus describes Emerson's unconscious as a "power brought into being by an enormous fresh influx of repression."[37] Elsewhere, Bloom argues that Emerson replaces original "absence" with a myth of "presence." Along these lines, a "deconstructive" reading of Emerson's writing would find "the precise location of its figuration of doubt."

Such an approach has been undertaken by critics like Barbara Packer and Carolyn Porter, who both emphasize the gaps between vision and being in Emerson's works. For example, Porter argues that in *Nature* "alienation resurfaces as a split between the I who sees nature and the I who inhabits it. He is content to unsettle his audience by forcing them to adopt a new point of view, but he entrusts Spirit with the course to be taken by the energy thus released. His theory fosters the act of building one's own world while limiting the means with which to construct it to the imaginative potential implied by vision, and assuming the moral ends already implicit in Spirit."[38] Although it draws attention to Emerson's portrayal of alienation, this stresses his self-consciousness at the expense of understanding the impact of his rhetoric. To argue, as Porter does, that Emerson's strongest desire is "to absent one's self from the world as physical being in order to view the world from the vantage point of the disembodied eye" is to eliminate almost entirely from consideration the dynamic aspect of his writing.[39] Perceiving around him the very split between "seeing and being" that Porter criticizes him for manifesting, Emerson offers to heal that split by transforming disembodied seeing into an active process of self-expansion. Unless we understand the emphasis that Emerson places upon activity, we obfuscate the wide appeal that his psychology held for nineteenth-century audiences— an appeal based upon his presentation of collective paradigms of regenerated being.

FIGURES OF SPIRITUAL ASPIRATION

Rather than viewing the portrayal of Emerson's "figuration of doubt" as a personal expression, we need to view that doubt as the occasion for a psychological fiction used to "patch" or weave over his sense of cultural dispossession. "In regard to the genesis of delusions," Freud was later to comment, "a fair number of analyses have taught us that the delusion is found applied like a patch over the place where originally a rent had appeared in the ego's relation to the external world."[40] Addressing the "rent" in his audience's relation to an increasingly secularized world, Emerson presents his interpretation of the self as a patch for the collective psyche. This reweaving appears as a delusion only if one withdraws the hermeneutic faith necessary for its operation. Instead of stressing—like Porter—the compensatory nature of Emerson's rhetoric, I shall focus upon its power, the radical claim that it makes upon the individual.

At the heart of this rhetoric is the conviction that vision and being must be conjoined. This "illusion" (a theological fiction) is the pattern of order that the auditor is motivated to impose upon the experience of Emerson's text. Emerson gives that myth persuasive power by dramatizing states of regeneration that embody the endpoint, the telos, of spiritual aspiration. In *Essays: First Series* he imagines this goal as an "internal ocean" (*CW*, 2:41), a "sea of light" (172), "the fountain of action and of thought" (37). A fluid and mobile energy, it animates the "common heart" (160) whose "blood rolls uninterruptedly an endless circulation through all men" (173). Each of these symbols evokes a common, transpersonal ground that unites all persons on the basis of their shared spiritual potential. Each one of us, Emerson asserts, can immerse ourselves in the same ocean of power by finding the right "avenues" (169) and "conductors" (79) into the collective unconscious.

Before one can release the divine energies buried in the mind, one must recognize that the distance between alienation and transfigured being defines a gap that must be bridged. Accordingly, Emerson's presentation of the difference between daily being and ecstatic vision constitutes the auditor's spiritual quest. From the beginning Emerson was forced to recognize that awareness of the self's circumscription precedes any vision of its expansion. "The characteristic theme of the early journals," Stephen Whicher writes, "is helplessness," while his affirmation of the "God within" attempts to cover over "the terrors of Unbelief."[41] The result, Whicher concludes, was the tempering of Emerson's faith by a lifelong "sceptical awareness."

Among the most disturbing aspects of this skepticism was the intermittence and variability of Emerson's inspiration. Consequently, his efforts to "hypnotize himself into rhapsody," F. O. Matthiessen observes, were chastened by "the realization that his kind of truth was to come through inaction and hope, through waiting for moments of illumination."[42] Despite his early Swedenborgian excesses, Emerson was no Swedenborgian. He quickly learned to differentiate the dream of correspondence in which "every appearance in nature corresponds to some state of mind" (*CW*, 1:18) from the realities of composition. His essays were the product of painstakingly accumulated and fused-together insights. This method of composition, based upon the accumulation of aphorisms, reflects what Roland Barthes describes as pleasure in "the edge."[43] Emerson's keen perception of discontinuity and limits shapes his psychological mythmaking by compelling him to portray both a vision of the self's transfiguration and the recognition of that vision as the object of spiritual aspiration, rather than as an achieved spiritual fact.

In his *Aids to Reflection* Coleridge had suggested that the use of aphorism (the hallmark of Emerson's style) is a process of drawing boundaries. He defines aphorism as "determinate position, from *aphorizein*, to bound or limit; whence our horizon." Then, in a homely but telling metaphor that cements the concept forever in our minds, Coleridge expands his definition:

> In order to get the full sense of the word, we should first present to our minds the visual image that forms its primary meaning. Draw lines of different colors around the different counties of England, and then cut out each accurately, as in the common play-maps that children take to pieces and put together—so that each district can be contemplated apart from the rest, as a whole in itself. This twofold act of circumscribing, and detaching, when it is exercised by the mind on subjects of reflection and reason, is to aphorize, and the result an aphorism.[44]

Emerson's psychological mythmaking depends upon such circumscription; it frames figures of spiritual aspiration through the prior evocation of absence. It imagines alienation as an area of reflection that is cleared and bounded so that new energies—discovered in the unconscious—can appear.

By defining the limits of his auditor's being, the index of alienation, Emerson can suggest the potential contour of faith. Circumscribing an image of existence within a limited horizon, his portrayal of alienation defines a space that is "cleared and free, namely, within a boundary." "A boundary," Martin Heidegger argues, "is not that at which something stops but . . . that from which something *begins its essential unfolding*."[45] Emerson's presentation of alienated self-consciousness defines such a boundary, establishing a horizon of awareness beyond which new energies can start to grow. "The health of the eye," Emerson comments in *Nature*, "seems to demand a horizon. We are never tired, so long as we can see far enough" (*CW*, 1:13). Defining the "horizon" of self-perception, Emerson's depiction of alienation creates a rift or tear in awareness that suggests the existence of deeper forces beyond conscious control.

The auditor's attention is thus focused upon his or her distance from unconscious inspiration, a self-division that Emerson's myth of the mind is designed to heal. Through such discrediting of ordinary habits of perception, he projects a curve of spiritual aspiration that his audience can follow by attending to the signs of power that surface from within. This pattern recreates the traditional form of the jeremiad. In Sacvan Bercovitch's words, it "advances a mode of personal identity designed as a compensatory *replacement* for . . . the ugly course of actual events."[46]

In order to assimilate unconscious energy to consciousness, Emerson finds it necessary to differentiate and project a spiritual goal, to posit for alienated consciousness an image of potential power. In his psychological terminology this involves translating the insight of "Reason" into the vocabulary of the "Understanding." *Reason* is Emerson's Coleridgean term for the spiritual insight intuited as rising from the unconscious. "Reason," he wrote to his brother Edward, "is the highest faculty of the soul—what we often mean by the soul itself; it never *reasons*, never proves, it simply perceives; it is vision" (*L*, 1:412–13). "The ideas of Reason," he noted in his journal, "assume a new appearance as they descend into the Understanding. Invested with space & time they walk in masquerade" (*JMN*, 5:272–73). Aware of the "short sight" of Understanding, which prevents it from "apprehending the truth," Emerson is compelled to use "all manner of fables"—a form that Understanding can assimilate. This use of fables commits him to mythmaking.

Emerson's presentation of the poet's song near the end of *Nature* clearly connects such mythologizing of the unconscious as a spiritual goal with the dramatization of alienation:

> "Man is the dwarf of himself. Once he was permeated and dissolved by spirit. He filled nature with his overflowing currents. Out from him sprang the sun and moon; from man, the sun; from woman, the moon. The laws of his mind, the periods of his actions externized themselves into day and night, into the year and seasons. But, having made for himself this huge shell, his waters retired; he no longer fills the veins and veinlets; he is shrunk to a drop. He sees that the structure still fits him, but fits him colossally. Say, rather once it fitted him, now it corresponds to him from far and on high. . . ." [*CW*, 1:42]

If we once existed within a mythic world, peopling the cosmos with gods that were our unconscious projections, those myths—Emerson complains—have become nearly lifeless objects. Because one "works on the world" with "understanding alone" (42–43), one is cut off from divine "Reason."

In this vision of the origin and history of consciousness, an original process of mythmaking led inexorably to an increased distance between human beings and divinity. Having "externized" the "laws" of the mind into divine images such as the sun and moon, we found that these external images then became alienated from us. The very act of worship, by setting up external images of God, signified an increased distance from divinity. Sooner or later, we become aware of this distance and feel "shrunk to a drop" compared to the magnificence of our icons; we see "that the structure still fits" but "fits . . . colossally." At this point, we slip from participation in divine being. Emerson's rhetoric in *Nature*, and throughout his early works, is designed to resist such secularization.

Attempting to articulate lost mythic power, Emerson defines the psychological effects that signify its elusive proximity. For example, impressions of "strangeness" half suggest what has been lost: "Yet sometimes he starts in his slumber, and wonders at himself and his house, and muses strangely at the resemblance betwixt him and it" (*CW*, 1:42). Because it is defined as the symptom of a transpersonal and divine unconscious, rather than as the index of private nightmares, such "strangeness" is not uncanny for Emerson. In his divine register, what might be uncanny becomes numinous; it awakens "the emotion of the sublime" (2:166). For beneath everyday consciousness, he finds the realm of "Instinct," an "elemental power" that "is not conscious power" and that "is not inferior but superior to his will." If myths exist in the nineteenth century, in other words, they will be found in the unconscious.

A comparison of Emerson's rhetoric in this passage with that of Sampson Reed, one of his sources, is instructive. Like Emerson, Reed argues in *Observations on the Growth of the Mind* for the expression of an inner spiritual energy that is revealed through the "correspondence" of mind and nature. But "correspondence" for Reed and Emerson means different things. Although both write for an age that they see as becoming increasingly secular, their strategies for defining and overcoming that decline are markedly dissimilar. Reed, unlike Emerson, unequivocally asserts that this declension is to be measured against God's revealed Word, which exists as an eternal standard. We must return to the "laws from which we have wandered," Reed proclaims; we must accept the "power of the Lord," realizing that "go where we will, the paternal roof, the broad canopy of heaven is extended over us."[47]

We can imagine that the man who criticizes his age for building "the sepulchres of the fathers" (*CW*, 1:7) would not follow Reed by invoking the "paternal roof" of divine authority. In contrast to Reed's evocation of an external spiritual standard, Emerson turns within. Since the Fall, Reed had observed, humans lack "the chart by which they might determine their moral longitude."[48] Reed defended the external authority of scripture as this "chart"; Emerson finds it within in an innate "moral sentiment" (*CW*, 1:77) revealed through successive stages of illumination, such as those embodied in the dialectical structure of *Nature*. Although Reed focuses upon the ideal, Emerson focuses both upon the ideal and the process of attaining it. This follows the Romantic quest pattern that M. H. Abrams documents throughout *Natural Supernaturalism*, for example in his discussion of Hegel's *Phenomenology of the Spirit*, whose "plot turns out to be the unwitting quest of the spirit to redeem itself by repossessing its own lost and sundered self, in an ultimate recognition of its own identity."[49] Both Reed and Emerson want regenerated vision, but in Emerson's discourse, as in Hegel's, it is the process of regeneration that occupies the center of attention. As a result, psychology begins to emerge as a separate field from within theology, for it is a short step from talking of the revelation of "God within" to exploring the dynamics of the unconscious. In Emerson's writing the object of faith shifts from God toward the psyche. But without the governor of an innate "moral sentiment," this shift—as Melville will amply illustrate—might lead to a dangerous inflation of the individual.

If a sense of alienation is central to Emerson's psychological myth-making, it also shapes his stance toward the act of writing. Despite his high admiration for Sampson Reed's "genius," Emerson found, when it came to writing *Nature*, that it was difficult to embrace Reed's metaphysical certainty. Nature, he discovered, was less tractable than Reed would have us believe; the gleams of the unconscious were more transitory and infrequent. Thus, after jotting down one of the most striking passages to be used in the utterance of his "poet" ("A man is a god in ruins"), Emerson paused to reflect upon the difficulties of composition, recalling in the process one of Reed's more inspiring precepts from his "Oration on Genius": "How hard to write the truth. 'Let a man rejoice in the truth and not that he has found it,' said my early oracle [Reed]. Well, so soon as I have seen the truth I clap my hands & rejoice & go back to see it & forward to tell man. I am so pleased therewith that presently it vanishes. Then am I submiss & it appears 'without observation.' I write it down, & it is gone" (*JMN*, 5:181). That language is limited and not perfectly suited to the needs of the spirit, despite the bravado of his contrary assertion in parts of *Nature*, is one of Emerson's more profound observations. In contrast to his yearning for correspondence, he recognizes that language will not, as Sampson Reed had asserted, always be "one with things." He realizes instead that "there are many things that refuse to be recorded, —perhaps the larger half. The unsaid part is the best of every discourse" (51).

Accordingly, Emerson places the most revolutionary aspects of his vision in *Nature* into the mouth of a fictive self, his Orphic "poet." Sampson Reed had no compunctions about ascending to prophetic levels of utterance, asserting the possibility of rending "the veil by which [the mind] would avoid the direct presence of Jehovah," but Emerson realizes that our imperfection circumscribes our vision and hence our rhetoric.[50] He, too, longs for that "apocalypse" of the mind in which the things of the world "shall reappear in their morning lustre" (*CW*, 1:21). But he also acknowledges, by placing within quotation marks "A man is a god in ruins," that this regeneration stands before him as an aspiration and not an accomplished fact.

Emerson's "poet" articulates a myth of human potential and our lapse from that ideal. But as myth, these Orphic assertions exist on a plane discontinuous with daily speech, discontinuous because—as Emerson observes, continuing to reflect upon the composition of this passage— often "the Reason refuses to play at couples with Understanding" (*JMN*, 5:181). This sense of a rift between the ideal and aspiration, between the noumenal intuitions of "Reason" and the phenomenal awareness of "Understanding," initiates Emerson's psychological mythmaking. It is the spiritual wounding that his writing attempts to heal. In *Nature* this gap opens a clearing for the unfolding of Emerson's vision. By defining our alienation from the original space in which his "poet" dwells, Emerson frames the voice of inspiration within a setting of potential interpretation. The ideal is established as a fiction demanding the reader's reinterpretation of the self for its validation. Only by accepting Emerson's revision of the self, his psychology of the unconscious, can the reader begin the process of spiritual unfolding that might culminate in regeneration.

We find a similar rhetorical strategy in "The American Scholar," where Emerson's presentation is designed to teach his audience how to recognize and interpret for themselves the lessons of the unconscious. For example, he discusses the interrelationship of unconscious projection and interpretive consciousness. "The preamble of thought," he explains, "the transition through which it passes from the unconscious to the conscious, is action" (*CW*, 1:59). By acting, the individual relates unconsciously to the world whose "attractions are the keys which unlock [one's] thoughts" (59). First, one "unfolds the sacred germ of his instinct" (61). Then afterward, in the calmness of reflection, the individual steps back to analyze the flower that has sprouted, the silk that has been woven: "A strange process too, this, by which experience is converted into thought, as a mulberry leaf is converted into satin. The manufacture goes forward at all hours" (59). The culmination of this mental alchemy is the moment of reflection, when the deed ceases to remain "immersed in our unconscious life" but instead "detaches itself from the life like ripe fruit, to become a thought of the mind" (60).

In such passages Emerson defines a pattern of reflection in which unmediated activity is so framed as to reveal previously unconscious energies. He assists this release of power by measuring his audience against symbols of regenerated being. The most striking of such emblems is his myth of "One Man," which constitutes the limit of transcendence toward which his audience is to aspire. Our lack of meaning, Emerson argues, results from our inability "to possess" ourselves (*CW*, 1:53). Our partiality is that of consciousness alienated from unconscious power. Consequently, our acts confront us as things, amputated limbs of the "One Man," fragments isolated from untapped psychic potential. Our goal, he suggests through this symbol, must be to reunite the broken god within, reconnecting his severed limbs. This transcendent image represents the joining together of isolated particles of energy, the scattered drops of the original "fountain of power" (53). It recalibrates individual being by aligning the disorder of random actions against an archetype of wholeness. Like magnetic particles falling into place, isolated persons have the potential to exhibit the contours of a collective energy, a patterning akin to Ezra Pound's "world of moving energies . . . magnetisms that take form, that are seen, or that border the visible."[51] Or, as Emerson himself observes in "Spiritual Laws" (in a passage that may have influenced Pound), a person's "genius" functions as a "selecting principle" like "the loadstone amongst splinters of steel" (2:84).

Through his evocation of such archetypes, Emerson sets up a gap between the alienated individual and an image of transfigured being. The distance between the individual and the ideal exists as an area to be traversed, a potential that must be bridged by the spark of spiritual aspiration. Emerson's auditor is taught to be aware of the gap between the Actual and the Ideal, then to aim toward a dream of a better self, the image of an ever-receding self-perfection. "The basis of Culture," Emerson later observed, "is that part of human nature which in philosophy is called the Ideal" (*EL*, 2:217). But no matter how fast one travels, "the ideal still craves a speed like a cannon ball, a speed like a wish" (218). Emerson awakens his audience to this quest by dramatizing their alienation and then by projecting before them myths that define the angle of spiritual desire toward the limit of transcendence. His discourse on the unconscious defines this process of regeneration, at the same time that it motivates his audience to express the power buried within.

This release of energy from the unconscious turns the individual into an "active soul" (*CW*, 1:56) capable of changing his or her world:

Every spirit builds itself a house; and beyond its house, a world; and beyond its world, a heaven. Know then, that the world exists for you. For you is the phenomenon perfect. What we are, that only can we see. All that Adam had, all that Caesar could, you have and can do. Adam called his house, heaven and earth; Caesar called his house, Rome; you perhaps call yours, a cobbler's trade; a hundred acres of ploughed land; or a scholar's garret. Yet line for line and point for point, your dominion is as great as theirs, though without fine names. Build, therefore, your own world. [44–45]

This passage (from the end of *Nature*) emphasizes the expression of unconscious energy through effective dwelling, an activity that Stanley Cavell calls "the accomplishment of inhabitation."[52] In this vision of existence things display what Heidegger was to call *Zuhandenheit*, a "readiness-to-hand" or human usefulness, that allows the individual to expand his or her "house," the scope of being.[53] It is striking that Emerson couples Adamic innocence with a figure of the history maker triumphantly at home in a world of his construction. Through productive activity, whether by naming the world's entities like Adam or by conquering its provinces like Caesar, one connects impulse with physical action, vision with being.

Activity, Emerson asserts, liberates unconscious energy and thus enables one to make a "world." Emerson's usage here is quite close to that of existential psychology. "World," Rollo May writes, "is never something static, something merely given which the person then 'accepts' or 'adjusts to' or 'fights.' It is rather a dynamic pattern which, so long as I possess self-consciousness, I am in the process of forming and designing. Thus Binswanger speaks of world as 'that toward which the existence has climbed and according to which it has designed itself. . . .'"[54] Elsewhere, Emerson's term for the world that one designs is *dominion*. "So much only of life as I know by experience," he observes in "The American Scholar," "so much of the wilderness have I vanquished and planted, or so far have I extended my being, my dominion" (*CW*, 1:59). Being-in-the-world ("experience") leads to the extension of one's world-design ("dominion"). The world in which one exists, Emerson reiterates, should be the world one constructs through the exercise of innate power. The alternative is to exist like Poe's characters in a world filled with obdurate and intractable objects.

Emerson's presentation of the unconscious as both divine source and as dynamic power confronts him with a potential contradiction. As "both teleological principle and ontological substratum, both final cause and energy source," Emerson's unconscious offers his audience the assurance that spontaneous action realizes the potential of an innate divinity.[55] At this stage of his career, *instinct* and *Spirit* are used as synonyms—both terms referring to the power expressed by the "divine oracle" within (*EL*, 2:304). Each person, Emerson asserts, needs to rely upon that spiritual energy as "the ground of his being" (298). But recognition of the arbitrary uniqueness of individual instinct (of the unconscious as personal) threatens faith in this divine source by narrowing the unconscious to the expression of individual will. The consequence would be the "grounding" of one's being upon what amounts to caprice or whim.

It is the threat that the unconscious might be personal, rather than collective, that haunts Romantic psychology in America. Emerson is largely able to repress this threat in his early works, but the writings of Poe, Hawthorne, and Melville demonstrate the psychological horrors that accrue from an unrestrained faith in what amounts to personal impulse. For these writers, the unconscious is *only* personal; there is no "correspondence" between its promptings and some larger, transpersonal whole such as Emerson's Oversoul or Nature. In effect, this redefinition of the unconscious cuts the individual adrift. Arthur Dimmesdale begins to experience this loss of bearings; Melville's Ahab and Pierre suffer the full consequences of an unrestrained libido divorced from any governor such as Emerson's innate "moral sentiment." Given the horrendous implications of faith in a merely personal unconscious, Emerson's evocation of the collective nature of the unconscious takes on a special urgency; for it represents the effort to maintain faith by displacing the ground of religion from church to psyche. Emerson offered his audience a means of securing individual identity to a transcendent mooring that, for a while at least, appeared stable. Although this secular religion eventually failed for most Americans, one must not deny its initial imaginative energy or its residual effects for later literary generations. In subsequent chapters I shall examine the appeal of this psychological myth for Thoreau, Whitman, and Fuller.

THREE

Thoreau's Landscape of Being

"SUBSTANTIVE BEING"

Emerson spent his life thinking about the mind; Thoreau spent his learning how to live economically. Explicit ethical imperatives, he came to see, are unnecessary for an individual attuned to his own nature. As a result Thoreau replaces the analogies of Emersonian "correspondence," as well as Emerson's moralizing, with symbolic action. "Thoreau recognized the importance of concrete ceremonial," Joel Porte comments, "because . . . he believed that religious experience was coterminous with the experience of the body and that he could make neither life nor art out of an abstraction."[1] In Thoreau's writing, not only images but the gestures of living itself become symbols expressing the contours of character. The centered individual, unfolding in a rhythm determined only by inner necessity, no longer needs signs of transcendent meaning, emblems pointing toward an Emersonian realm of archetypal ideas. Instead, he measures existence against the standard of simplified and economical being. Emerson imagines perfection as the purification of vision; Thoreau finds perfection in the simplification of life. As a result, his writing moves inductively, from being toward vision, instead of following the deductive curve of Emerson's idealizing rhetoric.

Emerson's sun, the Platonic glare of intellection, contrasts with Thoreau's fondness for dusks at Walden Pond. Existence, Thoreau knew, never comes in a pure form; it is imperfect and shaded. At the other extreme, Emerson had argued in "The American Scholar" for the "distillation" of "life into truth"—a process he described as creating a "perfect vacuum" from which "the conventional, the local, the perishable" has been excluded (*CW*, 1:55). Such a purification of existence refines away precisely the temporal and spatial phenomena that Thoreau focuses upon as the center of being. His interest is in history, in seasons passing—not in eternal perfection. Emerson's and Thoreau's views of time, as a result, are complementary, Emerson's heaven of eternal ideas contrasting with Thoreau's paradise of the specific. We might say that Emerson and Thoreau represent the Platonic and the Aristotelean strains of the American Renaissance; Emerson's *Nature*, a quasi-philosophical treatise, standing against Thoreau's "Natural History of Massachusetts." "When our river overflows its banks in the spring," Thoreau writes in the latter work, "the wind from the meadows is laden with a strong scent of musk, and by its freshness advertises me of an unexpected wildness" (*PT*, 42). In contrast to Emerson's tendency to shift from the particularities of existence toward the universal mind, Thoreau roots the reader more firmly in space and in time—in the world's "wildness."

Both Emerson and Thoreau confront, in different ways, a dilemma central to nineteenth-century psychological mythmaking: how to maintain a balance between light and darkness, rational spirit and physical energy. As this balance is upset, psychological models fragment into partial views that give spirit or the body supremacy. Spirit divided from matter degenerates into a lifeless and bodiless moralism—into spectral preachers delivering spectral sermons, to paraphrase Emerson's "Divinity School Address" (*CW*, 1:85). At the other extreme, bodily impulse isolated from rational control turns into destructive and violent energy. The goal is somewhere between—for example, in Emerson's vision of Christ who "saw that God incarnates himself in man, and evermore goes forth anew to take possession of his world" (81). By focusing upon the incarnation of spiritual energy through the body, Emerson balances spirit and physical nature. Spiritual energy, he argues, demands physical form for its articulation.

But at times we find even more radical attempts by Emerson to connect spirit and body. Perhaps the most famous of these occasions occurs in *Nature*, at the end of the section entitled "Idealism." Here, Emerson caps a long proof that "motion, poetry, physical and intellectual science, and religion, all tend to affect our conviction of the reality of the external world" by a seemingly willful affirmation of the physical life of the body: "I own there is something ungrateful in expanding too curiously the particulars of the general proposition, that all culture tends to imbue us with idealism. I have no hostility to nature, but a child's love to it. I expand and live in the warm day like corn and melons" (*CW*, 1:35). Although one cannot escape the impression that Emerson looks up, sees where his argument is going, and stops himself just short of a solipsistic abyss, it is also clear that this passage represents an attempt to preserve the phenomenal world and to elevate it into a symbol of spirit. If we read Emerson as denying idealism or as wavering between idealism and materialism, we invoke the either-or epistemology that he is trying to sidestep. In the face of a dualistic terminology partially obscuring his purpose, he attempts here to assert both nature and spirit—to lift nature up to the level of spirit, while retaining a grasp of physical qualities.[2]

Emerson states his intention in the following terms: "I wish only to indicate the true position of nature in regard to man . . . *as the ground which to attain is the object of human life, that is, of man's connexion with nature*" (*CW*, 1:36, italics mine). The problem is that we do not see nature clearly enough—our connection to it has become abstract and hence too loose, neither high nor deep. In contrast, Emerson's Unitarian contemporaries rested content with abstractions that impeded their "original relation to the universe" (7). As an antidote to such abstraction, Emerson asserts that "the mind is part of the nature of things" (37), that it is neither wholly spiritual nor wholly physical in its provenance, but a mixture of both. He attempts to bypass the "hypothesis" of "idealism" by insisting that "the demands of the spirit" include "the existence of matter" (37). Emerson's terms for the inextricable blending of spirit and matter are "substantive being" and "consanguinity" (37).

In twentieth-century terms Emerson strives here toward an "incarnate philosophy," as he attempts to put the mind "back into" the body. Maurice Merleau-Ponty defines this task in a passage that serves as an excellent commentary on Emerson's text:

> [O]nce man is defined as consciousness, he becomes cut off from all things, from his body and from effective existence. He must therefore be defined as a relation to instruments and objects—a relation which is not simply one of thought but which involves him in the world in such a way as to give him an external aspect, an outside, to make him "objective" at the same time he is "subjective." This can be accomplished by defining him as a being who "suffers" or "senses," that is, as a being with a natural and social situation but one who is also open, active, and able to establish his autonomy on the very ground of his dependence.[3]

This passage helps us to see that Emerson in *Nature* attempts to avoid a definition of the person solely as abstract consciousness, in terms of pure "light." Instead, he starts to define a being with a physical, "objective" aspect—one who is inextricably related to the world and others through productive activity. In this way, he turns away from the abstract realm of ethereal notions toward a philosophy of embodiment. This is not to deny Emerson's ever-present idealism, but to suggest that it is mixed with a position that partially foreshadows an existential vision of "being-in-the-world."

Without an appreciation of this existential motive, it is difficult to account for the fact that in Emerson's hands the "heart of light" starts to darken, to take on a shadow. This darkening is reflected in the widespread realization, among Emerson and his contemporaries, that life must regain depth, density, solidity, weight—not float off toward an unreal ideal. As we shall see, the fictions of Hawthorne and Melville take this process much further—by focusing both upon the opaque, social aspects of individual being and the psychological consequences of extreme emotional states. But Thoreau also attempts to put the mind back into the body. By reversing Emerson's equation, he gives greater weight to physical being than to spiritual presence. Although the Emersonian strain of idealism periodically surfaces in his writing, it is framed within dramatizations of bodily activity that constantly remind the reader of the need for physical discipline. As we have seen, Emerson slides easily into evocations of a timeless presence; Thoreau insists that such self-fulfillment depends upon careful attention to the body's requirements.

The danger of Emerson's approach to self-reliance, Thoreau suggests by counterexample, is that it is too easily misread. Although Thoreau reiterates the Emersonian faith in the divinity of our innate spiritual powers, he modifies that vision by grounding it upon the imagination of physical existence and labor. Thoreau's concreteness reminds one of Karl Marx's early dialogue with Hegelian idealism. "*Man* is a directly *natural being*," Marx wrote in 1844, in response to abstract conceptions of human being: "As a natural being, and as a living natural being he is . . . endowed with *natural powers* and *faculties*, which exist in him as tendencies and abilities, as *drives*. . . . The fact that man is an *embodied*, living, real, sentient, objective being with natural powers, means that he has *real, sensuous objects* as the objects of his being, or that he can only express his being in real, sensuous objects."[4] "Talk of a divinity in man!" we hear Thoreau exclaiming in similar terms to an internalized "Emerson," "Look at the teamster on the highway, wending to market by day or night; does any divinity stir within him?" (*Wa*, 7). Like Marx, Thoreau reminds us constantly of the physical side of life and of the dependence of spiritual expression upon a physical foundation. Despite his affirmation in *Nature* of "substantive being," Emerson frequently represses this embodied, sensuous aspect of human experience.

As a result, Emerson comes perilously close to that form of intellectual alienation in which "the subject knowing itself as absolute self-consciousness" turns "real man and real nature" into "mere predicates" of "*absolute spirit*."[5] If we see human activity as the function of a divine unconscious expressing itself from within, then doesn't "replete, living, sensuous, concrete activity" turn into "a mere abstraction"?[6] This is the Emerson that many critics have given us—the idealist who separated himself from lived experience and for whom nature itself became "an *entity of thought.*"[7] But Emerson was well aware that "abstract thought" might become alienated from "real sensuous existence."[8] "I expand and live in the warm day," he affirmed, "like corn and melons." To the extent that such an appreciation for concrete, physical process orients Emerson's writing, he escapes from the threat of intellectual alienation. We hear this assertion of the physical in his reiteration of the need for activity, relationship, and the spread of "dominion." For by showing us how "spirit" incarnates itself in concrete activities, he is able to replace the possibility of intellectual alienation with the image of productive labor.

Thoreau approaches this problem from a different angle. Rather than uniting spirit and body through the analysis of human activity as the predicate of unconscious power, he begins with a consideration of how decentered physical existence inhibits spiritual expression. Beginning with the body's needs and demands, he then works downward toward the spiritual center. Unlike Emerson, he does not "apprehend the absolute" and immediately escape all "affinity" with "time and space" and the "relations of matter" (*CW*, 1:35). In contrast to his mentor, Thoreau avoids portraying the natural world as "a great shadow pointing always to the sun behind us" (37), for he realizes that uncontrolled Platonism cancels the sensuous side of existence.

Like Marx, instead of Plato or Emerson, Thoreau reminds us that the condition of our senses can be an important index of spiritual fulfillment. Part of the human expense of physical alienation, Marx argues, is the corruption of the senses. That "human sensibility" which "can only come into being . . . through humanized nature" is damaged in a world of private property, where the products of labor turn into objects that are bought and sold.[9] The act of building up a bank account or accumulating valuable, fetishized objects becomes a substitute for living. "The less you *are*, the less you express your life, the more you *have*," Marx writes, "the greater is your *alienated* life and the greater is the serving of your alienated being. Everything which the economist takes from you in the way of life and humanity, he restores to you in the form of *money* and *wealth*."[10] In the process, all the "human relations to the world—seeing, hearing, smelling, tasting, touching, thinking, observing, feeling, desiring, acting, loving" are degraded.[11] Thoreau portrays an analogous process of sensuous degradation as a sign of alienation. "Most men," he complains, ". . . are so occupied with the factitious cares and superfluously coarse labors of life that its finer fruits cannot be plucked by them" (*Wa*, 6). Only by reforming one's life so as to escape those pressures that defer self-realization can the individual regain the "finest qualities of our nature," which "like the bloom on fruits, can be preserved only by the most delicate handling" (6).

In this regard, Thoreau demonstrates that "the senses"—as Fredric Jameson paraphrases Marx—are "the results of a long process of differentiation . . . within human history."[12] His writing thus becomes what Hans Robert Jauss describes as "a medium capable of forming and altering perception, in which the 'formation of the senses' chiefly takes place."[13] Attending to the subtlest of impressions, "a faint music from all the horizon" (J, 2:241), Thoreau demands of himself and others a constant alertness. "No method or discipline," he cautions, "can supersede the necessity of forever being on the alert" (357). The alternative is to sink back into a "dullness of sight, a stagnation of the vital circulations, and a general deliquium and sloughing off of all the intellectual faculties" (Wa, 105).

Thoreau's close attention to the degradation and refinement of sensibility should warn us of the danger of approaching his writing with any methodology predicated upon the split between spirit and matter. His reader is confronted with the challenge of interpreting moments of illumination without slipping into a critical methodology that privileges visionary presence over physical being, mental over bodily phenomena. "To make a perfect man—," Thoreau reminds us, "the Soul must be much like the body not too unearthly & the body like the soul. The one must not deny & oppress the other" (J, 2:240). The result of such views is a literary emphasis upon the process of existence. Rather than theorizing about the mind, Thoreau dramatizes the sensuous appropriation of reality. He focuses, in other words, upon ontology—the art of living, of being.[14] In order to see the dimensions of that subject, we need a new way of reading Walden. A good place to look for the tools we need is in the branch of psychology dedicated to bypassing dualistic terminologies—the field known as existential psychotherapy, or Daseinsanalyse.

RECONSTRUCTING THE WORLD

Rather than writing like Emerson about the unconscious, Thoreau describes how it feels to sense the approach of emerging powers. Consequently, his focus falls upon a person's concrete being-in-the-world, a perspective similar to that presented in Medard Boss's Psychoanalysis and Daseinsanalysis. "It would be inappropriate," Boss comments, ". . . to regard Daseinsanalytic statements as 'derived' from factors assumed to lie behind that which is described, or to expect that such statements can be 'proved' by reduction to imagined presuppositions."[15] Rather than reducing experience to an idea like the unconscious, Boss commits himself to exploring human existence as "a concrete occurrence."[16] His subject is *Dasein* (literally, "being there"), which he defines as "the manifold particular modes of human behavior and of . . . different ways of relating toward things and fellow beings." Instead of analyzing the *ego, consciousness*, or the *psyche*, Boss avoids terminology that presupposes a subject cut off from some separate reality. Following Heidegger, he bypasses such dualism by beginning with our intentional involvement with our world; thus Boss's emphasis falls upon patterns of relationship, not upon psychological functions.

Boss views human being as a "world-disclosing sphere of activity."[17] Each person, in his view, displays a different pattern of interest, a unique style of inhabiting the world. By describing the world a person experiences, Boss is able to draw an existential map of that person's world-design. This design is never viewed as a fiction or a delusion, but rather as the way the world exists for that specific individual. Each person, for example, experiences time and space uniquely. For some, like the characters in many of Poe's stories, space is constricted; others may live in a world of open horizons. Similarly, time may be perceived as fast or slow, as monotonous or as punctuated with ecstatic moments. By attending to the temporal and spatial patterns that an individual discloses, we can better understand the way that person unfolds being through relating to the world.

Boss's existential analysis suggests that, to understand Thoreau's vision of the psyche, we must analyze how he dramatizes experience, how he depicts the act of dwelling. Unlike many of his contemporaries, Thoreau does not create what Hawthorne terms "Allegories of the Heart." His images do not point toward some hidden psychological reality. Instead, Thoreau attends to how the changing aspect of physical reality indicates the proximity or distance of previously unconscious power. In Stanley Cavell's words, he is concerned with the act of "*placing* ourselves in the world."[18] Cavell's *The Senses of Walden* provides the groundwork for an existential reading of Thoreau, for Cavell shows us that the subject of Walden is "dwelling" or "habitation."[19] By depicting a range of inauthentic and authentic being, Thoreau demonstrates the need for self-awareness, for a centered existence that escapes mystification, the "disease of the imagination."[20] The dilemma of many persons is that they are not conscious of their alienation and hence are unable to begin "the recovery of the self, as from an illness."[21]

Thoreau's point of departure, in *Walden*, is the attempt to make us aware of the "fabulous" (95), the imaginatively fabricated, aspect of reality. "What painters of scenery we are," he exclaims in his journal. "We impart to the landscape the perfect colors of our minds" (*J*, 1:466–67). His goal is to emphasize the fabricated, imaginary aspect of reality by showing us how subservience to the "smoke of opinion" (*Wa*, 8) and "routine" (96) has clouded the world. "By closing the eyes and slumbering—and consenting to be deceived by shows—," he observes, "men establish their daily life of routine and habit everywhere—which however is built on imaginary foundations" (*J*, 2:246). Most of us, he suggests, have diminished the scope of being by pursuing life styles that retard attention to the world and interest in our experience. As a result, we become incapable of perceiving life's "glory" (*Wa*, 99), the "bloom of the present moment" (111).

Rather than theorizing about the depths of the mind, Thoreau studies the existential effects of liberating unconscious power. He describes how the world's appearance changes for one who is in the process of becoming self-reliant. Such self-conscious restructuring of experience depends upon the awareness that reality is partially a product of our preconceptions, that our sense of existence is shaped by what Heidegger calls "fore-sight."[22] "In interpreting," Heidegger observes, "we do not, so to speak, throw a 'signification' over some naked thing which is present-at-hand, we do not stick a value on it; but when something within-the-world is encountered as such, the thing in question already has an involvement which is disclosed by our understanding of the world, and this involvement is one which gets laid out by the interpretation."[23] Thoreau expresses essentially the same hermeneutic awareness when he writes that the "universe constantly and obediently answers to our conceptions" (*Wa*, 97). Since human potential is bounded by one's capacity to imagine existence, the challenge confronting Thoreau is to expand the horizon of his reader's self-expectation. Each of us, he observes, constructs a "space about us"—"familiar and worn by us, appropriated and fenced in some way, and reclaimed from Nature" (130). Dwelling involves constructing a "world," in the sense of *Lebenswelt* or "lived-world" of experience—or, as Thoreau phrases it, the "objects which we behold make a world" (225). In *Walden* Thoreau attempts to re-form his reader's sense of the world—to expand the "prospect" (112) or "horizon" (130) within which the reader dwells.

Only by transforming the "medium through which we look" (*Wa*, 90) can we attain self-reliant perception unfogged by the "smoke of opinion" (8). In order to escape the "stereotyped but unconscious despair" (8) that mars so many lives, we need to "awaken" to the sources of creative power within—an awakening that leads to a sense of our world's "freshness." Accordingly, much of *Walden* aims at inculcating a world-view that transcends "slumbering," "routine," "habit," and "ennui" (96, 112). Ennui (the bête noir of nineteenth-century consciousness, haunting—for example—Baudelaire's *Fleurs du Mal*) connotes an absence of interest, an incapacity to direct one's energies toward any effective project in the world. Thoreau aims at rousing us from such spiritual torpor, as well as from routine and drudgery, by evoking our sense of wonder. Instead of being the "slave" of a rigid "opinion of himself" (7), we are encouraged to emancipate our being-in-the-world by learning how to labor productively for ourselves rather than for others.

Attempting to enlarge the "horizon" of our existence, Thoreau dramatizes throughout *Walden* a range of experience that revises any sense of the world constructed upon commercial premises. The grasping "skinflint" (195) who "would carry the landscape, who would carry his God, to market" (196) has lost the capacity to perceive the world's freshness or wonder. He exists in a reality that has been "profaned" (197) by being subordinated to the profit motive. Such crass commercialism obscures the purity and transparency of the landscape within which Thoreau would have us dwell. It prevents the establishment of a dialogic, I-thou, relationship between self and world by defining reality solely as a marketable product. As a result, all sense of the world's "strangeness" (171) evaporates, to be replaced by the habitual repetition of preprogrammed scripts written only in terms of the business ethic.

Like Marx, Thoreau would have us escape from that "alienation" of labor that results when the productive "human world" is subordinated to the "world of things."[24] Existing in a world that values money and things over human productivity, the individual becomes a "commodity" who must sell himself or herself in order to live. Throughout the "Economy" section of *Walden* Thoreau appalled looks at his neighbors who eagerly exchange their lives for fine houses, excursions, and expensive clothes. Reminding us that "the cost of a thing is the amount of what I will call life which is required to be exchanged for it" (31), he argues that we can only regain life's "fragrance" and "wonder" by simplifying both social and economic relationships. If less of existence is objectified into marketable objects, we might become an active force that constructs, rather than mortgages, our world. Only then can we gain the psychological freedom that is the necessary ground for self-reliance.

Thoreau challenges us to see a world in which more authentic dwelling is possible, rather than the commercialized construction of existence. The key to this realignment of being is our acceptance of the existential premise that the world can be "fresh" (*Wa*, 99) instead of "routine" in its appearance. As Thoreau transforms his reader's vision toward an acceptance of that expanded horizon, the experience of reading his text becomes what Wolfgang Iser describes as "an extension or broadening of . . . reality."[25] He does this in part by providing the reader with dramatized moments that function as emblems of regenerated perception. As Thoreau watches the locomotive speeding by Walden Pond, for example, he reflects that the engineer and his crew become "better men for the sight": "The engineer does not forget at night, or his nature does not, that he has beheld this vision of serenity and purity once at least during the day. Though seen but once, it helps to wash out State-street and the engine's soot" (193–94). Thoreau would place his readers in the position of that engineer, by challenging them to find a mode of being in which perception can nourish a vision of the world's "serenity and purity."

In the memorable phrases of Coleridge, Thoreau's dramatization of the world's "glory" ultimately aims at "awakening the mind's attention from the lethargy of custom and directing it to the loveliness and the wonders of the world before us; an inexhaustible treasure, but for which, in consequence of the film of familiarity and selfish solicitude, we have eyes yet see not, ears that hear not, and hearts that neither feel nor understand."[26] Our achievement of this awakening, Thoreau emphasizes, involves an arduous physical preparation. We must recognize the alienation in our own lives and work to overcome it before the full wonder of experience can appear. Thus half of Thoreau's project in *Walden* is to evoke the psychological and spiritual consequences of alienation; the other half, closer in spirit to Emerson's rhetoric of regeneration, involves the dramatization of moments of spiritual expectation and fulfillment, moments that demonstrate how wondrous "the world before us" might look to one with cleansed eyes.

As Thoreau turns from his diagnosis of alienation toward the dramatization of regenerated existence, he engages in *psychological mythmaking* in the sense we have been using this term. Like Emerson, he offers the reader emblems of perfected existence as paradigms of being. But rather than reflecting upon the divinity of the unconscious, Thoreau dramatizes for us the existential dimension of an uninhibited and unalienated spirituality. In place of a theory of the mind and its dynamics, he examines the immediate, sensual consequences of self-reliant existence. Such an approach reflects Thoreau's conviction that we "should not *play* life, or *study* it merely . . . but earnestly *live* it from beginning to end" (*Wa*, 51). Thus, Emerson studies his life for signs of regeneration that he then theorizes about, but Thoreau portrays the appearance that the world acquires when one lives with an expanded "horizon."

Thoreau encourages us to view this reconstruction of reality as a dramatic process. Each of us, he suggests, stages a different "clearing" or "horizon" (*Wa*, 130). Although many persons live unconsciously, enmeshed and mystified by a cloud of unexamined assumptions, it is possible to become aware that our sense of reality is an imaginative construction, what Thoreau calls the "medium through which we look" (90). In order to gain some measure of control over this medium, he suggests that we need to be both actor and spectator of our lives and thus be "beside ourselves" (134), reflecting upon daily events as phenomena staged within the field of perception. "I only know myself," Thoreau comments, "as a human entity; the scene, so to speak, of thoughts and affections; and am sensible of a certain doubleness by which I can stand as remote from myself as another" (135). Similarly, he describes his life as "a drama of many scenes and without an end" (112). Although he manifests an engaging simplicity of being, Thoreau's Canadian woodchopper lacks just this capacity to understand the dramatic aspect of self-perception: "He would not play any part" (147). But only to the extent that we can see existence as a play that we both stage and act can we escape the primitive naïveté of the woodchopper, a natural man, and gain the self-consciousness necessary to reshape the role we are acting. Like Friedrich von Schiller's "sentimental poet," Thoreau "*reflects* upon the impression that objects make upon him"; he attempts "to restore out of himself that unity that has been disrupted by abstraction, to complete the humanity within himself, and from a limited condition to pass over into an infinite one."[27]

From this perspective, Thoreau's text enacts a play, a staging of self-consciousness, that proposes the assumption of a more authentic part. The "real reader," Wolfgang Iser argues, "is always offered a particular role to play, and it is this role that constitutes the concept of the implied reader"; "speech acts," he comments elsewhere, ". . . are successful to the degree in which the recipient is aware of and assumes the role intended for him by the speaker."[28] Throughout *Walden* Thoreau attempts to make us aware that our preconceptions, frequently unconscious, stage the "reality" in which we live. He aims to expand that existential "horizon," to widen our "prospect," so that we might exist more fully and realize more of our human potential. "The universe is wider than our views of it," he affirms (320), hoping through such assertions to project a different stage for us, one that is closer to the "wild" that lies outside of our prejudices. Slipping into the spiritual rhythms of Thoreau's "I," we see for a while through his eyes. In Wolfgang Iser's terms, this dramatization of regenerative potential is the "gestalt" that Thoreau constructs for us—the "living world" within which he stages our dwelling.[29]

Thoreau's dramatization of existence, in contrast to Emerson's, compels us to live in "front" of, in relation to, the natural world. Emerson, as we have seen, pieced together and collated individual perceptions into idealized structures, such as the ascending rhetoric of *Nature*. As a result, his arguments follow a dialectic that negates and elevates experience but does not actively preserve it. Deaths, like those of Emerson's first wife Ellen and his brother Charles, were compensated for by negating the permanent impact of experience in favor of ideal patterns. But lost entirely is the preserved memory, unchanged, recorded precisely as it happened or should have happened (if emotion has been "recollected in tranquillity"). In contrast, Thoreau's "Wordsworthian" landscapes—as Perry Miller describes them—retain significant details associated with specific moments of being.[30]

By preserving and reflecting upon actual experiences, Thoreau temporalizes and spatializes his imagination to the extent that it defines its own processes, not as an ascent back toward a lost perfection, but rather in terms of an actual existential geography. "Entomology extends the limits of our being in a new direction," he observes in "A Natural History of Massachusetts," "so that I walk in nature with a greater sense of space and freedom. It suggests besides, that the universe is not rough-hewn, but perfect in its details. Nature will bear the closest inspection; she invites us to lay our eye level with the smallest leaf, and take an insect view of its plain. She has no interstices; every part is full of life. I explore, too, with pleasure, the sources of the myriad sounds which crowd the summer moon, and which seem the very grain and stuff of which eternity is made" (*PT*, 35). Thoreau gains "a greater sense of space and freedom" by moving closer to the landscape; he "extends" his "being" by learning how to inhabit nature in a new way—in this case, like an insect. Reading a "Report on the Invertebrate Animals," Thoreau learns "to put a new value on space and time" (*PT*, 54–55). Orienting himself in different kinds of space and time—insect, animal, and human—he measures existence geographically, according to different styles of habitation and movement in given physical terrains.

Especially characteristic of Thoreau's writing is the sense of concrete movement through space and time. "Most of Thoreau's works," Lawrence Buell comments, "might be described as catalogues extended through time and space. His favorite form . . . is the romantic excursion: a ramble ("Walking") or trip (*Cape Cod*) or sojourn (*Walden*) which takes on overtones of a spiritual quest as the speaker proceeds."[31] Portraying himself as floating down the Merrimack River or drifting upon Walden Pond, Thoreau focuses upon the spatiality of existence. Similarly, a keen sense of temporal rhythm enables him to measure his development against the world's changes. Springtime and dawn, for example, become times of awakening and unfolding. Like Wordsworth's *Prelude*, Thoreau's writing is marked by a peripatetic and discursive narrative structure that is punctuated by heightened "spots of time." Both writers portray life as an arduous voyage or journey oriented in terms of occasional ecstatic moments.

Such concern with spatial and temporal placement leads Thoreau at times toward the projection of what Georges Poulet calls "the interior distance," a subjective landscape that parallels the distinctive gestures of being. "My thought," Poulet writes,

> is a space in which my thoughts take place, in which they take their place. I watch them arrive, pass on, wander aside or sink out of sight, and I distinguish them at spatial and temporal distances which never cease to vary. My thought is not made up solely of my thoughts; it is made up also, even more perhaps, of all the *interior distance* which separates me from, or draws me closer to, that which I am able to think. For all that I think is in myself who think it. The distance is not merely an interval; it is an ambient milieu, a field of union.[32]

Thoreau's writing exhibits a similar phenomenological concern with thinking as a field or stream of reflection. For example, in *A Week on the Concord and Merrimack Rivers*, ideas—as well as historical anecdotes and specific observations—float in and out of the narrator's consciousness as the reader is "subjected to the flux of events."[33] Thoreau establishes an imaginative milieu, an inner geography in which the "current of our thoughts made as sudden bends as the river, which was continually opening new prospects to the east or south" (*CMR*, 339).

Throughout *A Week* Thoreau imagines self-realization in geographical terms. "A man's life," he writes, "should be constantly as fresh as this river. It should be the same channel, but a new water every instant. . . . Most men have no inclination, no rapids, no cascades, but marshes, and alligators, and miasma instead" (*CMR*, 132). In the autumn, "behind the rustling leaves, and the stacks of grain, and the bare clusters of the grape," Thoreau becomes aware of "the field of a wholly new life, which no man has lived" (377). The challenge each man faces, he argues, is to "stand on such a bottom as will sustain him, and if one gravitates downward more strongly than another, he will not venture on those meads where the latter walks securely, but rather leave the cranberries which grow there unraked by himself" (387). Going "behind the ordinary" (383), attempting "to penetrate the spaces of the real" (386), Thoreau attempts to recover contact with a fresh and wild landscape, "an always unexplored and infinite region" that "makes off on every side from the mind, further than to sunset" (359). In such a place, he shows us, being regains both wonder and freedom.

In order to imagine the future unfolding of the self, Thoreau projects in *Walden*, as well, scenes of interior distance that map the extension of being in geographical terms. "It is a matter of great difficulty," Coleridge had observed, ". . . to fix the attention of men on the world within them, to induce them to study the processes and superintend the works which they are themselves carrying on in their own minds."[34] As a means to this end, Thoreau links his numerous descriptions of Walden Pond with corresponding bodies of "water" within. Human beings, he suggests, have their own interior "coves and inlets," a landscape that transforms according to the state of the soul: "When this bar is gradually increased by storms, tides, or currents, or there is a subsidence of the waters, so that it reaches to the surface, that which was harbored becomes an individual lake, cut off from the ocean, wherein the thought secures its own conditions, changes, perhaps, from salt to fresh, becomes a sweet sea, dead sea, or a marsh" (*Wa*, 291). The goal of the self-reliant individual, according to Thoreau, should be to explore this world within: "Be rather a Mungo Park, the Lewis and Clarke and Frobisher, of your own streams and oceans; explore your own higher latitudes. . . . be a Columbus to whole new continents and worlds within you, opening new channels, not of trade, but of thought" (321). In such passages Thoreau projects an interior landscape that parallels the world without. The exploration of "whole new continents and worlds within" finds its correlative in the capacity to inhabit more effectively the world in which one dwells.

At the center of Thoreau's landscape of being is the image of "presence"—of existence lived entirely in the present and present to, in contact with, the real. The *"past,"* he observes in *A Week*, "cannot be *presented"* (155) because "a distance of relation" makes the past "dusky" (156–57). His ultimate goal is to overcome such distance and to regain a sense of "what is" (155), of "the actual glory of the universe" (174). We cannot really *"know"* what we are *told* merely" (365), but rather what we experience and see. Sensing "faint revelations of the Real" (385), Thoreau leads his readers from a "common sense view of things" to "seeing them as men cannot describe them" (386). At the limit of this process is a sense of illumination and liberated being. Developing the "divine germs called the senses" (382), he aspires toward a *"natural* life" in which the "winds should be his breath, the seasons his moods" (379). "At rare intervals" in Thoreau's writing, such presence is attained as "we rise above the necessity of virtue into an unchangeable morning light, in which we have only to live right on and breathe the ambrosial air" (369). The following evokes such a moment of presence: "Whole weeks and months of my summer life slide away in thin volumes like mist and smoke, till at length, some warm morning, perchance, I see a sheet of mist blown down the

brook to the swamp, and I float as high above the fields with it" (295).
The challenge, for Thoreau's reader, is to explain the spiritual and existential dimensions of such moments—the exact nature of the promise
they hold forth.

Thoreau's scenes of presence realize in concrete terms Emerson's call
to immediate experience. "Why should we not have a poetry and philosophy of insight and not of tradition," Emerson had asked, "and a
religion by revelation to us, and not the history of theirs?" (*CW*, 1:7).
This attainment of insight and revelation, according to Emerson, involves a mode of existence that escapes deferral or anticipation by center-
ing itself totally in the present. But though Emerson theorized about the
need for presence, Thoreau's writing actively depicts what Emerson calls
life "in the present, above time" (2:39)—moments when we are "embosomed for a season in nature, whose floods of life stream around and
through us, and invite us by the powers they supply, to action propor-
tioned to nature" (1:7). Emerson supplies the theoretical description of
such moments, but Thoreau's writing dramatizes these scenes of presence—moments of self-realization in which aim and action, self-awareness and being, are conjoined. Yet if the heart of Thoreau's vision of self-
reliance is the image of pure, effortless being beyond the vicissitudes of
frustration or guilt, he frames that vision so as to emphasize both the
physical and spiritual discipline necessary for regeneration. We see this
especially in *Walden*, where Thoreau's imagination of timeless presence
is approached only through heightened sensitivity to the body's existence in space and time.

SCENES OF PRESENCE AND PROSPECT

The terminology of contemporary literary theory helps us to see more
clearly the mechanics of Thoreau's rhetoric of presence. In *Poetry and
Repression* Harold Bloom argues that Emerson's self-reliance depends
upon the repression of prior influence; its "Primal Lie" is the "denial of
Nachträglichkeit, of being as a nation 'after the event.'"[35] In other words,
Emerson attempts to eliminate from awareness what Bloom calls the
"anxiety of influence." Rather than defining the past as constitutive of
the present, he denies it as a "faded wardrobe" (*CW*, 1:7) that one can
dispense with. Such a position, Bloom observes, comes into direct opposition with Freud's view that the past forms an integral part of the
present, a part that each person revises and rearranges after the event in
the light of present concerns. Freud's concept of *Nachträglichkeit* entails
both an acceptance of historical conditioning and the analysis of such

belated revision; it sees the present moment as part of a larger system of "absent" forces that defer self-presence and self-fulfillment. One can never live entirely in the present because the past—in Freud's view—is always with us.

Thoreau, as we have seen, imagines existence as an ongoing river; Freud depicts it as a stream blocked by "unnavigable" repressions: "I begin the treatment . . . by asking the patient to give me the whole story of his life and illness, but even so the information I receive is never enough to let me see my way about the case. This first account may be compared to an unnavigable river whose stream is at one moment choked by masses of rock and at another divided and lost among shallows and sandbanks."[36] When interpreting his patients' dreams, Freud was struck by "gaps . . . in the content of the dream itself," "points" where "the content was, as it were, extinguished."[37] The process of psychotherapy involves the excavation and illumination of such gaps through the recovery and assimilation of material buried in the personal unconscious.

In contrast to the reconstruction of the psyche's fault lines and blind spots, Thoreau focuses instead upon the recovery and expression of a power that is imagined as eliminating absence and deferral. Unlike those many desperate persons who allow their lives to be determined by uncontrollable forces, he labors to achieve a self-aware existence oriented toward self-perfection. "My life," he observes in his journal, "will cut its own channel—like the mountain stream which by the longest ridges—and by level prairies is not kept from the sea finally" (J, 1:297). As Thoreau becomes aware of the power flowing through his life's "channel," he is able to visualize his psyche as a dynamic system with its own medium of exchange, equivalent to what Carl Jung later called "libido" or "psychic energy."

It is difficult, if not impossible, to discuss the mind's development without some concept of energy or force, whether Emerson's "spirit," Arthur Schopenhauer's "Will," or Henri-Louis Bergson's "élan vital."[38] Each concept allows the mind to perform operations on its own energy by treating it "as though it were hypostatized."[39] Focused into an image or a symbol, the mind's force can become the object of analysis and metamorphosis. Thus Jung writes about the "flow" of libido like electricity through "channels"; and Freud describes how libido can "flow backwards," be "dammed up," "find an outlet" through open "channels," even how it "bursts through its banks at the weakest spot."[40] Without such images of psychic energy, that energy itself would be inaccessible. With them, one is able to define what Jung calls a "disposable energy" within the self, an energy that can be directed into different projects and toward different goals.[41] Symbols of psychic energy thus facilitate the expansion of consciousness by defining a "pool" of creative potential that can be tapped.

At his most ecstatic, Thoreau uses the image of life's channel to suggest that existence might become a process of frictionless being, a completely fluid and unimpeded flow beyond repression. Thoreau's scenes of presence dramatize this potential escape from repression by embodying the antithesis of what Jacques Derrida calls *différance*. According to Derrida, the idea of presence is a fiction that later writers like Friedrich Nietzsche and Freud deconstruct by revealing "the temporal and temporalizing mediation of a detour that suspends the accomplishment or fulfillment of 'desire' or 'will.'"[42] But the fulfillment of desire or will is exactly what Emerson and Thoreau see as transpiring during moments of perfected self-reliance. At such times, temporal delay is imagined as disappearing as one feels immersed in an inexhaustible immediacy. "I was rich," Thoreau recalls, "if not in money, in sunny hours and summer days, and spent them lavishly" (*Wa*, 192). The ideal of being, as Thoreau expressed it elsewhere in *Walden*, is to live "in the present moment" (17).

In several important passages Thoreau dramatizes himself as having achieved such presence, as existing spontaneously beyond the pressure of time:

> There were times when I could not afford to sacrifice *the bloom of the present moment* to any work. . . . Sometimes, in a summer morning, having taken my accustomed bath, I sat in my sunny doorway from sunrise till noon, rapt in a revery. . . . I grew in those seasons like corn in the night. . . . I realized what the Orientals meant by contemplation and the forsaking of works. . . . My days were not days of the week, bearing the stamp of any heathen deity, nor were they minced into hours and fretted by the ticking of a clock. [*Wa*, 111–12, italics mine]

Time slows down and even seems to stand still in this passage, almost reaching a point of stasis as Thoreau becomes absorbed in a reverie of present existence.[43] In the words of Gaston Bachelard, he "re-enter[s] the world of confidence, of confident being, which is the proper world for reverie."[44] A representation of dwelling in a place "forever new and unprofaned" (88), such a passage functions as an emblem of regenerated being that is held up for the reader as a model. Evoking a vision of life beyond alienation, such a scene of presence embodies what John Carlos Rowe calls "a metaphysics of natural presence."[45]

"I grew in those seasons like corn in the night." Echoing Emerson's assertion that "I expand and live in the warm day like corn and melons"

(*CW*, 1:35), this image of spontaneous, organic growth evokes the presence of fully accessible energies that contrasts with the more homely image of Thoreau laboriously hoeing his beans. It idealizes the "substantive being" (*CW*, 1:37) that Emerson could achieve at only rare moments but that Thoreau saw as the basis of existence.

"We do not understand the notes of birds," Emerson had complained in *Nature*. "The fox and the deer run away from us; the bear and the tiger rend us" (*CW*, 1:39). Such an admission of estrangement from nature contrasts with Thoreau's assimilation of natural rhythm:

> The breams are so careful of their charge that you may stand close by in the water and examine them at your leisure. I have thus stood over them half an hour at a time, and stroked them familiarly without frightening them, suffering them to nibble my fingers harmlessly, and seen them erect their dorsal fins in anger when my hand approached their ova, and have even taken them gently out of the water with my hand; though this cannot be accomplished by a sudden movement, however dextrous, for instant warning is conveyed to them through their denser element, but only by letting the fingers gradually close about them as they are poised over the palm, and with the utmost gentleness raising them slowly to the surface. [*CMR*, 27]

This passage dramatizes the integration of physical gesture with mental impulse. Slowing himself to the tempo of fish, Thoreau imaginatively inhabits a fluid medium in which sense and will blend into a unity of being. As in Yeats's image of the dancer at the conclusion of "Among School Children," body and spirit are presented as moving together in a harmony beyond the vicissitudes of time.

Motivated to aim toward existence in the present, the reader of *Walden*—like Thoreau—becomes attuned to new energies within the self. Thoreau's emblems of frictionless being define the endpoint of this self-expression by evoking the presence of powers that forge new pathways— in the sense both of new avenues of dwelling and of new mental pathways. Wonder at the world stretching within toward an uncharted "interior" (*Wa*, 321) is matched by wonder at the world expanding without. More precisely, these two worlds are seen as merging, so that presence in the world is identified with self-presence. This is life without *différance*— a physical impossibility, yet a compelling dream. Attempting to live "in the direction of his dreams" (214), Thoreau commits himself to a self-perfection that finds its expression in such dramatized moments of frictionless being.

Thoreau's problem is that such moments of presence are impermanent. Most of the time we exist outside of presence and can only anticipate it in scenes of prospect that focus upon fulfillment before its appearance. Such scenes allow the imagining of a presence, not yet attained, but seen as the telos of a self-development rapidly becoming unimpeded. According to Lawrence Buell, "a strong but precarious sense of imminent fulfillment" is characteristic of Transcendentalist writing.[46] "Prospectiveness" is Buell's term for the moment that is "alive with vision, and strains eagerly toward its realization, but . . . cannot capture that ideal except momentarily."[47] Thoreau's scenes of prospect evoke the light that is about to dawn, the prophetic dream that is half-remembered, the seed that is beginning to sprout and unfold new forms. In order "to make my life of finer quality," he reflects in his journal, I have to be able "to transplant it into futurity" (*J*, 2:248). The note struck here is one of anticipation, an attitude of faith in powers that are approaching but have not yet arrived. The literary result of this attitude is the construction of scenes that momentarily bracket the sense of physical necessity while they define what Heidegger calls our "ownmost possibility of Being."[48]

An excellent example of a scene of prospect is Thoreau's portrayal of angling for elusive "nocturnal fishes," a passage that dramatizes the proximity of forces and possibilities just beyond the horizon. "These experiences were very memorable and valuable to me," Thoreau comments,

> —anchored in forty feet of water, and twenty or thirty rods from the shore, surrounded sometimes by thousands of small perch and shiners, with their tails in the moonlight, and communicating by a long flaxen line with mysterious nocturnal fishes which had their dwelling forty feet below, or sometimes dragging sixty feet of line about the pond as I drifted in the gentle night breeze, now and then feeling a slight vibration along it, indicative of some life prowling about its extremity, of dull uncertain blundering purpose there, and slow to make up its mind. [*Wa*, 175]

A phrase such as "dull uncertain blundering purpose" helps to give this passage a psychological, as well as a literal, reference. Its topic is partly the intuition of half-felt powers on the verge of articulation, what Thoreau terms the "prospect of awakening or coming to life" (134). Orienting the reader toward the possibility of future unfolding, it cultivates a stance of expectation and faith. At the same time it makes the reader aware of the edge of self-awareness, of the horizon separating consciousness from the "mysterious" unconscious.

A similar scene occurs at the beginning of "The Pond in Winter." There, Thoreau recounts how he awoke one morning with a sense of expectation, only to find prospect eliding into presence: "After a still winter night I awoke with the impression that some question had been put to me, which I had been endeavoring in vain to answer in my sleep, as what—how—when—where? But there was dawning Nature, in whom all creatures live, looking in at my broad windows with serene and satisfied face, and no question on *her* lips. I awoke to an answered question, to Nature and daylight" (*Wa*, 282). Thoreau imagines the "faint intimation" of presence as a dawn that merges into the daylight of a full being. This fulfillment is not imaginary; rather, it involves a re-awakening to one's habitation in the real, to a new mode of existing without alienation in the sensuous world.

The gap between approach and arrival defines the potential that Thoreau strives to activate within his reader. At times, this gap cannot be crossed; instead, "at the crucial moment, the wind stirs, the world is engulfed in darkness, and we are left with a keen sense of loss," as Joel Porte observes.[49] In the view of a theorist like Derrida, such disappointment is inevitable, for the prospect of future fulfillment reveals the dependence of presence upon "something other than itself." "Differance," he argues, "is what makes the moment of signification possible only if each element that is said to be 'present,' appearing on the stage of presence . . . retains the mark of a past element and already lets itself be hollowed out by the mark of its relation to a future element."[50] From this perspective, Thoreau's scenes of prospect, as well as his re-presentation of memories, reveals the fictionality of his image of presence.

But, as in the case of Emerson's evocation of unconscious powers, Thoreau's depiction of presence functions as the occasion for belief; it becomes a psychological myth. A deconstructive reading brackets such belief from critical awareness, eliminating completely the rhetorical impact of Thoreau's myth of presence. Indeed, throughout *Walden* Thoreau complains that the acceptance of deferral (or *differance*) undermines self-faith. His argument is predicated upon the assumption that most persons are alienated from themselves because they lead a deferred existence, depending upon external forces for self-definition. But at the same time that Thoreau's images of presence attempt to negate such deferral, they depend upon it in order to function. The force of his rhetoric is in direct proportion to his dramatization of the gap between our quotidian world of deferral and absence, the world in which the poor Irishman John Field lives, and an imagined realm of accessible being. The fact that this gap may never be permanently or perfectly closed adds to, rather than diminishes, the rhetorical power of Thoreau's myth of presence. Like any image of human perfection, those images point the way toward a self-improvement that has not yet been achieved.

Thoreau's dramatizations of presence and prospect awaken and direct our "attention" (from Latin: *ad* + *tendere*) by providing a model of how we might *stretch toward* the world, tending and anchoring our interest in its manifold attractions. Or, as Thoreau observes near the end of *Walden*: "I love to weigh, to settle, to gravitate toward that which most strongly and rightfully attracts me . . . not suppose a case, but take the case that is; to travel the only path I can, and that on which no power can resist me" (330). Uniting subject and object, attention—for Thoreau—is an "intentional experience"; it is, in the words of Edmund Husserl, "consciousness *of* something."[51] As a result, Thoreau does not attempt to change our idea of reality, but rather our experience of the world. By reading *Walden* in a "true spirit" (101), we entertain provisional faith in this new mode of attention, a transformation of vision that suggests the possibility of a more illumined and liberated existence by constituting in us a sense of wonder. Reading Thoreau's account of liberated being, we are "thinking the thoughts of" Thoreau, staging within ourselves the echo of his experience.[52] Reenacting his reconstruction of the world, our own world momentarily regains "bloom" (6); existence takes on a quality of "serenity and purity" (193).

Emerson's essay "History" provides the theory of interpretation behind this transformation of the reader's being. A writer, Emerson argues, re-forms his audience (reshapes their existence) by presenting to them an idealized model that defines their potential unfolding: "all that is said of the wise man by stoic or oriental or modern essayist, describes to each reader his own idea, describes his unattained but attainable self" (*CW*, 2:15). Entering into the spirit of a text, a reader finds "his own secret biography . . . in lines wonderfully intelligible to him, dotted down before he was born" (17). Paul Ricoeur's description of critical understanding serves as an excellent gloss on such passages. "Reading," he notes, "introduces me into the imaginative variations of the *ego*."[53] To understand a text, consequently, is "to understand oneself in front of the text," a process that involves "exposing ourselves to the text and receiving from it an enlarged self, which would be the proposed existence corresponding in the most suitable way to the world proposed."[54] In Thoreau's writing, the "world proposed" is one in which the pressures of temporality fall away as the individual regains a sense of productive being. At the heart of *Walden* is the vision of "an enlarged self" alive in a world, not of alienated objects but of unfolding power. Karl Marx imagines a similar recovery of full existence at the moment that private property is surpassed: "The supersession of private property is, therefore, the complete *emancipation* of all the human qualities and senses. . . . The eye has become a *human* eye when its *object* has become a *human*, social object, created by man and destined for him."[55]

For Thoreau, this achievement of existence in the "daylight" of "the present moment" involves the unimpeded articulation of creative energies emerging from within the self. Utilizing the vocabulary of Romantic organicism, he argues that the authentic life has its own "architectural beauty" that has "grown from within outward, out of the necessities and character of the indweller . . . out of some unconscious truthfulness" (*Wa*, 47). The self-reliant individual, he asserts, needs "time to take root and unfold" (132), as well as the "room to unfold" (141). The image of unfolding suggests the expression of an inner essence; it also focuses prospective attention upon the activity of unfolding as an existential thrust that roots both physical and spiritual fulfillment in the real world.

By reawakening us to "an infinite expectation of the dawn" (*Wa*, 90), Thoreau orients existence toward the future exfoliation of the self. This dawn is more than a subjective state, for it suggests the transformation of the world's appearance, its clarification. Awareness of "dawn" as a form of human potential orients one in a stance of self-faith; one becomes a person for whom dawn might appear. This alters one's preconceptions and hence the manner in which one exists in the world. A world in which there are dawns, in which dawning is possible, assumes an openness that frees the individual toward self-expression. There is a "space" or "clearing" in which being "begins its essential unfolding."[56] This process of illumination is described by Medard Boss as the act of "luminating and elucidating existence."[57] "Man," Boss writes, "is a light which luminates whatever particular being comes into the realm of its rays."[58] By achieving light, Thoreau's reader becomes more aware of the specific structure of his or her being-in-the-world.

From another angle, Thoreau's statement that "morning is when I am awake and there is a dawn in me" (*Wa*, 90) can be read as referring to the appearance of transfiguring spiritual energies. We might compare Thoreau's usage with the following from Coleridge's *Aids to Reflection*: "Awakened by the cock-crow—(a sermon, a calamity, a sickbed, or a providential escape)—the Christian pilgrim sets out in the morning twilight, while yet the truth . . . is below the horizon."[59] Like Coleridge, Thoreau perceives dawn as the emergence of a spiritual power that authenticates and orients the self. The presence of this light clarifies the world, giving existence a luminosity. But in contrast to Coleridge's dawning "truth," Thoreau's dawn evokes less the presence of divinity than the awakening of the self to its own nature. We find a similar awareness in Thoreau's symbolism of seeds and sprouting. Reflecting upon his labor in the bean-field, he observes that, in addition to beans, he sowed "seeds" of "sincerity, truth, simplicity, faith, innocence" (164). What sprouts here is the recognition that physical labor changes the shape of existence by facilitating self-recognition.

One of the most striking aspects of Thoreau's imagination of liberated being is his reflection upon movement along "channels" or "paths." At first, one has the impression that Thoreau uses such images to depict psychic pathways in a manner anticipating the later usage of Freud. Discussing Freud's successive representations of memory, Jacques Derrida analyzes how "Freud . . . forges the hypothesis of 'contact-barriers' and 'breaching' (*Bahnung*, lit. pathbreaking), of the breaking open of a path (*Bahn*). . . . Breaching, the tracing of a trail, opens up a conducting path. Which presupposes a certain violence and a certain resistance to effraction. The path is broken, cracked, *fracta*, breached."[60] Freud (as Derrida interprets him) uses the image of opening pathways to focus upon an internal difference underlying subjective phenomena, "the ungraspable and invisible difference between breaches," but Thoreau uses this image to define the existential dimension of renewed being in the objective world. His emphasis lies upon the exfoliation of new avenues of attention, of interest rooting the individual more firmly within an expanding realm of existence.

Accordingly, Thoreau uses the image of the repeated path to depict habitual activity with its stale, routine mode of perception: "For a week of even weather I took exactly the same number of steps, and of the same length, coming and going, stepping deliberately and with the precision of a pair of dividers in my own deep tracks, —to such routine the winter reduces us" (*Wa*, 265). The well-trodden path becomes a symbol of the life of custom, habit, and convention that Thoreau anatomizes throughout *Walden*. As one follows the same pathways over and over, one's energies lose their "bloom," while the perceived world takes on a shabby, worn quality. One finds a similar image of the routine repetition of old pathways in the essay "Life without Principle": "every thought that passes through the mind helps to wear and tear it, and to deepen the ruts, which, as in the streets of Pompeii, evince how much it has been used" (*RP*, 173). Thoreau's goal is to help his reader break out of such "ruts"—to regain the sense of wonder attendant upon the clearing of new avenues of attention and physical relation.

The antithesis of monotonous repetition, for Thoreau, is the act of "going abroad" (*Wa*, 265). For example, just after his description of winter routine, Thoreau describes how he broke a new pathway through "the deepest snow" to gain a closer view of natural phenomena. In passing, let us note that Thoreau must *break* through the snow; it doesn't effortlessly melt, as at the end of Emerson's *Nature*. But if one is able to escape from routine into a sense of wonder, one is again able to direct attention to the most minute details of existence (in this case, the gestures of a barred owl), details that had previously lacked interest. By breaking through what Coleridge in *Biographia Literaria* called "the film of familiarity," one uncovers a new world. "It is remarkable," Thoreau observes, "how easily and insensibly we fall into a particular route, and make a beaten track for ourselves" (323). His goal in *Walden* is to shake the reader out of such torpor, a goal John Carlos Rowe describes as the "systematic removal of barriers in order to open a path."[61] What results is the image of productive self-expression in which new pathways of attention can be broken into the physical world as one's existential prospect enlarges.

Such path breaking leads to existence outside of conventional boundaries: "I fear chiefly lest my expression may not be *extra-vagrant* enough, may not wander far enough beyond the narrow limits of my daily experience, so as to be adequate to the truth of which I have been convinced. *Extra vagrance*! it depends on how you are yarded. . . . I desire to speak somewhere *without* bounds; like a man in a waking moment, to men in their waking moments . . ." (*Wa*, 324). Here the exfoliation of existence passes into an image of freedom at the border of physical necessity. Like Marx's image of unalienated labor, this articulates hope in perfectly expressive, perfectly productive activity. Existence "without bounds" is a physical impossibility, but a compelling dream.

At its most ecstatic Thoreau's vision of "extra-vagrant" existence metamorphoses into a myth of Paradise regained, a "Golden Age." Such a transformation is enacted in "Spring," the penultimate chapter of *Walden*. After the repression and routine of winter, pent-up creative and spiritual energies are released in an explosion of paradisiac imagery. Winter had been portrayed as a time of psychic hibernation: "I withdrew yet farther into my shell, and endeavored to keep a bright fire both within my house and within my breast" (249). But if in winter "our human life . . . dies down to the root" (205), those roots retain the power to spring again into vital life, pushing their "green blade to eternity" (311). "Walden was dead and is alive again. . . . Suddenly an influx of light filled my house" (311–12). The "house" of Thoreau's being recovers clarity and illumination. This opening of "new channels," new pathways of being, presents itself as an expansive flourishing of vegetable life. Thoreau experiences the rejuvenation of "germs of virtues," of "holiness groping for expression . . . like a new-born instinct," of "innocent fair shoots preparing to burst from [the] gnarled rind . . . tender and fresh as the youngest plant" (315). Associated with this rebirth is a pure, bright light; the world is "bathed in so pure and bright a light as would have waked the dead" (317). Transfigured, apotheosized, existence takes on a sacred quality.

As the field of being becomes "innocent" again and "the sun shines bright and warm . . . re-creating the world" (*Wa*, 314), existence metamorphoses into paradise: "The coming in of spring is like the creation of Cosmos out of Chaos and the realization of the Golden Age" (313). Thoreau's imagination of paradise replants one in a pure presence beyond retrospective guilt and the need for atonement: "A single gentle rain makes the grass many shades greener. So our prospects brighten on the influx of better thoughts. We should be blessed if we lived in the present always, and took advantage of every accident that befell us, like the grass which confesses the influence of the slightest dew that falls on it; and did not spend our time atoning for the neglect of past opportunities, which we call doing our duty" (314). "We should be blessed"— Thoreau portrays a potential condition of transfigured being, one that shimmers before us if we live "in view of the future or possible" (324). *Walden* begins with evocations of the need for atonement; it ends with a vision of expanded being from which guilt and disunity might be eliminated.

Thoreau's reference to the Golden Age reminds us of the ongoing analogy that he constructs between existence close to nature and the being portrayed in classical mythology and Oriental philosophy. *Walden*, Robert D. Richardson argues, is "his major attempt to create a . . . new American mythology."[62] By casting his experiences into a mythical mode, Thoreau attempts to "mythicize . . . his own direct encounters with nature."[63] At the heart of this mythicizing of experience lies an equation between the freshness that Thoreau finds in ancient texts and the enlarged being that he imagines for both himself and his audience. Homer, the Vedas, and Confucius provide a model of regenerated perception that discloses a world of infinite possibility: "The oldest Egyptian or Hindoo philosopher raised a corner of the veil from the statue of the divinity; and still the trembling robe remains raised, and I gaze upon as fresh a glory as he did, since it was I in him that was then so bold, and it is he in me that now renews the vision" (99). This remarkable passage not only revives a sense of the sacerdotal, it turns the consciousness embodied in ancient literature into one of the "types already in the mind of man" (310).

Thoreau thus uses mythical allusion to evoke the perennial youth of Nature, its "indescribable innocence and beneficence" (*Wa*, 138). But more profoundly, he conflates his discovery of life in the present, a life of heightened attention, with the image of ancient wonder in the face of the sacred. "In the morning," he writes in a justly renowned passage, ". . . I lay down the book and go to my well for water, and lo! there I meet the servant of the Brahmin, priest of Brahma and Vishnu and Indra, who still sits in his temple on the Ganges reading the Vedas, or dwells at the root of a tree with his crust and water jug. I meet his servant come to draw water for his master, and our buckets as it were grate together in the same well. The pure Walden water is mingled with the sacred water of the Ganges" (298). Such a passage justifies Thoreau's perception that "in my brain is the sanscrit—Was not Asia mapped there before it was in any geography?" (J, 1:419). Asia already exists in Thoreau's brain because the ancient Hindu text and his record of contemporary experience share the same archetype of regeneration. They both dramatize a myth of psychological and spiritual rebirth; they both provide a paradigm of awakened and purified senses. Merging both himself and his reader with that ancient mythological voice, Thoreau uses it as an ideal that both measures and transfigures experience.

If, in the words of the English poet whom Thoreau quotes, "creation widens to our view" (Wa, 329), then our highest responsibility is to adopt the widest possible view of creation. The dream nourished by Emerson is that this transformation might take place without effort. "As fast as you conform your life to the pure idea in your mind," Emerson had written, "that will unfold its great proportions" (CW, 1:45). Proposing a more arduous vision of self-creation, Thoreau motivates his reader to reform his world by offering as a standard of measurement images of regenerated existence. Defining the limit of authenticity, these images mark the asymptotes of an infinitely expanding curve of being. Thoreau both details the kinds of resistance that might retard the renewal of existence and provides emblems of regenerated being aimed at convincing the reader to accept this ideal of self-perfection.

Emerson, Sherman Paul asserts, "discovered the continent of being."[64] By rooting himself in the real, Thoreau became one of its early explorers. Epitomizing Emerson's "active soul," the persona of Walden discovers how to exist in a world that appears as the result of his commitment to physical labor and authentic dwelling. This reconstructed world functions as an ontological model against which Thoreau's reader can validate his or her interpretation of existence. It constitutes a role, a model of being, that the reader is urged to assume. Ultimately, this strategy of measuring the self against an idealized vision of existence corroborates Ernst Cassirer's observation that "myth does not start from a finished representation of the I and the soul but is the vehicle which leads to such a representation; it is a spiritual medium through which spiritual reality is first discovered in its distinctiveness."[65] Let us revise this passage to emphasize Thoreau's portrayal of existence in *Walden*—his myth of dawning being is an existential medium through which being is discovered. Thoreau engages in psychological mythmaking because, in the words of Paul Ricoeur, he articulates "a *proposed world* which I would inhabit and wherein I could project . . . my ownmost possibilities."[66] Ultimately, he challenges us to expand the scope of our existence and thereby realize a new being at home in a renewed world.

FOUR

"Song of Myself": A Field of Potential Being

READING "SONG OF MYSELF"

Walt Whitman, Albert Gelpi notes, "cast himself in the role which Emerson had proclaimed."[1] Responding to the call for a bard who could express "the value of our incomparable materials" (*W*, 3:37), Whitman reflects both the democratic nationalism and the self-reliance promoted by Emerson. In all of its exuberance of discovery, the 1855 edition of "Song of Myself" constructs a central American archetype—an image of the self liberated within a field of expansive vision. From the start Emerson had shown the age that such self-liberation depended upon an intimate knowledge of the psyche and its rhythms. "It is a secret which every intellectual man quickly learns," he reflected in "The Poet," "that beyond the energy of his possessed and conscious intellect he is capable of a new energy (as of an intellect doubled on itself), by abandonment to the nature of things; that beside his privacy of power as an individual man, there is a great public power on which he can draw, by unlocking, at all risks, his human doors, and suffering the ethereal tides to roll and circulate through him" (3:26). In "Song of Myself" Whitman attempts to unlock "human doors" through a process of psychological mythmaking that—according to Robert D. Richardson, Jr.—"supplant[s] traditional 'objective' epic with 'subjective' epic."[2]

Although Emerson, by 1844, had started to call the mind's power "instinct" (instead of "Reason"), he maintained an idealism that celebrated "the divine *aura* which breathes through forms" (*W*, 3:26). Whitman, in contrast, takes Emerson's "aura" and demonstrates its rootedness in physical urge. Despite their shared concern with self-reliant expression, these two writers split over their respective conceptions of psychic energy. Both writers locate creative energy in the unconscious; both argue for the organic unfolding of that energy in unique personal forms; both write works designed to inspire their readers. But they differ in their sense of the energy that is released. Although Emerson was aware of a physical component to creative energy, he subsumes the body and nature under essentially theological definitions of the unconscious. If, as Perry Miller notes, the "relation of mind (brain) to object" defines a nineteenth-century intellectual "crisis," Emerson attempts to reconcile this epistemological dualism by defining nature in terms of spirit.[3] But instead of starting with the mind like Emerson, Whitman reverses the equation, defining spirit in terms of nature (or, more precisely, seeing the two as articulations of the same force). Thus, Emerson's vision of the mind seems at times strikingly close to that of Carl Jung, but Whitman's celebration of the body and its power anticipates Freud's later descriptions of the somatic bases of libido. By grounding poetic voice in the body, Whitman gives it emotional depth and a sensuality of tone.

"Outright sensuality," Gay Wilson Allen comments, "was always offensive to Emerson," who once remarked to a friend "that there were parts of *Leaves of Grass* 'where I hold my nose as I read.' "[4] In contrast to such fastidiousness, Whitman's exuberant affirmation of physical impulse carried beyond the bounds of decorum Emerson's plea for an active life in the world. Emerson's exhortation to lead a more substantial existence had stopped far short of violating the sexual mores of New England; but Whitman's imaginative energy arises from the act of violation itself, from transgressing the conservative standards of those who—in his eyes—inhibited their most natural drives. This contrast highlights a central question of morality, one that also haunts Hawthorne and Melville. Is the mind's energy, as Emerson had stressed, essentially moral? Or instead, is it amoral, beyond questions of good and evil? Like Friedrich Nietzsche, Whitman holds the latter view, asserting that the somatic bases of consciousness transcend moral valuation. According to D. H. Lawrence, Whitman was "the first to smash the old moral conception that the soul of man is something 'superior' and 'above' the flesh."[5] His celebration of the body directly challenges the moral assumptions of an age in which "the body was banished from polite society, and its external shape and structure were denied."[6]

Attempting like *Walden* to regain what Hegel had called "the substantial fullness of life," Whitman's "Song of Myself" defines a mode of being that transcends conventionalized categories inhibiting self-expression.[7] "Every thought," Emerson had reasoned, "is also a prison; every heaven is also a prison. Therefore we love the poet, the inventor, who in any form, whether in an ode or in an action or in looks and behavior, has yielded us a new thought. He unlocks our chains and admits us to a new scene" (*W*, 3:33). But if Emerson unlocks the chains of rationality only in order to forge them again, Whitman constantly moves beyond reason into what one critic calls "a larger erotic landscape."[8] Sidestepping definitions of human existence that oppose a thinking subject to a world of things, Whitman—much more than Emerson or even Thoreau—places the mind back into the body. In contrast to Emerson, Whitman's presentation of what Emerson called "substantive being" (*CW*, 1:37) avoids ethical perspectives that stigmatize bodily and sexual functions. Instead, his "democratization of the whole person" attempts to lift the repression that imprisons the "corporeal self."[9]

The nineteenth century, Nietzsche later observed, discovered the body. "More and more decisively," he noted, "the question concerning the *health of the body* is put ahead of that of 'the soul': the latter being understood as a state consequent upon the former."[10] Even more radically, Nietzsche suggested that "perhaps the entire evolution of the spirit is a question of the body; it is the history of the development of a higher body that emerges into our sensibility."[11] Behind the "I," Nietzsche argues in *Thus Spoke Zarathustra*, there stands "a mighty ruler, an unknown sage—whose name is self. In your body he dwells; he is your body."[12] Thoreau's writing started to flesh out Emersonian Transcendentalism, giving expression to the body and its senses. Whitman's poetry fully articulates the "mighty ruler" that transcends the "I"—the body.

Both the contemporary disciplines of phrenology and mesmerism supplied Whitman with psychological terminologies that stressed the physical side of the self. According to Arthur Wrobel, Whitman's recognition of the interdependence of mind and body is "fundamentally similar" to that of phrenologists such as Orson Squire Fowler, the distributor of the 1855 edition of *Leaves of Grass*.[13] Whitman frequented Fowler and Wells's "Phrenological Cabinet" and there learned "that outward bodily health and a well-developed physique are the signatures of a correspondingly robust soul."[14] Stressing the importance of careful diet and exercise, phrenologists argued that "every change in the state of the body is a change in the experience of the soul."[15] At the same time, they taught that self-knowledge depended not only upon the inner motions of the psyche, but also upon sensory impressions that reveal the self's immersion in the world. The result is a viewpoint that Wrobel characterizes as "subjective materialism" and that F. O. Matthiessen calls "material ideality."[16] In similar fashion, the terminology of mesmerism contributes to Whitman's view of the mind. "When he writes of the 'invisible magnetism dissolving and embracing all,'" Edmund Reiss comments, and when he "describes the underlying vitality of the universe as 'subtle, vast, electric,' he appears to be mentioning a force close to the vital physical fluid of the animal magnetists."[17]

Whitman's indebtedness to materialistic conceptions of the psyche is worth emphasizing as an antidote to readings of his poetry that tend to dismiss the physical altogether. A striking example of this tendency can be found in John Irwin's *American Hieroglyphics*. "Whitman," Irwin asserts, "makes the poetic self the sole referent of the poem."[18] "As a poet of the absolute self," Irwin argues, "Whitman is necessarily a poet of the will, and what we see in his poetry is the way in which the music of the will (the ceaselessly mobile energy of internal time-consciousness) strives to create its own phenomenal world, as if, to use Schopenhauer's phrase, when a person gives himself to this music, he 'seems to see all the possible events of life and the world take place in himself.'"[19] Such a reading focuses upon the motion of Whitman's will at the expense both of his relationship to his own body and to the world of solid physical objects (including the bodies of his audience). It emphasizes the imperialistic side of Whitman's sensibility without noting that such psychic imperialism defines itself through specific object-relations. What results is a "Whitman" imagined as a disembodied voice, a voice trapped within a subjective labyrinth that Irwin describes as "the self-referentiality of the Romantic self, the self as pure will, as pure motion/emotion."[20] While Whitman, as Irwin argues, did wish to achieve "the immediate intuitive conviction of music," he demonstrates over and over in his work that such immediacy is achieved only through the self's relationship to others.[21] Irwin's Whitman, by contrast, is an absolutely expressive voice singing in a perfect vacuum.

We can avoid such a tendency to idealize Whitman's poetic self by remembering what F. O. Matthiessen describes as his "efforts to master concreteness of statement."[22] Whitman, Matthiessen argues, "cannot use words" to express Adamic joy (Irwin's purely expressive will) "unless he has experienced the facts that they express, unless he has grasped them with his senses."[23] As a result Whitman "succeeds in endowing his poetry with the sensuousness that Coleridge held indispensable to insure a 'framework of objectivity.'"[24] In this view Whitman is not a poet who celebrates pure expression for its own sake, but rather the writer whose "greatest act of pioneering was in helping the modern sensibility feel at home in the natural world."[25] If one forgets this radical realism, one transforms Whitman's persona into a solipsistic egotist who writes for and about himself alone. The intentionality of Whitman's images, their anchoring in concrete existence, disappears.

One also forgets that Whitman's vision of the unconscious is radically different from Emerson's illuminated heart. By grounding the psyche in the body's energy, Whitman awakens his audience to a sense, not of the "God within," but of what he calls "it." "There is that in me," he writes,

". . . . I do not know what it is . . . . but I know it is in me" (*LG*, l. 1299). While Whitman's "it" refers to the life force (what he calls "procreant urge"), this term also articulates a sense of "being-with." The unconscious for Whitman, even more than for Emerson, is a relational force. Its energy, once released, adheres to the world, attaching itself to the manifold objects of attention. In Whitman's view human potential is released only through the act of relating to nature, to others, and to oneself. The terminology of existential psychoanalysis clarifies this process. "The existential analysts," Rollo May explains, "distinguish three modes of world, that is, three simultaneous aspects of world which characterize the existence of each one of us as being-in-the-world. First, there is *Umwelt*, literally meaning 'world around'; this is the biological world, generally called the environment. There is, second, the *Mitwelt*, literally the 'with-world,' the world of beings of one's own kind, the world of one's fellow men. The third is the *Eigenwelt*, the 'own-world,' the mode of relationship to one's self."[26] "Song of Myself" enacts, as its central concern, patterns of relationship in which the poet connects (or "merges") with all three aspects of world. If this act of relationship brings "the known world . . . into being," it also constitutes the reality of Whitman's reader, who is motivated to identify his or her being in terms of the poet's unfolding vision.[27] Ultimately, poet and reader merge together—the poet becomes an "itch" in our ears, a thought lingering on our tongues.

The challenge confronting the reader of "Song of Myself" is to find a model of the text that illuminates both its psychological rhythm and its rhetorical power. To date, most readings of the poem have emphasized the former concern at the expense of the latter. As a corrective to this situation, it is worth pursuing Roy Harvey Pearce's contention that "Song of Myself" enacts the release of a "procreant urge" both within Whitman's poet and his audience.[28] Despite this observation, few critics have discussed both the psychic rhythm followed by Whitman's persona and the radical effect that this figure has upon the receptive reader. Instead, many readings of "Song of Myself" provide an x-ray of the poem in which "the living energy of meaning . . . is neutralized" like "the architecture of an uninhabited or deserted city, reduced to its skeleton by some catastrophe of nature or art."[29] For example, James E. Miller, Jr., highlights the poem's structure at the expense of illuminating Whitman's involvement with the historical unfolding of his reader's being.[30] Such an approach reenacts what Paul Bové describes as the "disguised New Critical presupposition that language can magically free itself and its user from the immediate historical past either to return to some ahistorical scene which actually transcends time . . . or simply to begin again, free of historical consequences."³¹

A more serious distortion of meaning is created by those who turn away from the poem in order to view it as a symptom of Whitman's psychohistory. What results is an allegorized version of the text that turns it into an object exhibiting "infantile" and "homosexual" tendencies.³² Parodying the psychological rhythm of "Song of Myself," such readings avoid the impact of Whitman's rhetoric upon his audience by reading the poem solely in terms of authorial intention, whether conscious or unconscious. This approach ignores the fact that "the 'I' of [Whitman's] poems is generic: he celebrates himself as a representative man."³³ Rather than writing autobiography, Whitman creates "generic autobiography"—a first-person narrative presented to his audience as a possible course of being.³⁴ Whitman's "Ego-style," as he himself terms it, is designed to arouse his audience from the torpor of non-self-awareness (*NF*, 179). "Merely what I tell you is not to justify me," he asserts. "What I provoke from you and from ensuing times, is to justify me" (39). By "embodying the sentiment of perfect happiness, *in myself*" (104), "Song of Myself" dramatizes a model of potential being that his audience is motivated to emulate.

Although the psychological insight of "Song of Myself" has long been apparent to its readers, greater attention needs to be paid to the poem's self-dramatization as an act that constitutes the being of its audience. A celebration of the achievement of liberated vision, "Song of Myself" founds that vision upon the inclusion of energies buried in the unconscious. "I heat the hot cores within and fix the central point of the cores," Whitman once noted (*NF*, 34). This energizing of the self articulates a field of energy that radiates through the reader. Charles Olson's model of "projective verse" serves as a provisional account of this process. "A poem," Olson insists, "is energy transferred from where the poet got it . . . by way of the poem itself to, all the way over to, the reader."³⁵ Olson's comment reminds us of the danger of treating a work like "Song of Myself" as a critical object. Whitman's subject, like Olson's, is a force that changes the existential contours of anyone who encounters it. The challenge confronting Whitman's readers is to develop a model of reading that can account for this rhetorical exchange.

Before anything else, "Song of Myself" is an audacious work of self-dramatization. The voice that speaks to us is unlike anything encountered before in American literature. If we are to understand the impact of this voice upon Whitman's audience, we must attend to its psychological career as the radical representation of a possible course of being. "And what I assume you shall assume": this voice compels contact. It defines a matrix of energy—a field of vision—that we enter as we read. It doesn't teach us ideas but rather activates a model of being that energizes us as we move through the poem. Whitman teaches us that poems are not things, any more than music is a thing; they are processes alive with energy. His poetry, as a result, demands the reader's commitment to its patterning. By reading "Song of Myself," we allow it to shape our attention, to order our feelings. We enter the poem and inhabit it, trying on its vision of experience. Thus, as we talk about the poem's structure, we need to relate that discussion to how the poem works upon us, how it creates a psychological myth that aims to transform the reader.

To the extent that they turn us away from the poem, viewing it as a symptom of Whitman's own psychological history, readers of "Song of Myself" defuse its energy. The poem becomes an object held at arm's length, an artifact exhibiting "abnormal" tendencies. As a result, the reader defends himself against the poem's force by bracketing from discussion its rhetoricity. What disappears from discussion is consideration of how "Song of Myself" engages its readers, forcing them to recognize within themselves Dionysian energies. We can highlight the limitations of ahistorical readings by examining the reactions of James E. Miller, Jr., and Edwin Haviland Miller to the poem's climax—the "crucifixion" and "resurrection" of the poet in section 38. (Added by later editors, section numbers are used for the reader's convenience.) As a critical principle, let us assert that any adequate reading of this poem should be able to account for both the psychological and rhetorical logic of this moment.

The criticism of James E. Miller, Jr., exemplifies the strengths and weaknesses of a model of reading that attends to the poet's self-representation, at the expense of accounting for its effect upon Whitman's audience. In Miller's terms, the poem presents an "inverted mystical experience" that dramatizes the poet's passage through his own "Dark Night of the Soul" to a sense of godlike power.[36] In section 38 the poet "suggests his union with the Transcendent through imagery of the Crucifixion of Christ."[37] "As the Crucifixion of Christ," Miller continues, "resulted not in death, meaningless suffering, or shame but in eternal life and joy, so the poet's dark night results in renewed vigor and life."[38] Although Miller's analysis is extremely useful in formulating the emotional rhythm of "Song of Myself," it neglects to explain either the psychological logic or the rhetorical impact of the poet's transformation. Besides the fact that it culminates the poet's "Dark Night of the Soul," why exactly does the imagery of crucifixion enter the poem? And how are we to understand the poet's miraculous recovery, his rebirth to a renewed energy? What is the rhetorical force of this apotheosis? On these points, James Miller falls silent.

Edwin Haviland Miller's analysis of Whitman's "psychological" journey is not much more helpful. Having established the presence of a great deal of sexual ambivalence in Whitman's poem (expressed through moments of sexual affirmation and regression, images of life and death), E. H. Miller discusses section 38 as follows: "In the cyclical fashion characteristic of the poem and of the sexual rhythm upon which it is based, 'crucifixion' is (once more) followed by resurrection, doubt and vacillation (the Everlasting No) give way to affirmation (the Everlasting Yea), and death culminates in the birth (or rebirth) of the 'friendly and flowing savage' in the thirty-ninth section."[39] Like James Miller's treatment, this is more descriptive than analytic. Most readers of "Song of Myself" are aware of the poem's cyclic rhythms, but how these are to be attributed to Whitman's own psychology is a moot point. Greater success, one suspects, will result from a method of reading that attends to the transformations of Whitman's dramatized persona, and not to the alleged operation of Whitman's own psychological fixations.

Perhaps Albert Gelpi comes closest to capturing the inspirational force of "Song of Myself." In general, Gelpi's analysis provides the groundwork necessary for understanding the poet's transformation. The "dynamic" of Whitman's poetry, he argues, is "the comprehension and absorption of materials from the unconscious into consciousness."[40] This process leads to the discovery of a Self outside the boundaries of the ego: "As the 'inner divine spontaneities' of instinct and spirit become consciously acknowledged through the agency of the ego, the individual discovers that his ego concenters a Self more capacious and mysterious than he could ever have dreamed at the start."[41] Gelpi's discussion focuses primarily upon Whitman's presentation of this Self—a figure that Gelpi identifies as an androgynous "Cosmic Man," "one of the recurrent images of psychological wholeness in dreams and legends throughout history."[42] (Emerson's "One Man" at the beginning of "The American Scholar" is a similar figure.) But despite the psychological perceptiveness of his discussion, Gelpi's commentary also exhibits the disconcerting tendency to focus upon Whitman's imagined psychology instead of upon the career of his persona.[43]

Since numerous critics have by now related the development of "Song of Myself" to Whitman's personal psychology, let us try a different tack, one that suspends biographical questions. What happens if we concentrate instead upon the psychic career of Whitman's persona, not as an autobiographical figure, but as a dramatic creation designed to affect

Whitman's audience? To read the poem in this way takes seriously Whitman's assertion that its aim is to inspire his readers. How is that process of inspiration enacted? Is this an idle claim on Whitman's part, or does the poem have the desired effect: awakening us to "the origin of all poems" that we carry hidden within? To read "Song of Myself" rhetorically is to bypass the question of Whitman's personal psychology, which enters the poem in a disguised form. Instead of accepting at face value the self-assertions of "a poet who represents himself . . . in *Leaves of Grass* as growing up in Virginia and Texas and hunting polar bears in Alaska,"[44] one views his self-presentation as a "psychological ritual" that shapes the being of his audience.

EXPANDING THE WORLD

By calling "Song of Myself" a "psychological ritual," I wish to draw attention to the poem's function as a social drama that passes both poet and reader through a process of transformation. According to the anthropologist Victor Turner (following Arnold van Gennep's formulation), all rites of passage are marked by three phases: separation, liminality, and reintegration.[45] Separating the celebrant from conventional social structure, the rite reorients his existence by subjecting him to a "transitional period" when he is an outsider, beyond the normal categories of his culture.[46] During this "liminal period" the neophyte is "invisible," having passed beyond previous existential categories but not yet having achieved a reformulated identity. By directly challenging and overturning the previous cultural assumptions of his readers, Whitman places them in an analogous position. He destroys the "habitual life patterns" of his audience in order "to assure ongoing dis-closure."[47] Skewing and overturning the assumptions of his readers, Whitman forces them to move beyond conventionality into an intermediary space that enables him to reformulate their sense of world.

The first stage of this process in "Song of Myself" is the expansion of the reader's sense of world to include persons and activities ordinarily excluded as abnormal, immoral, or dirty. By moving the reader beyond conventional moral valuation, Whitman forces a redefinition of being in terms that eliminate ordinary social repressions. Entrance into such a "liminal period," according to Victor Turner, opens up the possibility of "a communitas of free and equal comrades—of total persons."[48] One of the primary functions of "Song of Myself" is to place its audience beyond social stratification into an imagined existential territory where such "communitas" is possible.

Starting in the third line, the poem forges connections between the poet and his readers. "For every atom belonging to me as good belongs to you"—this voice addresses us directly, affirming from the beginning that the "self" about to be unfolded belongs to reader as well as poet. We are not to be divorced from the poem that follows; instead, it will define a field of consciousness that we are invited to inhabit. Indeed, we must lend this field provisional faith as an "imaginative variation of our own ego," in order to understand it.[49] This understanding is not only a rational process but also an energizing activity. We shall learn, this speaker promises, not to "take things at second or third hand," nor to "look through my eyes either"; rather, "You shall listen to all sides and filter them from yourself" (ll. 27–29). Whitman's poem, in other words, will teach us "self-reliance" in Emerson's sense of unlocking the creative potential within.

Given this regenerative aim, the details of "Song of Myself" are best read in terms of their effect upon the reader. Section 3, for example, starts to delineate a sexual energy that the poet expects us to learn to recognize within ourselves without anxiety or repression: "Urge and urge and urge, / Always the procreant urge of the world" (ll. 36–37). Accordingly, many early passages are designed to suspend mental habits that distance the reader from the self as Whitman imagines it. For instance, we are asked to avoid thinking of existence as something that wears out or runs down. As in the opening of Emerson's *Nature* with its evocation of the "sun" that "shines to-day also," we are given an image of plenitude, a fullness of being available here and now, unexhausted by our precursors:

> There never was any more inception than there is now,
> Nor any more youth or age than there is now,
> And will never be any more perfection than there is now,
> Nor any more heaven or hell than there is now. [ll. 32–35]

This motif will be repeated throughout the poem. The message, as Arthur Lovejoy phrases it in his chapter on "Romanticism and Plenitude," is that "the human artist must, like the divine, make fullness in the expression of all possible modes of being and of experience the purpose of his activity."[50] Here such fullness is internalized; it becomes the function of a new habit of perception—a stance of openness toward inner and outer worlds. Equally central to Whitman's aim is his direct confrontation of attitudes that label certain bodily functions dirty or exclude from polite society a class of sexual or criminal outcasts. Such exclusivity, we see as we read "Song of Myself," inhibits the very energies that the poet is trying to liberate:

Welcome is every organ and attribute of me, and of any man hearty
and clean
Not an inch nor a particle of an inch is vile, and none shall be
less familiar than the rest. [ll. 49–50]

"I am satisfied," the next line begins. How few of us, Whitman's poet
asks, are truly satisfied? Instead, we judge and discriminate, separating
ourselves from others and cleaving our psyches into allowed and forbidden territories. "Our present ego-feeling," Freud reflects in *Civilization
and Its Discontents*, "is . . . only a shrunken residue of a much more
inclusive—indeed, an all-embracing—feeling which corresponds to a
more intimate bond between the ego and the world about it."[51] But
rather than accepting like Freud the restraints of civilization, Whitman's
poet exhorts us to return to that unbounded "oceanic feeling" in which
the ordinary borders between ego and world melt away.[52] However, we
must depart from Freud's view of this process as an infantile regression
to the "pleasure principle" as opposed to the "reality principle." For
Whitman it is much more; the field of consciousness that his poem
enacts liberates energies ultimately directed toward humanitarian and
creative aims.

In a moral sense, the poet takes us "beyond good and evil." Like
Nietzsche, he develops a perspective transcending egotism: "a thought
comes when 'it' wishes, and not when 'I' wish, so that it is a falsification
of the facts of the case to say that the subject 'I' is the condition of the
predicate 'think.'"[53] What "thinks" us, Whitman asserts, is a primordial
energy found in the unconscious. Writing from an awareness of amoral
forces buried in the psyche, Whitman thus shares with Nietzsche the
insight that "every morality is, as opposed to *laisser aller* (letting go), a
bit of tyranny against 'nature.'"[54] Given their respective visions of the
natural (i.e., physical) origins of psychic energy, both writers argue that
instincts should not be repressed, especially not out of some strict adher-
ence to religious dogma. Issues of right and wrong tend to bifurcate
human potential by consigning some urges to the region of the illicit. By
advocating the expression of physical and sexual energies over the drawing of moral distinctions, Whitman aligns himself with writers such as
Norman O. Brown who attempt to place the mind back into the body.[55]

Section 3 concludes with an image, "baskets covered with white towels
bulging the house with their plenty" (l. 53), that gives promise of the
richness, both physical and spiritual, to be gained from modes of cognition that eliminate such self-division. Section 4 further evokes the attitudes that inhibit perception of such plenitude—the stance of "Trippers
and askers" with their "mockings or arguments" (ll. 58, 72). Only after
this "exorcism" of self-divisive viewpoints does the poet's "soul" enter

the poem in section 5. However we interpret this quasi-mystical experience that leads to "the peace and joy and knowledge that pass all the art and the argument of the earth" (l. 82), we recognize this moment as defining a process of inspiration that the reader will be motivated to emulate.[56] The goal of our own regeneration, Whitman's poem ultimately suggests, should be a similar ecstasy. As in Emerson's famous epiphany in *Nature* of the "transparent eye-ball," we are given an emblem of regeneration, a model that helps direct the unfolding of our selves.

In section 6, perhaps the most beautiful and moving of the entire poem, the poet turns from us toward a tentative exploration of his newfound world:

> A child said, What is the grass? fetching it to me with full hands;
> How could I answer the child? . . . . I do not know what it is any
>   more than he. [ll. 89–90]

"How could I answer the child?"—we are addressed and engaged by this voice, who takes us along with him on his exploration of a freshly perceived world. We have the sense of a newly awakened self reaching out like the child in wonder, handling with delicate care its new awareness of experience. Connections are being discovered for the first time: white with black, life with death, life force with poetic utterance. Similarly, the concluding affirmation—"All goes onward and outward . . . . and nothing collapses" (l. 120)—enters our awareness (the poet's and the reader's simultaneously) as an insight that has been freshly earned. The tone of this passage suggests that psychic connections are being forged for the first time, that new pathways of libido are being laid down—channels that will open out into an expanding world, a *Lebenswelt*, that both poet and reader will share.

Defining himself as "the mate and companion of people" in section 7, the poet offers the reader an even more radical role:

> Who need be afraid of the merge?
> Undrape . . . . you are not guilty to me, nor stale nor discarded,
> I see through the broadcloth and gingham whether or no,
> And am around, tenacious, acquisitive, tireless . . . . and can never
>   be shaken away. [ll. 136–39]

He will be the reader's "lover," accepting us for what we are, tenaciously demanding sexual engagement, ultimately inseminating us with his meaning. If the poet here accepts the reader, forgoing moral judgment, in a more extreme sense, he also seduces the reader, forcing recognition of and involvement with sexual energy. If, unlike many of Whitman's contemporaries, one keeps reading beyond this point, one submissively accepts a bond with a being who holds—even fondles—one's attention. The effect of this is to place the reader in a classically feminine position, subject to the demands of a patriarchal voice that molds "her" consciousness. Contributing to the poet's hold on the reader is the shock value of his assertions. We must relinquish our inhibitions in order to continue. As the trainers of certain religious cults have discovered, such open confrontation and suspension of inhibition is an effective means of mind control. Relinquishing shame, the reader (like the cult inductee) is exposed, emotionally undressed. Made vulnerable to suggestion, the reader is opened to the new identity that is being forged.

Again, in section 8, the poet turns from us to explore the world he is laying down piece by piece, image by image, around himself and us. He connects birth ("The little one sleeps in its cradle"), love ("The youngster and the redfaced girl turn aside up the bushy hill"), and death ("The suicide sprawls on the bloody floor of the bedroom") in a pattern that encompasses the life cycle. From the perspective of the life force, moments and phenomena ordinarily seen as disparate become connected. This process of connection establishes for the reader an unfolding field of consciousness that functions as a model of regenerating vision. Images are engaged and juxtaposed in a perceptual mosaic that alters the reader's picture of reality. In particular, the poet fills in the reader's blind spots by including situations (like the suicide) that most people repress from awareness.

In section 9 such world construction is subsumed under the image of harvest. Here we see the poet as harvester, reaping the wealth of unloosed experience. The exuberance of his attitude—"And roll head over heels, and tangle my hair full of wisps" (l. 167)—conveys a sense of celebration. The "armfuls" that are "packed to the sagging mow" (l. 163) seem more than "dried grass." They suggest the images that poet and reader now find at hand everywhere. Having released the "procreant urge," we discover its tendency to invest itself in ever widening circles of lived experience. The world's wealth waits to be expressed. We might turn anywhere and find a new home for our energies, a new vehicle for the self's expression.

Section 10 graphically demonstrates the process of identification that typifies such participatory poetics. The reader's involvement in the poet's expanding circle of consciousness mirrors his or her involvement with the world. Starting as outside observers, we are drawn by the poet into his experience. In a similar fashion, he moves into the phenomena he starts to catalogue:

The Yankee clipper is under her three skysails . . . . she cuts the
    sparkle and scud,
My eyes settle the land . . . . I bend at her prow or shout joyously
    from the deck. [ll. 173–74]

Observation of the clipper as a distant object ("she cuts") merges into participation with the process of sailing ("I bend at her prow"). This transformation parallels the reader's growing submission to the rhythms of the poet's self-awareness. Taking over the stage of the reader's consciousness, the poet continues to feminize the reader, subordinating "her" experience to the spread of his masculine dominion.

Although the poet's representations of the "marriage of the trapper" and of the "runaway slave" seem somewhat heavy-handed examples of his identification with figures from all walks of life, in section 11 he more fully dramatizes an act of identification with another. Looking through the eyes of the "lonesome" lady, the poet empathically participates in her sexual frustration, at the same time that he provides the reader with a model of feminized desire. Just as the reader is learning to lie open to the poet's persuasive voice, the lady longs toward the potent bodies of the twenty-eight male bathers:

The beards of the young men glistened with wet, it ran from their
    long hair,
Little streams passed all over their bodies.

An unseen hand also passed over their bodies,
It descended tremblingly from their temples and ribs. [ll. 204–7]

What is especially striking here is that the act of perception itself has become sexualized; the poet's contact with both reader and world is presented in sexual terms.

The mind, Whitman shows us, invests its "procreant urge" onto first one object, then another. This awareness that attention involves the tending, the fixing, of libido onto various objects is a strikingly modern insight that anticipates Freud's view of object-relations. In section 12 the poet's attention (paralleling the reader's view of the poet) fixes itself momentarily upon the sexually attractive image of potent blacksmiths, upon the "lithe sheer of their waists" and their "massive arms" (l. 216). Then in section 13 the poet expresses in general terms this investment of psychic energy through the act of perception: "In me the caresser of life wherever moving" (l. 226). He *caresses* life—the verb is important, revealing Whitman's sexualizing of his relationship to world and reader. Similarly, in section 14 the poet is "enamoured of growing outdoors" (l. 248); he sees himself "spending" and "scattering" his seminal energy—an image that furthers his definition of the reader as the feminine vessel that will receive his meaning.

This energy, the poet shows us in the first great catalogue in section 15, bypasses the Apollonian distinctions that would separate the "bride" from the "opium eater" (ll. 300–301), a "prostitute" from the "President" (ll. 302, 305). The Dionysian impulse toward identification and merger eliminates the division of perceived reality into in-group and out-group, norm and outcast. Nothing and no one will be excluded from the poet's world. His primordial life force, an expansive energy that embraces the world's diversity, emerges from a level prior to the ego's categories and isolating differentiations. Having loosed this energy, the poet tends it indiscriminately. Like the impulse celebrated in Emerson's "Circles," this force has the tendency to expand freely in an ever-widening circumference. But in contrast to Emerson's identification of libido with the "moral sentiment," Whitman's sexualized energy is presented as being amoral. Moving through the poet's catalogue, we witness first his sense of time ("Seasons pursuing each other") and then of space rapidly enlarging. However, at this point, such psychic inflation (or should we say "world inflation"?) is still far from the critical point in section 38 where the poet's self starts to fly apart, and he can only maintain his vision by "dying" and being "reborn" as a god, an archetype of the self.

Sections 16 and 17 consolidate the poet's expansive gains through generalized expression of democratic acceptance: "I am of old and young, of the foolish as much as the wise" (l. 326); "These are the thoughts of all men in all ages and lands" (l. 353). Such statements establish a general pattern that the reader has been seduced into adopting, assimilating the insights of a democratic—but also patriarchal—consciousness. The poet molds us into a new form of identity, shaping our very souls.

REFLECTING UPON PSYCHIC PROCESS

By this point in "Song of Myself" the poet starts to reflect upon the special qualities of what he is giving us:

This is the grass that grows wherever the land is and the water is,
This is the common air that bathes the globe. [ll. 358–59]

What follows is a striking chain of metaphors that indicate both the substantiality of the poet's images, their rootedness in lived experience, and their energy. The poet characterizes his unfolding vision as "grass," "air," "breath," "water," and "sustenance" (ll. 358–61). In section 18 he tells us that his unfolding field of vision is a "trill" and a "march"; in 19, a "meal." By means of such metaphors, the poet moves toward conscious articulation of the force now passing both through him and us—a force that he will eventually term both "current" and "afflatus" (l. 506). Mixing images that evoke physical and spiritual qualities, he creates what Carl Jung calls "symbols of libido."[57] Such symbols are an important stage in the self's definition; for by naming the psyche's energy, they facilitate the operations performed by and upon it. Such symbols become a valuable psychological tool. "One of the most important attainments of consciousness," Erich Neumann argues, "is its ability to dispose at will of the libido supplied to its system, and to use it more or less independently of the source from which it came."[58] This disposition of psychic energy is made possible once libido has been named. At that point, symbols of libido become the "currency" of the psychic economy.

By the end of section 19 the poet—who has started to identify himself with natural processes ("April rain," "daylight")—takes the reader into his "confidence." We might pause to note the radical difference between Whitman's use of this term and Melville's, for this difference underscores the participatory poetics at the heart of Whitman's presentation. Enlisting his audience's trust, Melville's Confidence-Man exploits that faith through a series of charades that draw attention to the fictionality of social interaction.[59] Understanding the rules of the game, the confidence man can stand inside and outside, both participating and ironically controlling it. Before his transcendent union with the hidden self in section 5, this is the position of Whitman's poet: "Both in and out of the game, and watching and wondering at it" (l. 70). But by the end of section 19 his situation has changed; he not only moves entirely "within" the game, he places the reader inside as well.

By this point the poet's rhetorical and sexual domination of the reader turns into an act of trust. If the poet is able to discover his "self" by trusting in the self-representation that he is disclosing, we discover ourselves by trusting that figure as a model for the parallel identities forming within us. Whitman's poet confides in us the same way our inner mentor whispers in our ear—he spells out lessons of being that emerge from the hidden recesses of the psyche. Having assimilated the vocabulary of that voice (and hence, having mystified our original subordination to it), we learn to trust ourselves in an act of self-reliance. But, as in the case of Emerson, that self-trust paradoxically follows a period of submission in which the reader is placed in a passive, "feminine," position. One escapes from that subordination by "identifying with the aggressor," assuming as one's own his most intimate psychic rhythms.

During the next three sections (20–22) the poet gradually formulates the central sexual rhythm of "Song of Myself" as an alternating pattern of "influx" and "efflux" (l. 462). At the most active extreme of "efflux," Whitman's poet "is a person who 'infuses' a fresh consciousness in us" by constructing around us a "libidinized space" or "dream space."⁶⁰ This process involves world construction; the poet constructs our world, our worldview. Whitman's most shocking metaphor for this efflux is that of sexual outpouring: the poet "inseminates" us with his vision, impregnating us with it.⁶¹ Opposed to the creative "efflux" of the self is a "feminine" passivity (or "wise passivity," in Wordsworth's phrase) that allows the inflowing or "influx" of unimpeded experience. According to Quentin Anderson, Whitman frequently imagines this as "being immersed" or even of being sexually invaded by experiences that metamorphose into a pattern of rape in which the poet is the passive (although not unwilling) victim.⁶² At other times, Whitman multiplies oral images of ingestion, eating, sustenance, in which the poet is "fed by all the things seen."⁶³ In this state, sensory inhibitions are lifted, as the poet gorges himself with experience to (and sometimes, beyond) the point of satiety.

The poet's apostrophe to night in section 21 is an instance of this second movement, "feminine" influx: "Press close barebosomed night!" In this section the poet becomes the world's "lover," filling himself with sensuous experience. But at the same time, this immersion is matched by "masculine" efflux, the reciprocal outpouring of his vision:

Prodigal! you have given me love! . . . . therefore I to you give
     love!
O unspeakable passionate love!

Thruster holding me tight and that I hold tight!
We hurt each other as the bridegroom and the bride hurt each other.
[ll. 447–50]

Similarly, in 22 the poet and the sea exchange sexual outpourings: "Dash me with amorous wet . . . . I can repay you" (l. 456). During the course of this section we have the impression that what addresses us is the impersonal life force itself, a force that can take form as sea or poet: "I moisten the roots of all that has grown" (l. 472). This voice has transcended individual identity. If we continue to label it as the poet's, it is for want of a better term.

By the end of section 23 and the beginning of 24, Whitman gives us two terms that characterize the voice that we are hearing. In section 23, this voice tells us that it uses facts to "enter by them to an area of the *dwelling*" (l. 494, italics mine). In 24, it assumes a name—"Walt Whitman, an American, one of the roughs, a *kosmos*" (l. 499, italics mine). "Song of Myself" is about dwelling, in Heidegger's sense of dwelling as existential habitation. To dwell is to exist, to unfold one's being. This poem constructs a dwelling, in the form of a model of regenerated existence, that becomes a habitation for vision—first Whitman's, then the reader's. By characterizing himself as a "kosmos," the poet evokes our awareness that one's lived-world, one's *Lebenswelt*, constitutes a cosmos through which being transpires. "One world is aware, and by far the largest to me, and that is myself" (l. 416). Bracketing the moral judgment of reality, Whitman allows this world to appear within the phenomenological field of his poet's reflection. The universe, he shows us, exists anew in each conscious incarnation, in each person's awareness of existence. Whitman's "kosmos" suggests the bubble of experience that each individual constructs as his or her image of reality. This construction is an existential field that includes bodily "image," as well as mental image. It can widen or—as in the case of Whitman's "trippers and askers"—contract. "Song of Myself" attempts to widen the reader's "kosmos," to liberate the energies that connect being to an expanding reality.

Section 24 portrays this liberation of the self from inhibition and repression as the escape of Dionysian energy:

> Unscrew the locks from the doors!
> Unscrew the doors themselves from their jambs! [ll. 502–3]

Like the uncontainable god in Euripides' *The Bacchae*, a divinity who escapes the chains of King Pentheus and shatters his palace, this being expresses an energy that cannot be bound or tied down. Both "afflatus" and "current" (l. 506), this power combines spiritual vision and physical impulse. Obliterating the barriers that divide norm from outcast, it connects both poet and reader with "many long dumb voices" (l. 509), "forbidden voices" (l. 518): the voices of "slaves," "prostitutes," "deformed persons," "the diseased and despairing," "thieves and dwarfs" (ll. 510–12). Evoking the spirit behind the age's lust for reform, Whitman portrays that liberating power as an energy that transcends, and hence removes, "the veil" (l. 519) of physical and sexual shame. Taboo subjects—"the bowels," "copulation," "death," "the flesh and the appetites" (ll. 522–24)—now enter the field of awareness. Transgressing the civilized impulse to separate, to dissociate, to distinguish, this power displaces the psychic economy from egotism to an inclusive and "primeval" (l. 507) sense of self. In the process Whitman suspends reification of the body— a self-division manifesting itself in the repression of physical urges— and replaces it with a vision of the human body as a moving pattern of Dionysian energy. Such energy, according to Norman O. Brown, "breaks down the boundaries; releases the prisoners; abolishes repression, and abolishes the *principium individuationis*, substituting for it the unity of man and the unity of man with nature."[64] Emerson's Apollonian reflection, discovering the unconscious and then sublimating its energy, finally meets its ecstatic double in Whitman's celebration of the body's sexual power.

Inflated by this power, the poet's image of the body phallically expands—metamorphosing into a landscape. The "body's world" and the "world's body" merge into a figure of archetypal dimensions: "Trickling sap of maple, fibre of manly wheat" (l. 538), "Broad muscular fields, branches of liveoak" (l. 543). If the American poet, as Whitman asserts in his 1855 Preface to *Leaves of Grass*, "incarnates [the] geography and natural life and rivers and lakes" (*LG*, 7), here this geographical motive transforms into a mythologized image of the body as libidinized field of natural energy. As a result, the drive of "manifest destiny"—the imperative to explore and tame the wilderness—is displaced to the self, which has its own wild and fecund energies waiting to be cultivated and harvested. Standing in awe of his own body, the poet imagines sublime vistas within that parallel vistas without. The self's movements are mysterious: "I cannot tell how my ankles bend . . . . nor whence the cause of my faintest wish" (l. 547). The mystery of human impulse, like the mystery of nature, occasions celebration and wonder—not fear and shame.

By the end of section 24 the poet, having returned to a less deific form, reflects upon the dual process of experience (influx) and expression (efflux):

Hefts of the moving world at innocent gambols, silently rising,
   freshly exuding,
Scooting obliquely high and low.

Something I cannot see puts forth libidinous prongs,
Seas of bright juice suffuse heaven. [ll. 555–58]

"Hefts of the moving world," in all their cloudlike and lamblike spontaneity, suggest blocks or chunks of sense impressions moving freely through the poet's field of perception. Receptive influx is paired with the efflux of his response—his sense of an unseen psychic urge toward expression, stretching forth "libidinous prongs." The "sense organs," Freud comments in a relevant passage, "may perhaps be compared with feelers which are all the time making tentative advances towards the external world."[65] Whitman's "libidinous prongs" capture this sense of psychic extension as a tending of libido, a stretching outward of attention. "The ego," Freud notes elsewhere, "is a great reservoir from which the libido that is destined for objects flows out and into which it flows back from those objects. . . . As an illustration of this state of things we may think of an amoeba, whose viscous substance puts out pseudo-podia."[66]

Like Freud, Whitman eroticizes this activity by portraying vision (the fulfillment of attention) as a transforming insemination that pours throughout perceived reality and the reader's consciousness. Here Whitman manifests the phallocentric imagery analyzed by Sandra Gilbert and Susan Gubar; he portrays the poet as "a father, a progenitor, a procreator, an aesthetic patriarch whose pen is an instrument of generative power like his penis."[67] This organ, Gilbert and Gubar continue, has both "the ability to generate life" and "the power to create a posterity to which he lays claim." By feminizing the reader and subjecting "her" to the power of his pen, Whitman enforces the imperialistic claims of his vision. But at the same time he is starting to compel a liberating identification with the orgasmic and Dionysian release of phallic power.

Sections 25 through 29 display this erotic rhythm of tension and discharge on a larger scale. However, before transposing this phallic imagery to a more expansive key, the poet pauses to reflect upon the sexual rhythm of influx and efflux that he has just experienced. By alternating passages of self-dramatization with such moments of commentary, Whitman enables himself to detach scenes of expression (like that in section 24) as signs exemplifying the creative process that he is unfolding. He both portrays and "psychoanalyzes" the rhythms of the self by alternating scenes of self-dramatization and self-analysis—a process that allows the reader both to experience vicariously the poet's libidinous creative energy and then to assimilate that power into an ongoing process of psychological reflection. But as Whitman stands back in order to comment upon his psychological mythmaking, he begins to mystify the sexual foundation of his rhetoric. At the beginning of section 25, for example, his poet translates sexual energy into the vocabulary of creativity and vision. If he receives "the sunrise" into himself (influx), he must "always send sunrise out" of himself (efflux). "Speech," he tells us, "is the twin of my vision" (l. 568). Receptive understanding is paired with the urge to "let it out" (l. 570). The source of "articulation" (l. 571), he reminds us, is found in the dark recesses of the self, in the "gloom" where "the buds beneath are folded" (ll. 572–73). Sublimating sexual urge into an image of the unconscious, the poet evokes a creative potential that we share with him. But we can only discover this creative power by imitating him, embarking on our own voyage of self-discovery:

"whoever hears me let him or her set out in search of this day" (l. 577). Like Thoreau, Whitman emphasizes that creative energy roots being more firmly in the sensuous apprehension of the present.

After such self-commentary, sections 26–29, which dramatize even more graphically the sexual rhythm of experience and expression, serve as a psychological model of the creative process. Like William Butler Yeats, who multiplies arcane diagrams of the psyche's oscillating creative rhythm in *A Vision*, Whitman presents emblems of the self's movement toward and away from ecstatic moments of insight. These are not autobiographical statements, as many readers assume, but paradigms demonstrating both the joy and potential vulnerability of unrepressed creative being. Thus when section 26 returns us to the pattern of influx, it is imagined now as the passive reception of the world's sounds:

> I think I will do nothing for a long time but listen,
> And accrue what I hear into myself . . . . and let the sounds
>   contribute toward me. [ll. 584–85]

As this section progresses, the aural attractions of reality resolve into the image of the "trained soprano" whose music "convulses" the poet "like the climax of my love-grip" (l. 602). Experiencing what Nietzsche calls "the rapture of the Dionysian state with its annihilation of the ordinary bounds and limits of existence," the poet transcends ordinary cognition.[68]

But the poet's receptiveness to the word's attractions, his tending of unloosed libido as attention, leaves him feeling "exposed" (l. 607) and vulnerable. Having removed the normal barriers impeding self-expression, he has also eliminated the restraints that ordinarily limit attention before it passes over into fascination or even fixation. Meditating upon what he calls "the puzzle of puzzles . . . Being" (ll. 609–10), the poet focuses in sections 27 and 28 upon the potential danger of unrestrained libido. The tendency of the psyche's energy, he shows us, is to be drawn out and to adhere indiscriminately to things:

> I have instant conductors all over me and whether I pass or stop,
> They seize every object and lead it harmlessly through me. [ll. 614–15]

For a moment, the word *harmlessly* forestalls the poet's sense of danger. But in the next section his adhesiveness threatens to stretch him too far, to pull him apart (the fate he nearly suffers in section 38). He succumbs to the seductive advances of even more enticing experiences:

> Is this then a touch . . . . quivering me to a new identity,
> Flames and ether making a rush for my veins,
> Treacherous tip of me reaching and crowding to help them. [ll. 618–20]

Whitman's attentiveness here to the vulnerability resulting from unleashed attention is perhaps rivaled only by passages in Theodore Roethke's poetry. Like Whitman, Roethke in "The Lost Son" and "The Far
Field" considers the possible extinction of the conscious self. Unlocking
the body's ecstatic motives, Roethke as well portrays similar moments
when "prurient provokers"—an intense ingathering of impressions—invade the self, seducing it toward a climactic release of pent-up energies.

   Finally in section 29, the moment of orgasmic release arrives—a "Rich
showering rain" (l. 644) that creates "Landscapes projected masculine
full-sized and golden" (l. 646). At this point, Whitman's phallocentric
model of the creative process is complete. Thus he can allow the poet to
stand back again in sections 30 and 31 in order to reflect upon what has
transpired. Shifting to the level of generalization, the poet now consoli-
dates the psychological rhythm he has just experienced, at the same time
that he continues the sublimation of sexual energy into a generalized
vision of the self's relation to world:

> All truths wait in all things,
> They neither hasten their own delivery nor resist it,
> They do not need the obstetric forceps of the surgeon,
> The insignificant is as big to me as any,
> What is less or more than a touch? [ll. 647–51]

This affirmation of the "truths" to be elicited by a "touch" (both physical
caress and mental embrace) begins to articulate Whitman's view of object-relations. Contact with the world, he asserts at the end of section 30,
facilitates the unfolding of the self; it leads to insight and delight that
"branch endlessly out of that lesson" (l. 660).

   Section 31 continues the poet's affirmation of his newly discovered
psychic economy. Wonder at existence is matched by his incorporation
and reinvention of reality. "Now the poet can both believe in and be
everything in his world," Roy Harvey Pearce writes, "for its being is
grounded in his relation to it."[69] As the poet asserts in section 32, the
world's entities "bring me tokens of myself" (l. 693); they allow him to
discover the contours of his being through the act of relation. This
section closes with an example of such "correspondence" as the poet
ponders "a gigantic beauty of a stallion" (l. 702)—a blatant masculine
image that correlates with his newfound sense of creative potency. But
he then realizes that even this image reflects but one facet of his emerging psychic reality: "I but use you a moment and then I resign you
stallion" (l. 707). From this point on, an accelerating impulse toward
inclusion starts to take precedence over sexual bonds with individual
objects. "My ties and ballasts leave me," the poet proclaims near the

beginning of section 33. Unleashed once again, his omnivorous mind starts to attach itself to and devour the things of this world. But the next wave of influx (stretching from sections 33 to 38) carries the poet over the edge into psychic catastrophe. He ingests too much; he expands the field of vision until it explodes, flying apart into dismembered fragments of Dionysian energy. The fate of Dionysius, let us remember, was to be torn apart by the ecstatic energies he embodied.

INFLATION AND APOTHEOSIS

Like the earlier catalogue in section 15, section 33 exhibits an unrestrained "oral" ingestion of experience.[70] His energy unleashed, the poet revels in his newfound ability to adhere to and assimilate any experience. Floating aloft in his "pear-shaped balloon" (l. 739), he fills himself with the manifold sights and sounds of the American landscape. "I fly the flight of the fluid and swallowing soul," he exclaims (l. 799). "No guard can shut me off, no law can prevent me" (l. 802). But as his influx expands, a new note enters the poet's reflection. Like the Dionysius of classical myth, he associates himself with wild beasts: "the panther," "the rattlesnake," "the alligator," "the black bear" (ll. 720–23), "winter wolves" (l. 766). Along with such wildness, images of suffering, victimization, and death enter the poem in full force: "my man's body . . . dripping and drowned" (l. 816), the "rudderless wreck of the steamship . . . death chasing it up and down the storm" (l. 820), "martyrs" (l. 828), the "mother condemned for a witch and burnt with dry wood" (l. 829), "the hounded slave" (l. 834), "the mashed fireman" (l. 842). Moving toward a Christlike role, the poet—according to James E. Miller, Jr.—"assumes the agony and despair of the world," a self-identification that moves him into his "dark night of the soul."[71] While Miller's adaptation of mystical terminology clarifies the psychological rhythm of this passage, it does not entirely explain why such an abrupt transition should take place at this point.

We can start to understand the poet's transformation by examining his changing relationship to his own creative energy. Like Goethe, Byron, and Melville, Whitman dramatizes here the potentially tragic fate of an overextended Romantic self who has started to lose control over his creative power. Identifying themselves too closely with the ecstatic energies emerging from within, Faust, Manfred, and Ahab all risk being torn apart by irrational urge. Expanding the scope of his self-image to the verge of dissolution, Whitman's poet risks being sucked into a maelstrom of unrestrained passion (a fate that threatens many of Poe's charac-

ters). Images of dismemberment—the "whizz of limbs heads stone wood
and iron high in the air" (l. 860)—evoke the potential explosion of the
self into pieces. Like Ahab, the poet is in danger of being branded and
ripped apart by the powers with which he is dealing. Unable to halt its
own progress, the impulse toward influx starts to overstrain the poet's
capacity to maintain his psychic center. According to Albert Gelpi, "he
finds himself in the danger opposite to the 'egotistical sublime'; namely
the rapid catalogue and, more urgently, through the depth of empathic
identification with . . . vivid and painful particulars."[72] Models of this
process are provided by the Dionysian myth of ecstasy leading to dismemberment and by the Jungian account of psychic "inflation."

John Irwin suggests the first model when he notes that Whitman's
model of self-development enacts a "Dionysian impulse": "if the *expressed* purpose of the Dionysian impulse in Whitman's poetry is the
reabsorption of the individual self into the cosmic float, we as readers
should never forget that the actual method of the poetry is just the
opposite, in that the generic 'I' of Whitman's poems is based upon the
absorption of the cosmos into the individual, the identification of the
world with the self."[73] In our terms, *both* movements—expansion of self
into world and absorption of world into self—involve a Dionysian sur-
render. The poet's identification with reality, his adhesion to things,
pulls him ecstatically "out of himself," but identification becomes ab-
sorptive "influx" at the moment the poet recognizes the correspondence
between the objects of his interest and his own self-awareness. Altering
Irwin's emphasis, let us focus not upon Whitman's "purpose" but upon
the psychological effect of his "Dionysian impulse." To risk an anachro-
nistic metaphor, Whitman shows us that the motive energy fueling correspondence threatens to reach a critical mass analogous to that achieved
in an out-of-control nuclear reactor. The poet's rapidly accelerating adhesion to things packs the field of his reflection with the combined
radiation of their respective emotional charges. At some point he will
reach a sensory and emotional overload, blowing his mind.

Such fragmentation of the self, imagined as dismemberment, is central
to Dionysian myth. One of the most striking aspects of Dionysian rituals, H. J. Rose notes, was the "tearing in pieces and devouring of an
animal or even human victim."[74] Such was the fate of King Pentheus in
The Bacchae. According to legend, Orpheus himself—the archetypal
poet—was torn in pieces by the women of Thrace during a Dionysian
frenzy.[75] Intoxication and ecstasy, the Dionysian myth teaches, elide
easily into the annihilation of identity by overpowering forces. Yet, as
Richard Chase noted years ago, Whitman's evocation of Dionysian

frenzy serves a larger reintegration of the self: "Do we not have a ritual celebration of 'Nature without check with original energy,' of the cycle of death and rebirth, the *agon*, sacrifice, and *gamos* of the protagonist, i.e. the self? Do we not have in Whitman's image of the diffusion of the self in nature a religious feeling akin to that engendered in the Dionysian mysteries by the dismemberment and assimilation of the sacrificial victim?"[76] The self's *agon* (conflict between the "I" and overpowering unconscious forces) gives way to a *gamos* (marriage) in which "I" and other are harmoniously recombined. Following such a pattern, Whitman's poem enacts a ritual that gives mythical form to the emotional response of its readers. We might term this pattern a "ritual of psychic inflation and apotheosis."

"Song of Myself," Malcolm Cowley notes, flirts with "self-inflation."[77] Carl Jung describes psychic "inflation" as a feeling of "godlikeness" that can result from the "process of assimilating the unconscious."[78] Identifying this psychic phenomenon as the fate of Goethe's Faust, Jung argues that inflation manifests itself in two ways—either as a sense of superhuman power or as "a sense of powerlessness," "a 'godlikeness' in suffering."[79] Psychic inflation, as Jung defines it, "involves an extension of the personality beyond individual limits, in other words, a state of being puffed up. In such a state a man fills a space which normally he cannot fill."[80] Elsewhere, Jung argues that inflation of the personality causes a dangerous overextension of the self, an excess of psychic energy that can "dismember" or "crucify" the individual: "it is just the inspired soul . . . that becomes god and demon, and as such suffers the divine punishment of being torn asunder like Zagreus [Dionysius]. This is what Nietzsche experienced at the onset of his malady."[81] As he slipped into madness, Nietzsche signed his final letters "Dionysius" and "The Crucified."[82] Nietzsche's "crucifixion" resulted from his being torn apart psychologically by unconscious forces that he could no longer control; a similar fate is experienced momentarily by Whitman's poet: "O Christ! My fit is mastering me!" (l. 933).

During "Song of Myself," the poet follows a course of Dionysian expansion that nearly leads to a fragmentation of the self into dismembered pieces. By the end of section 37 the poet is "so sensitively exposed that he feels himself on the verge, once again, of losing his ego-center in circumference."[83] Faced with the potential dissolution of his persona, Whitman exerts artistic control in two different ways. Ultimately, in section 38 his poet transcends disintegration by assimilating his experience to a Christian model of crucifixion and resurrection. Having "assume[d] the agony and despair of the world," he overcomes the threatened loss of the self by metamorphosing into a creative god.[84] This apotheosis raises self-awareness from human to superhuman dimensions. Giving the Oversoul voice, it sublimates sorrow and passion to the serene self-assurance of a deified being. The psyche's energy, as a result, no longer threatens the "I" with dissolution, for that power is focused and controlled by an archetypal model of being that ensures the transference of energy from self to other. We can conclude from this that one avenue of escape for the tormented Romantic hero is to assume the mantle of prophecy and step from self-destructiveness into a certified public role. This is what Whitman's poet does. By donning the role of "crucifixion," he accepts an interpersonal model of suffering predicated upon the sublimation of pain into self-awareness.

This dialectical maneuver (roughly analogous to the movement of Emerson's "compensation," his affirmation of the educative value of hardship) is prepared for in sections 34 to 36. In these sections Whitman reveals his second means of artistic control over potentially disruptive Dionysian energies. Before identifying himself as a creative god, his poet transposes his psychic experience into the emotional rhythms of American patriotism through his accounts of the Texas martyrs' defeat and of John Paul Jones's famous naval victory. As in the pattern of crucifixion and resurrection, images of death give way to a celebration of power. Whitman's conflation of patriotic and religious rhythms is revealed by the way he reverses the chronology of the historical events that he portrays. The massacre of four hundred and twelve Texans in 1836, the "tale of a jetblack sunrise" (l. 866), is followed by the account of John Paul Jones's heroic victory over the British *Serapis* in 1779. The account of the Texas massacre arouses feelings of bitterness and defeat; the succeeding portrayal of Jones's triumph reframes defeat within the context of a self-aggrandizing patriotism that dates back to the founding of the American Republic. By portraying the defeat first, Whitman sets up the emotional release provided by Jones's model of heroism. Manipulating his audience's response, Whitman shifts from a distancing third-person narrative when recounting the Texas massacre to the first person when he turns to the naval victory. His poet moves from detached observation of defeat back into a mode of identification that celebrates individual heroism: "*We* closed with him" (l. 895, italics mine), "*I* laughed content when *I* heard the voice of *my* little captain" (l. 904, italics mine).

But as we have seen, the underside of heroism—for Whitman—is the danger of inflation and hence self-fragmentation. By the end of section 36, as the poet evokes the casualties of naval warfare, this underlying pattern of Dionysian dismemberment is made explicit by the imagery of amputation:

The hiss of the surgeon's knife and the gnawing teeth of his saw,
The wheeze, the cluck, the swash of falling blood . . . . [ll. 930–31]

But if this imagery suggests the impending disintegration of the heroic self, that dissolution is partially negated by the context of military victory. Section 37 repeats this recuperative elevation of the self by shifting from a patriotic to a Christian frame of reference. This section opens with the poet on the verge of losing control over the Dionysian forces of self-expansion: "O Christ! My fit is mastering me!" (l. 933). But it ends with the confident assertion that "I rise extatic through all" (l. 953). Again, the pattern of self-expansion—threatened dismemberment—apotheosis marks the career of the poet. Before he reaches the triumphant resurrection of his persona in section 38, Whitman rehearses this pattern of transformation twice.

By the climax of "Song of Myself" in section 38, Whitman has effectively politicized the psychological career of his poet. Much more than a passage through "the dark night of the soul," the preceding sections lay the groundwork for the poet's apotheosis into a voice keyed both to the rhythms of religious awakening and patriotic fervor. As he expands into a messianic bard, Whitman's persona has been authorized to articulate both the spiritual and the political desires of the American people. No longer singular in his identity, the poet emerges as part of the mass, as the voice of American democracy. From here to the end of the poem, Whitman tries on a series of "archetypal roles" as he explores the dimensions of this newly constituted poetic being.[85]

LEAVING CHARGES

Mediating his image of the transfigured self through images of natural power, divinity, and cosmic being, Whitman in the final sections of "Song of Myself" portrays a figure with the capacity to inspire each reader with the creative power that he has been incarnating. In section 39 we see the poet as noble savage; in 40, the poet as phallic god and inspirer; in 41, the poet as god of reality; in 42, the poet as sublime orator. These figures combine into a composite "god of self-reliance" who fills each one of us with an energy that unlocks our own being:

You there, impotent, loose in the knees, open your scarfed chops till
    I blow grit within you . . . . [l. 993]

I dilate you with tremendous breath . . . . I buoy you up. [l. 1009]

"I have embraced you," he tells us at the end of section 40, "and henceforth possess you to myself, / And when you rise in the morning you will find what I tell you is so" (ll. 1013–14).

Emerson exhorted his congregation to listen to "the voice" whispered within by "the Father" (*YES*, 200); Whitman's poet starts to become "the Father"—a figure representing forces now becoming audible within his readers' own minds. By this point the poet's patriarchal power over the feminized reader is obscured, for he is completely internalized by the reader, able to assert that "I act as the tongue of you" (l. 1244). From here to the end of the poem the poet turns from his own development back toward the reader, addressing him or her in terms designed to facilitate self-possession. In the process the poet turns himself into an exemplary persona, becoming a symbol of the process of inspiration that he is promulgating. Presenting himself as a god, "becoming already a creator" (l. 1048), he devotes himself to the creation of his audience's being. This model of regeneration parallels Emerson's "rhetoric of regeneration," except that Whitman hopes to inspire his audience with a different kind of energy. The form of self-reliance is maintained, but the content of self-awareness has been changed.

Speaking as a sublime orator in section 42, the poet presents himself as a "performer" who "has passed his prelude on the reeds within" (l. 1054). Having completed his psychological apprenticeship, educated in the ways of authentic being, he is now authorized to teach his audience how to distinguish "buying or taking or selling" from "the feast" (l. 1067). This lesson is facilitated both by the poet's identification with the crowd and by his "egotism." On the one hand, he asserts his common identity with the other citizens of the city: "Every thought that flounders in me the same flounders in them" (l. 1078). His self-portrayal depicts a universal psychological model. But at the same time the poet admits that his aggrandized self-dramatization, a sign of his difference, has served a rhetorical aim:

> I know perfectly well my own egotism,
> And know my omniverous words, and cannot say any less,
> And would fetch you whoever you are flush with myself. [ll. 1079–81]

Presenting himself both as identical with his audience and as a model of superior attainment, the poet aims at compelling his reader to recognize "you yourself." Opposing "sermons and creeds and theology," he teaches his reader to see the dimensions of the self—the truth embodied in the "human brain," in "reason," "love," and "life" (l. 1091).

In the next three sections (43–45) Whitman's psychological mythmaking is most apparent, as he turns to religious imagery in his attempt to label the poet's creative power. The poet's faith surpasses all previous forms of worship, but the center of that belief is not a conventional image of divinity, but rather what Whitman calls "it." Like Nietzsche and

Freud after him, he resorts to the neuter third-person pronoun in order to evoke the otherness of the psyche's core of energy. (Poe and Hawthorne, by contrast, frequently use "she.")

> I do not know what is untried and afterward,
> But I know *it* is sure and alive and sufficient.
>
> Each who passes is considered, and each who stops is considered,
>   and not a single one can *it* fail.
>
> *It* cannot fail the young man who died and was buried,
> Nor the young woman who died and was put by his side . . . .
> [ll. 1120–24, italics mine]

Evoking an infinite life force, the plenitude of the world's power, "it" grounds being on a secure ontological base. Like Emerson's Oversoul or Wordsworth's Nature, "it" signifies an expansive power found both in the psyche and outside the self. "I turn and talk like a man leaving charges before a journey" (l. 1108), the poet comments. Teaching us to recognize the power within, he leaves "charges": duties to be performed, electrical impulses, potential insights that might explode into self-awareness.

"What is known I strip away . . . . I launch all men and women forward with me into the unknown" (l. 1134). Orienting each reader toward the future unfolding of his or her self, the poet cultivates the stance of self-faith necessary to release unconscious power. Aiming toward the unknown, each individual must relinquish the security of past ties, the defenses provided by conventionalized categories of perception. For James E. Miller, Jr., this unknown represents "that which is not perceived by the senses, known only to the mystic, and designated by him the 'transcendent reality.'"[86] But Whitman's goal throughout "Song of Myself"—like Thoreau's in *Walden*—has been to immerse us in our senses, not to turn us away from them. More precisely, the unknown evokes the horizon of each person's being, the limit beyond which new forms of experience can appear. Like Emerson and Thoreau, Whitman forces us to see the horizon and hence to recognize the ways in which our lives have been bounded. "In the tranquil landscape, and especially in the distant line of the horizon," Emerson wrote in *Nature*, "man beholds somewhat as beautiful as his own nature" (*CW*, 1:10). Only when one can perceive the horizon can one clear a space for new growth of the self. The "quiet desperation" of most people (to use Thoreau's phrase) is that they have no horizon, no sense of personal scope.

Although the poet—in the rest of section 44—expands his horizon to encompass "eternity," his use of that term does not tie his vision to any traditional religious dogma. Instead, the evocation of infinite time and space enlarges his consciousness until it expands to fill the cosmos: "I am the acme of things accomplished, and I am encloser of things to be" (l. 1148). This "I" is no longer an identifiable person, but rather a field of vision that can stretch from "the apices of the stars" (l. 1149) back to "the huge first Nothing" (l. 1153). Despite this massive enlargement, the "I" avoids dismemberment by assimilating all imaginable experience back to the present moment. Although the poet's reflection can expand to cosmic dimensions, that expansion no longer dangerously inflates the self because he has moved once and for all beyond egotism. He speaks from a vantage point outside self-interest, beyond the demands of personal identity. Although Whitman was not able to maintain such disinterest in his later poetry, in "Song of Myself" at least he is "careful to distinguish the external self or personality from the deeper Self."[87]

"The victory is won," Emerson once observed, "as soon as any soul has learned always to take sides with reason against himself; to transfer his *Me* from his person, his name, his interest, back upon Truth & Justice .... Keep the habit of the observer & fast as you can, break off your association with your personality & identify yourself with the Universe" (*JMN*, 5:391). The final sections of "Song of Myself" serve such a relocation of self-awareness to a point halfway between the "I" and the unconscious, the "it." But Whitman finds neither Truth nor Justice in the "deeper Self." Instead he discovers an infinite power, an energy that "promulges what grows after and out of itself" (l. 1180):

> Wider and wider they spread, expanding and always expanding,
> Outward and outward and forever outward. [ll. 1184–85]

Life, the poet asserts, is an unstoppable power; a rich reality stretches as far in every direction as the eye and the mind can see. But if the poet tells us that "God" waits at the end of the open road, at the horizon of experience, the vocabulary of religion can only suggest the expansive power of the self, the potentially infinite curve of being. In this poem, Malcolm Cowley explains, "God is neither a person nor, in a strict sense, even a being; God is an abstract principle of energy that is manifested in every living creature, as well as in 'the grass that grows wherever the land is and the water is.' "[88]

Finally, in section 46 the poet is able to articulate fully the rhetorical aim behind his long self-affirmation. Like Emerson, his goal has been to remake the reader's self, to open for each one of us a field of potential being:

But each man and each woman of you I lead upon a knoll,
My left hand hooks you round the waist,
My right hand points to landscapes of continents, and a plain public
    road.

Not I, not any one else can travel that road for you,
You must travel it for yourself. [ll. 1204–8]

Donning the role of spiritual guide, the poet points out to each of us
"the way." Two literary analogues demonstrate the function of this passage. In books XI and XII of *Paradise Lost* Adam ascends a mount with
the archangel Michael, who then teaches him the Christian fortitude
necessary in a fallen world by revealing to him the future history of
mankind. Wordsworth's *Prelude* culminates in a similar moment, when
the poet interprets his epiphany on Mount Snowden as an emblem of the
mind's imaginative power. Both passages serve pedagogic aims. Dramatizing ideals of selfhood, they teach their respective audiences the kind of
ethical and psychological response that each poet most desires. In radically more intimate terms than either Milton or Wordsworth, Whitman
solicits our transformation: "Shoulder your duds, and I will mine, and
let us hasten forth" (l. 1212). Opening "the gate" for your "egress" (l.
1224), he orients you toward an existence in which you discover "the
dazzle of the light and of every moment of your life" (l. 1227).

At the center of the self's transformation is a buoyant and athletic
sense of being. "Now I will you to be a bold swimmer" (l. 1229), exclaims
the poet, who describes himself as "the teacher of athletes" (l. 1231).
Anchored in a newfound awareness of the self's potential, each male
reader "becomes a man not through derived power but in his own right"
(l. 1234). In section 47 the poet openly addresses the paradox of such self-
reliance—that it cannot be learned by slavish copying yet depends upon
a process of imitation. Ultimately, imitation must leave the model behind:

I teach straying from me, yet who can stray from me?
I follow you whoever you are from the present hour;
My words itch at your ears till you understand them. [ll. 1240–42]

Locating himself now within the reader's self, the poet becomes the
voice that echoes within us as we read and remember his poem. He
identifies himself with the internal mentor who guides each person.
More than the voice of conscience, he becomes the expressive sound of
our own tongues (ll. 1244–45).

Whitman's term for this self-awareness is the sense of "me":

No shuttered room or school can commune with *me* . . . . [l. 1251, italics mine]

The young mechanic is closest to *me* . . . . he knows *me* pretty well,
The woodman that takes his axe and jug with him shall take *me* with
    him all day . . . . [ll. 1253–54, italics mine]

To know "me" is to be self-aware, to have the capacity to stand both "in
and out of the game" (l. 70)—a perspective that allows one to perceive
the motions of one's being. This kind of awareness is analogous to
Heidegger's *Dasein*; it is a "being there" that illuminates the dimensions
of being, of one's relationship to self, others, and environment. Made
aware of "me," the reader—according to Paul Bové—is driven "out of
. . . habitual life patterns in order to . . . assure ongoing dis-closure
which is the definition of truth and authenticity."[89] As a result, the individual becomes able to distinguish the self's ultimate interest, which is
not to rehearse the melodramas of public opinion, but rather to unfold
the unique personal dimension of one's own life. Such individuated being is lost by all those who fail to differentiate their selves from parental
injunctions and social codes. Like many of Hawthorne's characters, such
persons always find their voices mingled with the accents of others; they
reiterate the "language of the 'they,'" which is "inauthentic precisely
because it solidifies and covers up," because "it preempts the possibility
of individual discovery."[90] By detaching the reader's sense of "me" from
the decentering demands of others, Whitman awakens instead faith in
the inner rhythms of the self.

Speaking for an age that had not yet discovered the full pleasures of
narcissism, who had little inkling of today's "me-generation," the poet is
able to assert without irony that "nothing, not God, is greater to one
than one's self is" (l. 1264). A few lines later he wonders "who there can
be more wonderful than myself" (l. 1275). Whitman's later poems (as
well as the autobiographical misreadings of generations of critics) demonstrate how easily such assertions can blend with self-aggrandizement.
Whitman, Roger Asselineau writes, "kept on trying to approximate
more and more closely the model he had set for himself"—"the ideal
being of whom he dreamed."[91] But by investing the psyche's energy in
the self, he runs the risk of overestimating the self's importance. The
ego, Hawthorne and Melville were quick to show the age, can easily be
contaminated by an unrestrained celebration of the unconscious. But in
"Song of Myself" this danger is avoided, first by a ritual exorcism of the
self's inflation, and then by the fervent assertion of the poet's transpersonal spiritual and political aims.

"A life process is the more powerful," Paul Tillich once observed, "the more non-being it can include in its self-affirmation, without being destroyed by it."[92] If, as Tillich goes on to argue, power "is the possibility of overcoming non-being," Whitman demonstrates the expanse of his power in the concluding sections of "Song of Myself" as he imagines his own physical dissolution. Fundamental to his acceptance of nonbeing is his capacity to embrace the otherness within:

> There is that in me . . . . I do not know what *it* is . . . . but I
>   know *it* is in me. [l. 1299, italics mine]
>
> I do not know *it* . . . . *it* is without name . . . . *it* is a word
>   unsaid,
> *It* is not in any dictionary or utterance or symbol. [ll. 1302–3, italics
>   mine]

The self awakes through embracing "it," a power that can be found throughout reality: "To *it* the creation is the friend whose embracing awakes *me*" (l. 1305, italics mine). If Martin Buber overcomes self-imprisonment through an "I-thou relationship," Whitman advocates an "I-it relationship." Inculcating in us a sense of the "it" within, he promotes the self-faith necessary for an authentic unfolding.

In the final two sections the poet assumes his ultimate identity by metamorphosing into the other who waits for each one of us as the mirror-image that awakens self-reflection.[93] He is the stranger lingering to meet us: "I wait on the door-slab" (l. 1317). He becomes the very elements underfoot, the sense impressions that constitute our awareness of physical being:

> I bequeath myself to the dirt to grow from the grass I love,
> If you want me again look for me under your bootsoles.
> You will hardly know who I am or what I mean,
> But I shall be good health to you nevertheless,
> And filter and fibre your blood.
>
> Failing to fetch me at first keep encouraged,
> Missing me one place search another,
> I stop somewhere waiting for you. [ll. 1329–36]

Each person's "me"—the undiscovered self—waits to be recognized in the phenomena that he or she attends to. Seeing the poet of "Song of Myself" in the very substance of our lives, we learn to interpret and hence attach ourselves more fully to our own existence. Ultimately, this poetry, as its most famous reader noticed years ago, "has the best merits, namely, of fortifying & encouraging."[94]

FIVE

Recovering the "Idea of Woman": *Woman in the Nineteenth Century* and Its Mythological Background

EXORCISING THE "PHANTOM MARGARET"

American audiences are finally in a position to appreciate Margaret Fuller. The object of sexual prejudice during her own lifetime, she found her literary reputation in large part shaped by those who shared Emerson's opinion that "a masculine woman is not strong, but a lady is" (*W*, 11:425). Emerson's definition of a lady included the familiar virtues of beauty, passivity, and personal influence. As "civilizers of mankind" (409), women—according to Emerson—are "more delicate mercuries of the imponderable and immaterial influences" (405–6). Marked by "religious character" (414), they are the guardians of spirituality. Public action, however, is closed to woman, who is to "find in man her guardian" (426). Female identity, Emerson concludes, depends upon relationship to men: "Every woman being the wife or daughter of a man, —wife, daughter, sister, mother, of a man, she can never be far from his ear, never not of his counsel, if she has really something to urge that is good in itself and agreeable to nature" (425). Ironically, these comments were addressed to the Woman's Rights Convention in Boston, September 21, 1855. Although Margaret Fuller did not live to hear them, she was always acutely aware of the ideal that Emerson and his contemporaries took for granted as "natural" feminine behavior. The index of Fuller's genius was her capacity, both in her life and her writing, to engage that ideal in a constructive dialogue.

Commenting on Emerson's address to the Woman's Rights Convention, Margaret Vanderhaar Allen writes, "Emerson discoursed on women's lack of self-control, their excessive moodiness, their narrowness, their variable constitutions, and the necessity for them to accept men as their guardians."[1] The ideal woman, Emerson told his audience, exhibits the "humility" of Chaucer's Griselda (one of Emerson's favorite literary characters, according to Edward Waldo Emerson) (*W*, 11:413, 626). Earlier, in his journals Emerson had written, "Woman should not be expected to write, or fight, or build, or compose scores: she does all by inspiring man to do all."[2] From such evidence, Margaret Allen concludes that Emerson "makes clear that [his] Transcendentalist stance on the broadening of human possibility, human rights, and equality stopped far short of women."[3] Self-reliance, one is forced to conclude, was seen by Emerson and his generation as largely a male virtue. No respectable woman of his time could live alone for two years at Walden Pond; few of them would emulate Emerson's model of heroic action—Napoleon. The fascination of Fuller is that she believed Emerson when he preached the divine potential of the individual, and in her writing she attempted to put Emerson's radical ideas into action. Eventually, that commitment to self-reliance led her to an active involvement in reform movements, first in New York City, then in revolutionary Italy.

At the heart of Fuller's vision of self-reliance was a commitment to female identity and what she termed "femality" (*WNC*, 102). That a "masculine woman" (or for that matter, a "feminine man") might be strong was one of the points that she defended. In his Boston address Emerson alluded to Swedenborg's doctrine that "the difference of sex . . . run[s] through nature and through thought" (*W*, 11:415–16); in *Representative Men* he mentioned Swedenborg's belief that "in the brain are male and female faculties" (*W*, 4:108). But a more profound recognition of androgyny animates Fuller's writing. "Plato," she asserts, "sometimes seems penetrated by that high idea of love, which considers man and woman as the two-fold expression of one thought. This the angel of Swedenborg, the angel of the coming age, cannot surpass, but only explain more fully" (*WNC*, 90). Whitman sexualized the psychological assumptions of his age by defining the mind's motive power as "procreant urge"; here Fuller goes a step further. She argues that both social and psychological economies reflect an innate sexual bipolarity. As a result, prejudice against "femality" represses half of the human mind. The "idea of Man" and the "idea of Woman"—in her terms—are intimately linked. Since they "are the two halves of one thought," the "development of the one cannot be effected without that of the other" (*WNC*, vi). Fuller's most extensive work of psychological mythmaking, *Woman in the Nineteenth Century*, analyzes the expense—for both men and women—of repressing the female.

Despite his acquaintance with Swedenborg, Emerson fails to consider the radical implications of androgyny. Instead, in "The American Scholar" he protests against what Ann Douglas has called "the feminization of American culture" by asserting an aggressive masculinity.⁴ Commenting upon the political isolation of the scholar, Emerson observes: "It is a shame to him if his tranquillity, amid dangerous times, arise from the presumption that *like children and women*, his is a protected class; or if he seek a temporary peace by the diversion of his thoughts from politics or vexed questions, hiding his head like an ostrich in the flowering bushes. . . . So is the danger a danger still: so is the fear worse. *Manlike* let him turn and face it" (*CW*, 1:64, italics mine). The goal of self-culture, Emerson emphasizes, is "the upbuilding of a man" (65). Action, as the exercise of power, is an essential part of this process; without it, the scholar "is not yet a man" (59). Four years later, characterizing the age in "Man the Reformer," Emerson complains: "Instead of masterly good humor, and a *sense of power*, and fertility of resource in himself; instead of those *strong* and learned eyes, that supple body, and that *mighty* and *prevailing* heart, which the *father* had, *whom nature loved and feared*, whom snow and rain, water and land, beast and fish seemed all to know and to *serve*, we have now a puny, protected person guarded by walls and curtains, stoves and down beds, coaches, and men-servants and women-servants from the earth and the sky" (151, italics mine). The import of such remarks is clear. In Emerson's view, the age is slipping from an ideal of masculine power toward an otherness to be avoided and feared—feminine passivity and domesticity. Man's proper role, Emerson's comments imply, is to dominate that otherness—to control nature both at home and in the field.

According to Barbara Berg, this identification of the feminine household with nature was typical of antebellum America. "Emphasis upon woman's essential domesticity," she observes, "completed the transfer of the pastoral legend to the urban environment. The insistence that woman's sphere be limited to the home became a prevailing dogma of the nineteenth-century faith."⁵ "In her domestic role," Berg continues, "idealized and fantasized, woman embodies all the attributes of bountiful nature"—her image replacing "nature as the sole repository of goodness and ethicality."⁶ Through an analysis of "sexual politics in the language of Emerson," Eric Cheyfitz also has explored the psychological dimensions of such attitudes. In Emerson's *Nature*, he argues, self-awareness is mediated by two figures—"the sacred realm of the FATHER" and "the profane realm of a 'beautiful mother.'"⁷ "If *Nature* is a revolutionary call to 'face' the FATHER," Cheyfitz continues, "it includes in this call an apparently nostalgic summons to lie 'embosomed for a season in nature,' the realm of the feminine, or sensuous, mob, the realm of material well-being." Dramatizing the relationship between consciousness and the unconscious, Emerson relates "an apparently masculine 'will' and an appar-

ently feminine 'intuition,' 'instinct,' or 'inspiration.' "[8] The ideal form of
this relationship is one in which the mother "becomes transparent, or
effaces herself, to reveal the FATHER to the child," a relationship in which
"feminine form" is made "transparent to the pure content of the father."[9]

Cheyfitz reveals the sexual dimensions of a mind-body split that is
typical of male writing in the nineteenth century. To the extent that any
male writer defines himself in terms of a divine Logos or Spirit, he
identifies with an essence that is superior to feminine matter. As a result,
Susan Griffin argues, he "sets himself apart from woman and nature."[10]
Although Emerson establishes a dialogue between masculine spirit and
feminine nature, this dialogue is weighted in favor of male mastery and
power. In *The Lay of the Land* Annette Kolodny documents the ambivalence that resulted for many men because of the exploitative quality of
this kind of relationship. The "essence of the pastoral paradox," she
observes, is that "man might . . . win mastery over the landscape, but
only at the cost of emotional and psychological separation from it."[11]
Nineteenth-century theology reinforced this separation. While conservative circles worshiped God the Father, more liberal thinkers celebrated
the manly perfection of Christ or the expansion of masculine spirit. The
result of such views, Mary Daly asserts, is the casting of woman in the
role of "the Other" (a position she occupies in the fiction of Poe, Hawthorne, and Melville). Not only does "masculine symbolism for God . . .
reinforce sexual hierarchy," it leads to the identification of woman in
terms of "demonic power structures which induce individuals to internalize false identities."[12]

The most familiar of such false identities in the nineteenth century was
the image of woman as fallen Eve. "The myth of the Fall," Mary Daly
observes, "can be seen as a prototypic case of false naming. . . . It mis-
names the mystery of evil, casting it into the distorted mold of feminine
evil."[13] The obverse of such otherness was what Barbara Berg describes
as "the image of a passive, porcelain being whose immaculate delicacy
made her willing to submit to the superior wisdom of her worldly,
knowledgeable husband or father."[14] This "cult of purity," Berg continues, repressed the female body by denying that "women had natural sex
drives." The result was the creation of an "imaginary woman" who was
defined as "pious and pure, fragile and weak, submissive and domestic,
passive and unintellectual."[15] Commenting on this familiar type, Emerson commends those women who "give entirely of their affections, set
their whole fortune on the die, lose themselves eagerly in the glory of
their husbands and children" (*W*, 11:407). "Man stands astonished," he
reflects, "at a magnanimity he cannot pretend to."

The effect of Margaret Fuller's writing is to call into doubt the "imagi-

nary woman" that the age took for granted. "Fuller was and is so disqui-
eting," Ann Douglas writes, "because she does not lend herself to the
fantasy life, to the essentially fictional identity, associated with women."[16]
Instead, Fuller contended with what she called the "phantom Margaret,"
the mirage that nineteenth-century America mistook for female reality.[17]
An obsession with personality stands at the center of that illusion; for in
the case of nineteenth-century women, personality was indistinguishable
from stereotype. The sweet homebodies who manifested docility, submissiveness, and domesticity acted out roles whose arbitrariness had
been forgotten. Fuller's great accomplishment—her "crime" in the eyes
of many—was that she showed the age that female personality was a
fabrication and, hence, could be changed and strengthened. In this, she
was only following Emerson, who had advocated a deliberate artistry in
living. But few suspected the explosive potential of Emerson's insight
when displaced to the realm of sexual identity.

The problem for any student of Fuller is that her literary reputation
has been distorted by the very sexual stereotypes that she challenged.
The "Margaret ghost" (as Henry James termed the figure) haunted the
nineteenth century.[18] By now it is well known that the imaginations of
both Hawthorne and James were profoundly touched by this personage.
Frequently relegated to the role of footnote illuminating the background
of *The Blithedale Romance* and *The Bostonians*, the figure of Margaret
Fuller has frequently come to stand for a type—the overly intellectual
woman, the feminist bluestocking who threatens most of the men
around her. Until the recent revision of Fuller's literary reputation by
Bell Gale Chevigny and others, the only Fuller we had was the Fuller that
such men imagined. In perceiving her life, as well as editing her *Memoirs*,
even Fuller's friends "chose what fit the image they wished to project
and ignored or destroyed the rest."[19] Subsequently, students of American
literature have been more interested in Fuller's personality and sexual
history than in her writing. Excluded from F. O. Matthiessen's *American
Renaissance* (except in her roles as Emerson's correspondent and as the
probable model for Hawthorne's Zenobia), Fuller has never occupied
a central position in the American literary canon. In place of serious es-
timations of her work, most "critical commentary on Margaret Fuller," Joel Myerson notes with telling understatement, "has always been
marked by a degree of personalism, for few writers have been able to
judge Fuller's works without bringing in her personality as well."[20]

As a result, one of the most prominent literary figures of her age has
been held to a standard of judgment that would be deemed inappropriate for her male contemporaries. "One factor in our settling a public

image of Margaret Fuller," Perry Miller writes, "is that she cannot be dissociated from the hyperbolically female intellectualism of the period, the slightest invocation of which invites our laughter."[21] Such a comment graphically illustrates the kind of blind spot that continues to mar the commentary of many of Fuller's male readers. The time has come to dissociate ourselves from the prejudice behind such statements, to exorcise the "Margaret ghost," and to view Fuller's work for what it is: an explosive effort to free the psychological and social images of woman from inhibiting patriarchal assumptions. By necessity, Fuller's dialogue with the dominant male culture of her time was incomplete. How could it be otherwise when her writing represents the opening move in an American feminist discourse that has not yet reached completion? Much of the interest of that writing resides in the ways Fuller develops a sexual critique of the dominant culture in order to find a place on which to stand. To begin with, she had to show her audience that the very terms used to construe human identity, terms that ignored femininity as a source of strength, were biased and destructive.

RECOGNIZING THE GODDESS

In order to revise the self-estimation of women, Margaret Fuller had to transform the very gods that they worshiped. By locating divinity within, Emerson opened the door for the celebration of individual perfection. But Emerson's God was masculine. What would happen, Fuller must have asked herself, if the "God within" were feminine as well? *Woman in the Nineteenth Century* pursues the implications of this insight. Originally entitled "The Great Lawsuit.—Man *versus* Men; Woman *versus* Women," it measures both men and women against an androgynous ideal of self-perfection. In order to understand Fuller's achievement in that work, we must comprehend her ongoing efforts to recover the other side of "divine thought"—forgotten images of the Goddess within.

Our analysis of Margaret Fuller's commitment to female mythmaking supplements Bell Gale Chevigny's discussion of her psychological unfolding. Chevigny interprets Fuller's career as an attempt to balance within herself qualities that she, along with her age, defined as masculine and feminine. Fuller's "sexual confusion," Chevigny argues, led to "the coupling of her desire to fulfill that ill-defined instinct she considered 'womanly' and her relentless hunger to know and achieve as only men seemed to do."[22] She was successful in this attempt, according to Chevigny, only when "her mental and emotional gifts joined in real historical action," allowing her to discover power that "would become hers in her active and intelligent concern for those who lacked it."[23] In this view, Fuller's growing social awareness, culminating in her active involvement with social reform, enabled her to achieve an identity transcending stereotyped sexual categories.

Although Chevigny's analysis provides the most coherent reading we have of Fuller's inner life, it has one major blind spot. "I now believe," Chevigny later revealed, "that identification at times led me to distort a side of her nature I found difficult to accept. Perhaps because I had repudiated adolescent mystical tendencies in myself, I felt distaste for Fuller's vocabulary of mysticism and in my book either underplayed it or smothered it in an analysis that argued it was not what it seemed. While I believe my analysis has some merit, I also think it was governed by failure to appreciate the role of mysticism in Fuller's period."[24] As we shall see, Fuller's "vocabulary of mysticism" is intimately linked to her imagination of female myths orienting identity. Just as H. D.'s poetry, in the words of Susan Friedman, "turned Freud's categories upside down" through its exploration of "a new mythology of womanhood," Fuller's writing challenges the androcentric assumptions of Transcendentalism by developing a body of female archetypes.[25] Indications of Fuller's growing appreciation of female myth can be found in the letters of 1840 documenting her emotional break from Emerson, in several evocative sketches that she printed in the *Dial*, in her "Conversations on Mythology," and in her choice of the sistrum of Isis as a personal talisman.

Margaret Fuller's commitment to a psychological mythmaking founded on female myths dates from the summer and autumn of 1840. This period, Bell Gale Chevigny writes, was "a season of crisis for Fuller. Sam Ward and Anna Barker, each of whom had roused tumultuous feelings in her, were in the last stages of problematic courtship, and Fuller was probably struggling to feel a generous joy in their union."[26] In love with both Ward and Barker, Fuller was deeply shaken by their engagement. "Partly as a result," Robert Hudspeth observes, Fuller "turned to Emerson, challenging him to become a better friend" (*LMF*, 2:6). From the letters that survive, it is evident that over the next two months Emerson and Fuller debated the grounds of their friendship in their correspondence. Finally, in September and October they reached a crisis. "If you have not seen this stair on which God has been so untiringly leading me to himself," Fuller wrote to Emerson on September 29, "you have indeed been wholly ignorant of me. Then indeed, when my soul, in its childish agony of prayer, stretched out its arms to you as a father, did you not see what was meant by this crying for the moon?" (*LMF*, 2:160).

"Our moods were very different," Emerson notes in the *Memoirs of Margaret Fuller Ossoli*, "and I remember, that, at the very time when I, slow and cold, had come fully to admire her genius, and was congratulating myself on the solid good understanding that subsisted between us, I was surprised with hearing it taxed by her with superficiality and halfness" (*M*, 1:288).

Although a basic ambivalence in Fuller's relationship to Emerson seems to have contributed to this estrangement, an even more important factor seems to lie at its base. The "halfness" that Fuller found in Emerson reflects not only a judgment of his personality but also of his beliefs. "I need to be recognized," Fuller had written to Emerson (*LMF*, 2:160). But the desire for his approval was counterbalanced by an even more powerful motive—by "certain mental changes" that Emerson saw in Fuller during the autumn of 1840 (*M*, 1:289). Emerson later characterized these changes as "certain religious states, which did not impress me as quite healthy, or likely to be permanent" (289). "She made many attempts to describe her frame of mind to me," Emerson adds, but "she was vexed at the want of sympathy on my part, and I felt that this craving for sympathy did not prove the inspiration" (308–9). "All things have I given up to the central power, myself, you also," Fuller had written Emerson (*LMF*, 2:160). The nature of that "central power" we can infer both from Fuller's and Emerson's letters.

For the only time during his career, Emerson's letters to Fuller during the few months preceding their break were filled with references to archetypal female myths. Returning a number of *Dial* manuscripts to Fuller on August 4, Emerson writes, "I hasten now at last to restore them before the moon shall fill her horns" (*L*, 2:322). In the same letter he imagines that the *Dial* might become "a sort of fruitful Cybele, mother of a hundred gods and godlike papers." In his letter written to Fuller on August 29, Emerson characterizes her as "the holiest nun" (*L*, 2:327), an epithet that—in the extraordinary letter of September 25— expands into "divine mermaid or fisher of men, to whom all gods have given the witch-hazel wand, or caduceus" (336). In this same letter, after asserting his "difference" from Fuller, Emerson makes the following concession: "Nothing is to me more welcome nor to my recent speculations more familiar than the Protean energy by which the brute horns of Io become the crescent moon of Isis, and nature lifts itself through everlasting transition to the higher and highest" (337). Margaret Fuller, we can surmise, was the source for much of this mythical material. Typically, Emerson sees in the myth of Isis a pattern of sublimation. But that he also recognized deeper and more troubling currents of meaning in female myth is evident from his letter to Fuller of October 7. Commenting upon the "wild element in woman," Emerson observes, "I suppose we are not content with brightest loveliness until we discern the deep sparkle of this energy which when perverted & outraged flashes up into a volcano jet, & outdares, outwits, & outworks man" (345). Clearly, Fuller was working with a body of material that had the capacity to disturb even the most self-assured of men.

Referring to Fuller's "restlessness and fever" during this period, Emerson attributed to her "an occasional enthusiasm, which gave a religious dignity to her thought" (*M*, 1:309). For Fuller's side of things, we might turn to her ecstatic letter of September 8. "I live, I am—," she exclaims to Caroline Sturgis, "*The carbuncle is found* And at present the mere sight of my talisman is enough. The hour may come when I wish to charm with it, but not yet" (*LMF*, 2:157). Fuller's "talisman" had not been provided by Emerson. In her letter of renunciation, written September 29, Fuller observes that she had hoped to receive from him "the clue to the labyrinth of my own being" (159), but that he had mistaken her intentions. Hoping to "be my truest manlike self" with Emerson, Fuller found that his brand of intellectualism touched only half of her being.[27] Ultimately, as a result of Emerson's failure to comprehend her, Fuller was able "to understand herself in a more meaningful way, with her mental and emotional gifts joined in real historical action."[28] However, before Fuller could rejoin her divided self and engage in "historical action," an important step intervened. She supplemented the conventional patriarchal religion of her day with the imagination of female objects of worship, images of the Goddess that returned her to herself. Fuller's mystical experiences of 1840 revealed to her the possibility of a psychological mythmaking founded on female myth. If Fuller lost her Osiris in Emerson, that loss helped her to find Isis.

From this point on Fuller's worship of the Father is joined by a "crying for the moon" (*LMF*, 2:160), a yearning for the archetypal feminine. Her letters of October 1840 document how the marriage of Ward and Barker along with the failure of her friendship with Emerson led to an intense meditation upon female archetypes. Writing again to Caroline Sturgis, Fuller both laments her break from Emerson and dedicates herself to the work of self-transformation. Once an "Amazon" (*LMF*, 2:168), Fuller now imagines herself as being "like the holy Mother" (167), a "nun" who is "shrouded in a white veil" (168). Her condition, she observes, has become wintry: "Winter is coming now. I rejoice in her bareness, her pure shroud, her judgment-announcing winds. These will help me to dedicate myself" (169). But this emotional winter promises a rebirth in which "Phenix like rises the soul into the tenderest Spring" (169). Committing herself to chastity and sublimation, Fuller writes, "I am not yet purified. Let the lonely Vestal watch the fire till it draws her to itself and consumes this mortal part. Truly you say I have not been what I am now yet it is only transformation, not alteration. The leaf becomes a stem, a bud, is now in flower. Winds of heaven, dews of night, circles of time, already ye make haste to convert this flower into dead-seeming seed—yet Caroline far fairer shall it bloom again" (167). Embarking on a spiritual quest (like the pilgrims seeking the magical gem in Hawthorne's tale "The Great Carbuncle"), Fuller "would now steal away . . . into the very heart of the untrodden mountain where the carbuncle has lit the way to veins of yet undreamed of diamond" (168). Like Thoreau in *Walden* divining "the richest vein," Fuller orients spiritual discovery in terms of a hidden core of energy.

A biographer characterizes Fuller's "prolonged ecstasy of nunlike self-denial" during this period as "the sticky remains of an outworn idiom."[29] But the archetypal quality of Fuller's reflection begs for more precise analysis. On the one hand, Fuller longs to be reabsorbed into the Father. "Father, I am weary!" she exclaims in her journal, "Reassume me for a while, I pray Thee. Oh let me rest awhile in Thee, Thou only Love!"[30] "I have no child," she laments, "and the woman in me has so craved this experience that it has seemed the want of it must paralyze me."[31] But at the same time that Fuller defines herself in terms of male-female relationships (as daughter or wife), her reflection is marked by the emergence of powerful female archetypes that promise self-sufficiency. During October of 1840 she begins to discover the body of female myths that forms the imaginative core of the earliest material she published in the *Dial*. For example, in her letter of October 19, Fuller records the interview with William Eustis that supplied her with the material for "The Magnolia of Lake Pontchartrain" (published January 1841) and "Yuca Filamentosa" (published January 1842). Eustis's description of the Yuca, Fuller notes, evokes "the type of pure feminine beauty in the moon's own flower" (*LMF*, 2:166). "How finely it harmonizes with all legends of Isis, Diana," she exclaims (166). Struck by Eustis's account of his "rapture" at the unfolding of a "flower . . . made for the moon" (165), Fuller later expands his material into two revealing sketches that comment both upon the failure of male-female relations and upon the power of compensating female myths.

Together, "The Magnolia of Lake Pontchartrain" and "Yuca Filamentosa" explore the psychological dimensions of female being forced to withdraw from heterosexual society and to rely upon her own resources.

On one level, both sketches document the emotional aftershocks of Margaret Fuller's estrangements from Samuel Ward and Emerson. But more important is their exploration of a female power released by an enforced distance from male influence. Presented as the account of an unnamed male traveler, "The Magnolia of Lake Pontchartrain" portrays the effect upon him of an encounter with an "imperial vestal" who has discovered self-reliance in solitude: "I found her at last, the Queen of the South, singing to herself in her lonely bower. Such should a sovereign be, most regal when alone; for then there is no disturbance to prevent the full consciousness of power" (*D*, 1:299). The Magnolia tells her story to a man whose "life bears no golden fruit" (302). "Blighted without," he explains, "I was driven back upon the centre of my being, and there found all being" (302). The Magnolia's history is similar to the traveler's and reflects Fuller's recent experiences with Emerson.

Discussing the latest issue of the *Dial* with Fuller in his letter of January 19, 1841, Emerson praises "the Magnolia" and then exclaims: "Depart ye profane this is of me & mine" (*L*, 2:377–78). But Emerson's comments also indicate that Fuller's sketch has hit home; "but be it known unto you O woman of little faith, that I can read affectionately," he adds defensively (378). Then, after exclaiming over the Magnolia's "fervid Southern eloquence," Emerson "wonder[s] as often before how you fell into the Massachusetts" (378). Despite the assertion of kinship, the tone of this letter bespeaks Emerson's increasing sense of distance from Fuller's new mythological sensibility.

Rejected by the "inaccessible sun" who would not release the "one smile sacred to me alone," the Magnolia turned within and discovered the existence of a neglected female power. Stirring to mysterious sympathies, she (like Fuller in October 1840) could "but retire and hide in [the earth's] silent bosom for one calm winter" (*D*, 303). Turning inward, she attempted to discover "what was hid beneath the perpetual veil of glowing life" (303). In the process, she found herself cut off both from the sun and from the blossoming orange, symbols of male approval and motherhood: "I felt that I had been that beauteous tree, but now only was— what—I knew not; yet I was, and the voices of men said, It is dead; cast it forth and plant another in the costly vase" (303).

At this moment of rejection the Magnolia must either accept this negation of her being or move outside of male-defined categories of existence. She does the latter, experiencing a vision of "the queen and guardian of the flowers." "Of this being," she tells her male auditor, "I cannot speak to thee in any language now possible betwixt us. For this is a being of another order from thee" (*D*, 303–4). At this moment, in

Marie Urbanski's words, Fuller announces the presence of "the occult power of the female," a power that transcends and threatens male identity.[32] This "goddess," the Magnolia asserts, "is not such a being as men love to paint" (304). "All the secret powers," she continues, "are 'Mothers.' There is but one paternal power" (304). Dedication to the power of the "Mothers" involves "a step inward"; for one must "become a vestal priestess," a being who is "purer, of deeper thought, and more capable of retirement into [her] own heart" (304).

Fuller concludes her sketch by turning the tables upon Emerson and other male exponents of self-reliance. The Magnolia, she suggests, provides a lesson in female power that they have yet to learn. "The Magnolia left me," the male traveler concludes, "I left not her, but must abide forever in the thought to which the clue was found in the margin of that lake of the South" (D, 305). Even as it initiates a dialogue with masculine culture, "The Magnolia of Lake Pontchartrain" ends by imagining that culture's need to accept female existence on its own terms. For women to achieve true self-reliance, the men around them had to listen to and acknowledge the validity of their insight as women. Later, in *Woman in the Nineteenth Century*, Fuller advocates a stage of female separatism; but here, male-female dialogue is still a possibility. Yet, Fuller's sketch contains the seeds of her later position. Never again, the Magnolia asserts near the end, "shall I . . . subject myself to be questioned by an alien spirit to tell the tale of my being in words that divide it from itself" (304–5). Margaret Fuller's writing between 1840 and 1845 records her struggle to elaborate this insight by finding a new language adequate to her sense of herself as a woman.

A year later, in January 1842, Fuller published in the *Dial* her second flower-sketch, "Yuca Filamentosa." In that work Fuller continued the lifting of the "Isis veil" (D, 2:235) as she examined the "living hieroglyphic" of "the Diana-flower" (286). Staging another encounter between a female persona and a male character, Fuller explores here "that class of emotions which the moon calls up" (286). "The belief that there is a peculiar connection between woman and moon," Esther Harding observes, "has been universally held from the earliest times. . . . These beliefs were naturally related to the fact that women's physical rhythms corresponded with the periodic changes of the moon."[33] The "Moon Mother," Harding continues, was one of the most powerful and popular of female myths. Diana of Ephesus (whom Fuller mentions in her 1841 Conversations) was just one of many similar figures, including Artemis, Cybele, and Isis.

Particularly striking is the universal association of such goddesses with virginity. "The Great Mother," Harding writes, "is always represented as *Virgin*, in spite of the fact that she has many lovers and is the mother of many sons."[34] The "virginity" of these goddesses is understandable in light of the different meaning that ancient cultures assigned to that term: "It may be used of a woman who has had much sexual experience; it may even be applied to a prostitute. Its real significance is to be found in its use as contrasted with 'married.'"[35] A married woman was considered to be "the property of her husband," but a virgin "belonged to herself alone, she was 'one-in-herself.'"[36] Thus the "virginity" of Diana or Isis refers not to their state of sexual experience but to their self-reliance. As a "Vestal" dedicating herself to female power in the 1840s, Fuller begins to associate the image of virginity with such self-sufficiency. In the process, she discovers one of the major symbols of *Woman in the Nineteenth Century*.

Like "The Magnolia of Lake Pontchartrain," "Yuca Filamentosa" again analyzes the female power drawing Margaret Fuller outside the orbit of male domination. In the light of her experiences with Ward and Emerson, this sketch reads like a dismissal of those men unable to appreciate the "emotions which the moon calls up" (*D*, 2:286). "Often, as I looked up to the moon," it begins, "I had marvelled to see how calm she was in her loneliness" (286). By the end of this piece the moon's solitude and calmness become signs of female independence. Like the Yuca plant, the speaker learns to "wait and trust." Paralleling the speaker's emotional situation, "the flower brooded on her own heart; while the moon never wearied of filling her urn, for those she could not love as children" (288). After commenting in a journal entry upon her paralyzing desire to have a child, Fuller notes, "But now as I look on these lovely children of a human birth what slow and neutralizing cares they bring with them to the mother. The children of the muse come quicker, with less pain and disgust, rest more lightly on the bosom and have (not on them the taint of earthly corruption)."[37] Fuller's "children of the muse," this sketch reveals, were born under the moon's light, quickened by the gracious influence of Diana.

In place of the word *woman*, Barbara Berg observes, the nineteenth century used "the fragmenting, identity-negating terms 'wife,' 'mother,' and 'daughter.'"[38] In "Yuca Filamentosa" Fuller steps outside such male-determined categories by suggesting the presence of archetypal female powers that only women can perceive. The speaker records how two Yuca plants, in what seems a "nuptial hour," bloom together. But this union is marred by the "friend" (presumably a male Yuca plant) who "retired into silence" (*D*, 2:288). The situation of the female speaker and her male friend, Alcmeon, parallels that of the flowers in its emotional

estrangement. Dragging Alcmeon outside to share with her the blossoming of the moon-flowers, the speaker realizes that he "could travel
amid the magnificent displays of the tropical climates, nor even look at a
flower" (287). Although Alcmeon seems momentarily roused from "ob-
tuseness" by the flowers' nuptial bliss, he fails to respond to the speaker's
solitude. Turning her back on the comforts of marriage or motherhood,
she thus chooses to "fill her urn" with moonlight.

Buried in "Yuca Filamentosa" is an echo that confirms Fuller's dedication to an ascetic life beyond conventional female roles. "As I looked on
this flower," her speaker exclaims, "my heart swelled with emotions never
known but once before. Once, when I saw in woman what is most
womanly, the love of a seraph shining through death. I expected to see
my flower pass and melt as she did in the celestial tenderness of its smile"
(D, 2:287). In order to understand this strange passage, we must turn to
the letter that Fuller wrote to Caroline Sturgis three days after her discovery of the Magnolia and Yuca material. This letter, which marks
Fuller's "nun-like dedication" to independent female power, we have
already cited.

Immediately after Fuller's evocation of "the very heart of the untrodden mountain where the carbuncle has lit the way to veins of yet undreamed of diamond," there occurs an extraordinary passage. Fuller
records how a night-long deathbed vigil over a woman who had tried to
abort her fetus led to a moment of religious ecstasy: "One day that I
once lived at Groton rises on my thoughts with charm unspeakable. I
had passed the night in the sick chamber of a wretched girl in the last
stage of a consumption. It was said that she had profaned her maiden
state, and that the means she took to evade the consequences of her stain
had destroyed her health and placed her on this bed of death" (LMF,
2:168). Staring "into that abyss lowest in humanity of crime for the sake
of sensual pleasure," Fuller sensed the presence of a "star, pale, tearful . . .
mirrored from the very blackness of the yawning gulf" (168). At that
moment, "unheard of assurance came to me." "O, it has ever been thus,"
Fuller continues,

> from the darkest comes my brightness, from Chaos depths my love. I returned
> with the morning star. No one was with me in the house. I unlocked the door
> went into the silent room where but late before my human father dwelt. It was
> the first winter of my suffering health the musings and vigils of the night had
> exhausted while exalting me. The cold rosy winter dawn and then the sun. I
> had forgotten to wind up the clock the day marked itself. I lay there, I could
> not resolve to give myself food. The day was unintentionally a fast. Sacredest
> thoughts were upon it, and I comprehended the meaning of an ascetic life.
> [168]

In the face of female sinfulness and paternal death, Fuller finds a self-reliant asceticism. Like Emerson, who compensated for the deaths of father, brother, wife, and son with a fierce independence, she locates the "morning star" within. Its cold and serene light, akin to the moonlight drawing forth the hidden radiance of the Yuca, pulls Fuller outside the roles of dutiful daughter and procreative woman. It illuminates instead an area of female experience largely unseen by the nineteenth century: the image of woman as Diana, dedicated to her own spiritual needs.

"O these tedious, tedious attempts to learn the universe by thoughts alone," Fuller exclaims several days later in a letter to Caroline Sturgis (*LMF*, 2:170). Dwelling almost entirely in the world of thought, Emerson expresses for her only one half of being. At times, Fuller confesses, she feels the "desire to teach this sage all he wants to make him the full-formed Angel" (170), i.e., the androgynous "angel of Swedenborg, the angel of the coming age" (*WNC*, 90). "But that task is not for me," she realizes. "The gulf which separates us is too wide" (170). Moving beyond the reach of androcentric models of the self, Fuller has begun to explore that area of being left out of Emerson's thought—the rich, nurturing domain of the Goddess.

THE SISTRUM OF ISIS

To understand the sources of Fuller's female archetypes, we must examine the Conversations for women she conducted between 1839 and 1844. These gatherings not only offered Boston women an opportunity for serious intellectual exercise, they also provided Fuller with a forum in which to shape a myth of the psyche that uses Greek myths as "types of various aspects of human character."[39] As early as the 1839 Conversations, Fuller's interest in psychology was apparent: "Under the mythological forms, room was found for opening all the great questions, on which Margaret and her friends wished to converse. Prometheus was made the type of Pure Reason; Jupiter, of Will; Juno, the passive side of the same, or Obstinacy [*sic*]; Minerva, Intellectual Power, Practical Reason; Mercury, Executive Power, Understanding" (*M*, 1:333). In her letter of January 21, 1840, Fuller repeated part of this scheme, associating Jupiter with "Creative Energy, Will" and Apollo with "Genius" (*LMF*, 2:118). By the end of her first series of Conversations, she had started to use the figures of classical mythology "to illustrate traits of mind or spirit"; but her reflection on the significance of goddess-images had only just begun.[40]

In March of 1841 (after Fuller's spiritual crisis during the autumn of 1840) the situation has changed. Admitting men to her Conversations for the only time, Fuller again discusses the subject of Greek mythology. She found "Greek and even Egyptian mythology . . . much more useful and inspiring" than "Christian mythology," Robert D. Richardson suggests, because "the Christian and Jewish religions gave women a far less important place in the scheme of things than most other religions and mythologies."[41] As one reads Caroline Healey Dall's account of the 1841 Conversations, *Margaret and Her Friends*, one notes that the discussion revolves around myths that either develop feminine archetypes or mediate questions of sexual difference. For example, on May 6, Fuller compares the "vivifying power" of Apollo and "genial glow" of Bacchus with the powers of Persephone and Ceres: "Persephone was the hidden energy, the vestal fire, vivifying the universe. Ceres was the productive faculty, external, bounteous. They were two phases of one thing. It was the same with Apollo and Bacchus" (Dall, 159). By attributing energy and productivity to female deities, Fuller—in Mary Daly's words—challenges "exclusively male symbolism for God, for the notion of divine 'incarnation' in human nature."[42] In place of the worship and emulation of distant paternal images, she offers her female auditors a framework of belief in which salvation does not only come "through the male." She makes the radical suggestion that women can perfect themselves by realizing the essential power of female ideals.

Fuller reveals her commitment to female images of self-perfection by finding in the story of Cupid and Psyche an account of "the pilgrimage of a soul" (Dall, 97). The story of Cupid and Psyche occurs in *The Golden Ass* by Apuleius, a book that Fuller later cites in *Woman in the Nineteenth Century* as the source of her image of Isis. Turned into an ass as the result of his lasciviousness, the protagonist of that work, Lucius, wanders the world in search of the rose that will enable him to return back into human form. On his wanderings Lucius overhears the story of Cupid and Psyche. Both that tale and the narrative frame present what one scholar describes as "a record of the journeys of the soul through carnal adventures into mystic peace."[43] Significantly, this pilgrimage involves the acceptance of the spiritual authority of powerful goddesses—of Venus, in the story of Cupid and Psyche; and, finally, of Isis, who appears to Lucius in a dream-vision and promises a return to human form if he becomes her votary.

In Apuleius's account Psyche is a beautiful royal daughter who offends Venus because she is worshiped as her successor. Full of fury, Venus instructs her son Cupid to wound Psyche so that she will fall in love with the basest of mankind. But instead Cupid falls in love with Psyche and installs her in a sumptuous palace where he visits her each night as an invisible lover. Eventually, Psyche is discovered by her two malicious sisters, who convince her to find out the identity of her lover by reminding her of the oracle that her husband was to be a winged serpent. Despite Cupid's express warning that such an action would force him to leave her, Psyche takes a lamp one night and looks upon his face. Awakened by a drop of burning oil that spills from her lamp, Cupid flees. Grief-stricken, Psyche searches the world over for her lover. After Ceres and Juno refuse to aid her, she is taken to Venus, who sets a series of seemingly impossible and fatal tasks that include visiting Proserpina (Persephone) in the Underworld. But with the assistance of various beasts Psyche survives these ordeals and is reunited with Cupid as an immortal in heaven.

To the shock of some of the clergymen attending the 1841 Conversations and of Caroline Healey Dall, Margaret Fuller interprets this tale as a "story of redemption" which "contained the seeds of the doctrine of election, —saving by grace, and so on!" (Dall, 118). In place of the orthodox account of Christian redemption, Fuller here replaces the suffering Christ with a female substitute, a heterodox suggestion that she offers in response to William Story's comment that "it was a Paternal power that *ruled*, not an autocratic power which *fathered* us" (Dall, 118). The exchange between Fuller and Story forms part of a significant digression. "Margaret wanted to pass on to Diana," Dall reports, "but there were too many clergymen in the company" (117). When Fuller finally does bring the Conversation around to Diana,

> Her pure and sacred character with the Athenians was compared to that of Diana of Ephesus, whose orgies were not unusual, and who was considered as a bountiful mother.
>   IDA RUSSELL said that *her* mythology accused Diana of being the mother of fifty sons and fifty daughters!
>   MARGARET laughed, and said that certainly was Diana of Ephesus! [119]

Here Fuller's image of Diana affirms her sexuality as a prolific childbearer. But a year later, in "Yuca Filamentosa," Fuller emphasizes the virginity of the Goddess—a sign of her self-reliance. This change in emphasis measures the rapid rate at which Fuller was assimilating powerful goddess-images in order to express her developing sense of female identity.

At the same time that Fuller begins to mediate her discourse through goddess-images, she begins to articulate the idea of androgyny that later forms the center of *Woman in the Nineteenth Century*. Discussing the figure of Orpheus as an archetype of creativity, she quotes Thomas Taylor's commentary on Plato's *Republic*:

Mars . . . requires the assistance of Venus, that he may bring order and harmony into things contrary and discordant.

Vulcan adorns by his art the sensible universe, which he fills with certain
natural impulses, powers, and proportions; but *he* requires the assistance of
Venus, that he may invest material effects with beauty, and by this secure the
comeliness of the world. [Dall, 144]

In addition to Thomas Taylor's commentaries on Plato, Fuller was
probably also familiar with his 1824 edition of *The Hymns of Orpheus*, a
work that Emerson refers to in a letter of 1842 (*L*, 3:106). In this book
Taylor, one of the central nineteenth-century sources for a theory of
androgyny, translates the following passage from "Ficinus, on Plato's
Theology": "Those who profess . . . the Orphic theology consider a
two-fold power in souls and in the celestial orbs: the one consisting in
knowledge, the other in vivifying and governing the orb in which that
power is connected. Thus in the orb of the earth, they call the nostic
power Pluto, the other Proserpine. In water, the former power Ocean,
and the latter Thetis. In air, that thundering Jove, and this Juno."[44] The
import of this passage, Taylor explains, is that "all souls and the celestial
spheres are endued with a two-fold power, nostic and animating; one of
which is male the other female."[45] In her 1841 Conversations, Fuller's
terms for nostic and animating powers are "Indomitable Will" (associated with Jupiter and Juno) and "Productive energy . . . variously represented at different times by Isis, Rhea, Ceres, Persephone" (Dall, 26–28).

Of particular interest are Fuller's comments upon the goddess Isis.
Emerson remembers that Fuller "had a taste for gems, ciphers, talis-
mans" (*M*, 1:219) and that she "surrounded herself with a little mythology of her own" (221). "She chose the *Sistrum* for her emblem," he
continues, "and had it carefully drawn with a view to its being engraved
on a gem" (221). This gesture bespeaks the selection of a personal talisman. As we shall see, the sistrum of Isis, a rattle used in the goddess's
cult, becomes perhaps the central symbol in Fuller's psychological mythmaking. Fuller was familiar with this instrument from her reading in
Plutarch's *Morals*, which she borrowed from Emerson in 1837 (*LMF*,
1:277). In Plutarch's "Isis and Osiris" the sistrum is discussed in the
following terms: "The sistrum likewise (or rattle) doth intimate unto us,
that all things ought to be agitated and shook . . . and not be suffered to
rest from their motion, but be as it were roused up and awakened when
they begin to grow drowsy and droop. For they tell us that *the sistrum
averts and frights away Typhon*, insinuating hereby that, as corruption
locks and fixes Nature's course, so generation again resolves and excites
it by means of motion."[46] "I have a great share of Typhon to the Osiris,
wild rush and leap, blind force for the sake of force," Fuller is recorded as

saying (*M*, 1:230). On one level the sistrum of Isis seems to represent a talisman of psychic control—an emblem that "frights away Typhon," taming otherwise unruly moods.

But at the same time the sistrum is a symbol of the power of Isis. The first appendix to *Woman in the Nineteenth Century* reveals the extent of Fuller's acquaintance with the archetypal dimensions of this figure. Fuller quotes the following passage from Thomas Taylor's translation of *The Golden Ass*—the moment of Lucius's dream-vision of "a divine form emerging from the middle of the sea":

> A multiform crown, consisting of various flowers, bound the sublime summit of her head. And in the middle of the crown, just on her forehead, there was a smooth orb, resembling a mirror, or rather a white refulgent light, which indicated that she was the moon. Vipers, rising up after the manner of furrows, environed the crown on the right hand and on the left, and Cerealian ears of corn were also extended from above. Her garment was of many colors. . . . Glittering stars were dispersed through the embroidered robe, and through the whole of its surface, and the full moon, shining in the middle of the stars, breathed forth flaming fires. A crown, wholly consisting of flowers and fruits of every kind, adhered with indivisible connection to the border of conspicuous robe, in all its undulating motion.
>
> What she carried in her hands also consisted of things of a very different nature. Her right hand bore a brazen rattle, through the narrow lamina of which, bent like a belt, certain rods passing, produced a sharp triple sound through the vibrating motion of her arm. [*WNC*, 167–68]

The importance to Fuller of this portrait of Isis and her sistrum can be measured by looking at the 1822 edition of Apuleius she cited.

In his notes Thomas Taylor quotes Plutarch's analysis of the sistrum and provides an illustration that must have served as the model for the emblem that Fuller "had . . . carefully drawn with a view to its being engraved on a gem." But Taylor's notes provide something more. Two pages earlier he concludes a discussion of Apuleius's theology with the following: "all the other mundane Gods subsist in the twelve abovementioned . . . and . . . the first triad of these is *demiurgic* or *fabricative*, viz. Jupiter, Neptune, Vulcan; the second, Vesta, Minerva, Mars *defensive*; the third, Ceres, Juno, Diana, *vivific*; and the fourth, Mercury, Venus, Apollo, *elevating* and *harmonic*."[47] In *Woman in the Nineteenth Century* Fuller cites this passage *without attribution* as the mythological foundation of her discussion of androgyny (*WNC*, 105). Thus Taylor's edition of Apuleius provides Fuller with both a personal talisman and with the pantheon that she uses to substantiate the psychological mythmaking in her most famous book. At this point Fuller's comments on Isis take on considerable interest.

During the Conversation of March 8, 1841, the story of Isis was perhaps the central topic. In Caroline Dall's words, Fuller asserted that the "pilgrimages of . . . Ceres and Isis seem to indicate the life which loses what is dear in childhood, to seek in weary pain for what after all can be but half regained. Ceres regained her daughter, but only for half the year. Isis found her husband, but dismembered" (Dall, 42). In a moment, we want to consider Fuller's understanding of the Isis-Osiris myth, which she read in Plutarch's *Morals*. But first, as an index of her tendency to psychologize myth, it is instructive to contrast Fuller's reading of Persephone with that of Thomas Taylor. In an extended footnote to the Cupid and Psyche episode of *The Golden Ass*, Taylor argues that "this fable . . . was designed to represent the lapse of the soul from the intelligible world to the earth."[48] According to Taylor, Psyche's descent into the Underworld "indicates that the soul, through being enslaved to a corporeal life, becomes situated in obscurity, and is deprived of the light of day."[49] "But Psyche," Taylor continues, "in returning from Hades, is oppressed with a profound sleep, through indiscreetly opening the box given her by Proserpine. . . . This obscurely signifies, that the soul, by expecting to find that which is truly beautiful in a corporeal and terrene life, passes into a profoundly dormant state."[50] In support of this reading Taylor quotes from his translation of Plato's *Republic*, book VII: "he who is not able, by the exercise of his reason, to define the idea of *the good* . . . we must say . . . that in the present life he is sleeping, and conversant with dreams, and that before he is roused, *he will descend to Hades, and there be profoundly and perfectly laid asleep.*"

In contrast to Taylor's Neoplatonic allegorizing of the Persephone myth, Fuller argues that "Persephone's periodical exile shows the impossibility of resuming an unconsciousness from which we have been once aroused, the need thought has, having once felt the influence of the Seasons, to retire into itself" (Dall, 41–42). Like Emerson, Fuller transposes Neoplatonic allegory into a psychological frame of reference. Rather than discussing the soul's descent into the realm of matter, she considers the relationship between consciousness and the unconscious. Although Fuller, like most of her contemporaries, does use myth in the service of a sublimating idealism, she tempers this movement toward spiritual insight with a concern for the emotional life as well. By commenting upon the "weary pain" of the questing Ceres and Isis and upon the lost "unconsciousness" of Persephone, she uses myth to develop a psychological vocabulary of suffering and loss. Clearly, what interests Fuller in these fables is their representation of female figures alienated from their families and themselves.

Along these lines, Plutarch's account of "Isis and Osiris" represents a central fable of female alienation and compensating power. In the Egyptian myth Typhon (associated by Plutarch with irrationality) tricks Osiris into being entombed in a chest, which he then casts into a river. The chest floats out to sea and eventually comes ashore. It is enclosed within the trunk of a tree that the local king has cut down as a pillar to support his house. This is where Charles Wheeler, in the Conversation of March 8, picks up the story; he "related the story of Isis, of her hovering in the form of a swallow round the tree in which the sarcophagus of Osiris had been enclosed by Typhon; of her being allowed to fell the tree; of the odor emitted by the royal maidens whom she touched, which revealed her Divinity to the Queen; of the second loss of the body, as she returned home, and its final dismemberment" (Dall, 54–55). "There was little success in spiritualizing more of this story than the pilgrimage," Dall comments, "and R. W. E. [Emerson] seemed to feel this; for when MARGARET had remarked that even a divine force must become as the birds of the air to compass its ends, and that it was in the carelessness of conscious success that the second loss occurred, he said that it was impossible to detect an inner sense in all these stories." In response, "MARGARET replied, that she had not attempted that, but she could see it in all the prominent points" (Dall, 55). At this moment the subject changes, and we are left wondering what further significance Margaret Fuller saw in the story of Isis and Osiris.

This consideration is greatly complicated by a passage omitted from the story of Isis and Osiris during the 1841 Conversation. Charles Wheeler refers to the "final dismemberment" of Osiris. In Plutarch's text, which both Emerson and Fuller had read, this dismemberment is described in the following terms: "But of all Osiris's members, Isis could never find out his private part, for it had been presently flung into the river Nile, and the lepidotus, sea-bream, and pike eating of it, these were for that reason more scrupulously avoided by the Egyptians than any other fish. But Isis in lieu of it, made its effigies, and so consecrated the phallus for which the Egyptians to this day observe a festival."[51] Some indication of Emerson's acquaintance with this passage is given in a journal entry of 1833. Commenting upon his anxiety during a violent storm at sea, Emerson noted: "A long storm from the second morn of our departure consigned all the five passengers to the irremediable chagrins of the stateroom, to wit, nausea, darkness, unrest, uncleanness, harpy appetite & harpy feeding, the ugly sound of water in mine ears, anticipations of going to the bottom, & the treasures of the memory. I remembered up nearly the whole of Lycidas, clause by clause, here a verse & there a word, as Isis in the fable the broken body of Osiris" (*JMN*, 4:102–3). Here, "the broken body of Osiris" is used as an image of dismemberment, dissolution, and of castration.

The nineteenth century, of course, assiduously avoided nonmedical references to the genitals, especially in mixed company. But we can surmise that part of the "inner sense" of the story of Isis includes the recognition by Fuller of a male principle rendered powerless, even impotent. This conjecture is substantiated by Plutarch's identification of Isis with Minerva, a goddess who also plays a central role in Fuller's *Woman in the Nineteenth Century*. The Egyptians, Plutarch notes, "oftentimes call Isis by the name of Minerva, which in their language expresseth this sentence, 'I came from myself,' and is significative of a motion proceeding from herself."[52] Isis, in other words, represents a self-sufficient female power who generates herself. Given the mores of the age, with their emphasis upon female dependency, such a figure threatens male identity. At the heart of Fuller's vision of the self is a female myth powerful enough to steal the energy of the phallus.

THE SELF AT ELEUSIS: IMAGES OF FEMALE UNION

We can measure Margaret Fuller's commitment to images of the Goddess from a sketch she published in the *Dial* in April, the month the 1841 Conversations ended. Marie Urbanski describes this work, entitled "Leila," as Fuller's "fullest exploration of the feminine principle."[53] Given the central role played by female archetypes in Fuller's thought, this work becomes a central document. According to Bernard Rosenthal, "Leila" is a "tale of psychological investigation" that portrays the encounter between a female persona and a goddess-figure characterized as a "Saint of Knowledge" (*D*, 1:465).[54] As a "bridge between me and the infinite" (463), Leila resembles Demeter of the Eleusinian myth, the Great Mother who seeks and is reunited with her wayward daughter. "The one essential motif in the Eleusinian mysteries and hence in all matriarchal mysteries," Erich Neumann writes, "is the *heuresis* of the daughter by the mother, the 'finding again' of Kore by Demeter."[55] But like the mythical material used by Emerson, the Eleusinian rituals had shifted, by the nineteenth century, from being an external ritual. According to Nor Hall, they "no longer have visible structures, symbols, or spaces to manifest in, but rather have turned themselves inward so that the initiation is an active entry into the dark terrain of an unknown self where we still search for the lost daughter, the feminine source of life."[56] This quest within necessitates "divesting oneself of the outer layer, the *persona* or mask by which the world recognizes us."[57] Thus, for Fuller, Leila "ever seemed to me a spirit under a mask" (*D*, 1:463), a double embodying the creative energies that had long lain fallow within.

Some indication of the powers that Fuller was rediscovering is given by the fragmentary "autobiographical romance" that she composed in 1840. Confined by her father's rigid common sense and his severe academic discipline, Fuller recounts the split of her being into an intellectual facade and buried emotion: "My own world sank deep within, away from the surface of my life; in what I did and said I learned to have reference to other minds. But my true life was only the dearer that it was secluded and veiled over by a thick curtain of available intellect, and that coarse, but wearable stuff woven by the ages, —Common Sense" (*M*, 1:18). In contrast to her father's stern intellectuality, Fuller opposes the "dear little garden" of her mother, the one place as a child she "felt at home" (23). The imaginative importance of this locale for Fuller has been demonstrated by Bell Gale Chevigny and, most recently, by Annette Kolodny, who documents how the image of her mother's garden becomes an index of female existence in *Summer on the Lakes*.[58] According to Chevigny, the contrasting images of mother and father helped Fuller analyze her divided self: "the self nurtured by her father was public, while that like her mother was private, even invisible."[59] Fuller's task is to resuscitate that invisible, female presence, to create the image of a "mother" who "might act as companion, guide, and interpreter for Fuller herself."[60] "Leila," along with a later *Dial* sketch entitled "Bettine Brentano and Her Friend Gunderode," enables Fuller to imagine such a nurturing female presence.

If paternal and maternal images in the "autobiographical romance" mediated Fuller's sense of her "masculine" consciousness and "feminine" unconscious, she elaborates this contrast through her discussion of Rome and Greece. Drilled in Latin by her father, Fuller came to associate his stern authority with the Roman world of "discipline in heroic common sense" (*M*, 1:18). This world, she notes, is characterized by "a single thought, an earnest purpose, an indomitable will, by hardihood, self-command, and force of expression" (18). She sees the Roman "commanding nature too sternly to be inspired by it" (19). "The ruined Roman," she adds, "sits among the ruins; he flies to no green garden; he does not look to heaven" (19). In contrast, Fuller associates Greece with "the enchanted gardens" of its mythology (21). She "loved to creep from amid the Roman pikes to lie beneath this great vine," "to get away from the hum of the forum and the mailed clang of Roman speech, to these shifting shows of nature" (21). Greece, for her, is a place of "sunny waters, where there is no chill, and the restraint is from within out" (22). It is the analogue of her mother's garden, a place where she gathered the most beautiful flowers and "pressed them to my bosom with passionate emotions, such as I have never dared express to any human being" (24). Recovering the image of this nurturing clime in "The Magnolia of Lake Pontchartrain," Fuller analyzes its personification in "Leila."

A figure leading to "a perception of boundlessness, of depth below depth" (*D*, 1:462), Leila exists outside of male understanding. Most men are left "baffled," if not "angry," by her and, as a result, call her "mad, because they felt she made them so" (462). Leila "transcends . . . all the human barriers behind which man entrenches himself from the assaults of Spirit," but to women she opens a realm of insight (463). "At the hour of high moon," Fuller's speaker conjures her to rise from "a little lake" at "the centre of the park" (463). Responding to this "prayer," she "rises and walks on its depths." A dream-figure, Fuller's Leila belongs to the same category as the feminine archetypes studied by Erich Neumann, Nor Hall, Annis Pratt, and others. "In the patriarchal development of the Judaeo-Christian West with its masculine, monotheistic trend toward abstraction," Neumann writes, "the goddess, as a feminine figure of wisdom, was disenthroned and repressed."[61] Fuller's "Leila" represents an attempt to recover what Neumann calls the "unity of Demeter and Kore."[62] Reunited with "the Great Goddess as the female self," Kore "in conjunction with Demeter becomes the Olympian Kore, the immortal and divine principle, the beatific light."[63] This reunion, Annis Pratt reminds us, carried an especial emotional resonance for women. Symbolizing the "rebirth of the personality," the Eleusinian rites expressed a "transformational power" that "derived from the relationship of women to each other."[64] "Leila" portrays such a reunion of woman with her female double.

If she is "given space," Nor Hall argues, the Goddess "will come into consciousness and culture positively"; but if she is rejected, she "will break the doors down and come in to individual or cultural consciousness in a negative, devouring . . . way."[65] Fuller's Leila embodies both aspects. In the face of resistance she is "lava" that "shakes the thoughts" (*D*, 1:465) and a "Demon" (466). But for the speaker, she is a transforming and life-giving power. A bringer of light to those who accept her, she is a "Star" drawing one "into religion" (465). She "showers down . . . balm and blessing"; flowers spring from her glance; "rivers of bliss flow forth" at her touch, which metamorphoses "prison walls" into "Edens" (466). Her influence redeems "matter," making each "serpent form soar into a Phenix" (466).

The image of the "Phenix" recalls Fuller's letter of October 22, 1840, to Caroline Sturgis, where she links the image of herself as a "lonely Vestal" (*LMF*, 2:167) with the coming rebirth of the soul "Phenix like . . . into tenderest Spring" (169). "Leila" picks up this theme of nunlike dedication to the rebirth of the self. The "condition of this ecstasy," the speaker comments, is "a moment of frail virginity," a "purity" that men can only see as "the seal of death" (*D*, 1:464). "Into my single life," she comments, "I stooped and plucked from the burning my divine children. And ever, as I bent more and more with an unwearied benignity . . . more beauteous forms, unknown before to me . . . were born from that suddenly darting flame, which had threatened to cleave the very dome of my being" (466). If Fuller's "divine children" are her inspired thoughts, here she again mediates inspiration through the figure of Isis. In Byblus, before she recovered the body of Osiris, Isis was the nurse of the queen's infant whose mortal parts she used to burn away at night. This allusion suggests that virgin dedication necessitates purification, a burning away and sublimation of desire. Such a process is made familiar by William Butler Yeats's poem "Sailing to Byzantium." "Consume my heart away; sick with desire," he writes as he invokes "God's holy fire."

At the conclusion of Fuller's metaphysical sketch, Leila prepares herself, like the unborn Christ in Milton's *Paradise Lost*, for incarnation. In response, the speaker wonders if she might meet Leila, "who hast taken into thyself all my thought," on "the radius of humanity" (*D*, 1:467). She wishes for Leila and herself to "be impersonated," united, so that they might "traverse the regions of forms together" (467). Like Demeter and Kore, the speaker and Leila will form an ecstatic couple, a merger of self and archetype that pulls together the divided halves of the female psyche.

"Leila" projects the image of female healing onto a metaphysical plane; Fuller's incomplete "autobiographical romance" brings this process down to the realm of interpersonal relations. The two works are linked by their imagery. As Leila spreads her gracious influence over the earth, "the thorn glows with a crown of amaranth" (*D*, 1:466). Amaranth was a flower with a special meaning for Fuller, for it was associated with her first friend (Ellen Kilshaw), whose presence for the young Fuller was "a gate of Paradise" (*M*, 1:34). Fuller's "guardian spirit," the "first angel" of her life (35), Ellen pledged her friendship with "a bunch of golden amaranths or everlasting flowers" (36). In Fuller's account this gift assuages her childhood grief at a scene of estrangement modeled on Sir Walter Scott's *Guy Mannering*: "I was the little Harry Bartram, and had lost her, —all I had to lose, —and sought her vainly in long dark caves that had no end" (36). Fuller's imagined loss of her first friend merges with the image of her long-dead sister, "who would have been the companion of my life" (14). In opposition to such losses, Fuller places the idealized image of female companionship, friendship most fully realized as friendship between women. Disappointed in 1840 by her male friends, Samuel Ward and Emerson, Fuller is freed psychologically to explore the dimensions of female intimacy.

According to Carroll Smith-Rosenberg, women's friendship in the nineteenth century took on a central function in providing emotional support and defining female identity. Since "American society was characterized in large part by rigid gender-role differentiation," "most nineteenth-century Americans assumed the existence of a world composed of distinctly male and female spheres, spheres determined by the immutable laws of God and nature."[66] Although Fuller later attempts a psychological rapprochement between these two spheres in *Woman in the Nineteenth Century*, first she explores in her writing the contours of female being. Her "autobiographical romance" and her *Dial* essay "Bettine Brentano and Her Friend Gunderode" define her idea of friendship between women. Writing them, Fuller was able to extend her "idea of woman."

Members of what Elaine Showalter refers to as "a *muted group*, the boundaries of whose culture and reality overlap, but are not wholly contained by, the *dominant (male) group*," nineteenth-century women frequently found that their experience fell outside of the purview of patriarchal consciousness.[67] Showalter characterizes this area of exclusively female awareness as a "wild zone," a psychological and existential region beyond male "civilization."[68] In "Bettine Brentano and Her Friend Gunderode" Fuller steps over into that territory by suggesting the ultimate insufficiency of male companionship for female self-development. In Fuller's view Brentano's relationship with Goethe, like her own friendship with Emerson, initially facilitated her development but ended up confining her being. Although Brentano "had grown up in the atmosphere he created" (*D*, 2:315), "her progress" was retarded by "boundless abandonment" to Goethe's paternal influence (317). Ultimately, Goethe did not reciprocate Brentano's feelings: "there being no response from the other side to draw her out naturally" (317). In contrast, Brentano's friendship with the woman Gunderode stirs emotional and spiritual depths; it "comes like the *moonbeam* to transfigure the landscape, to hush the wild beatings of the heart and dissolve all the sultry vapors of day into *the pure dewdrops of the solemn and sacred night*" (319, italics mine). Fuller's language here connects the image of female friendship with her ongoing exploration of female archetypes. If "true intimacy," in her terms, reveals "two souls prophesying to one another" (322), her imagination of intimacy between women carries her well beyond the failure of such prophecy with Emerson. Instead, it helps Fuller to imagine that area of female spirituality left out of Transcendentalism. Like "Leila" and her human avatar, the relationship between Bettine Brentano and her friend Gunderode evokes a domain in which women can be reunited with each other and with female ideals.

"TIDES THAT BETOKEN A WAXING MOON"

Woman in the Nineteenth Century completes Fuller's sexualizing of Transcendentalist psychology. As David M. Robinson illustrates, this work "uses the central intellectual commitment of the transcendentalist movement, the belief in the possibility of 'self-culture,' or the continual spiritual growth of the soul, to diagnose, and prescribe a remedy for, the condition of women."[69] In the process Fuller illustrates the interdependency of self-culture and social reform. "Could you clear away all the bad forms of society, it is vain," she argues, "unless the individual begin to be ready for better. There must be a parallel movement in these two branches of life" (*WNC*, 65). Thus, on the one hand, Fuller's book develops a model of self-culture that takes Transcendentalism as its point of departure; on the other, it exemplifies what Robinson calls "transcendental politics."[70] Both aspects of Fuller's argument exemplify an impulse toward reform. But Robinson stops short of exploring the sexual implications in Fuller's redefinition of identity. Where Emerson imagines spirit or thought in "neutral" (i.e., male) terms, Fuller explicitly analyzes the psychological expense of such unexamined assumptions upon both men and women. As a result Fuller carries Emerson's idea of self-reliance into the realm of sexual politics.

The root of Fuller's difference from Emerson and the other Transcendentalists lies in her "idea of woman." Translating Emerson's image of "universal man" into images both of universal woman and universal androgyne, Fuller aims at a radical revision of the ideals orienting self-awareness. This enterprise deeply disturbed her contemporaries. As Robinson comments, Emerson's radicalism was "readily accepted into the canon of American values while Fuller's was regarded as dangerous."[71] The question that Robinson does not address is, what made Fuller's "idea of woman" so upsetting?

We can begin to gauge the nature of Fuller's disturbing originality by considering contemporary reactions to *Woman in the Nineteenth Century*. The most virulent of these reviews attacked her attempts to redefine sexual identity. "It is the law," Charles F. Briggs wrote in response, "that woman shall reverence her husband, and that he shall be her head."[72] "Woman is nothing but as a wife," Briggs continues. "How, then, can she truly represent the female character who has never filled it? No woman can be a true woman, who has not been a wife and mother."[73] Orestes Brownson buttresses similar views with scripture: "She says man is not the head of woman. We, on the authority of the Holy Ghost, say he is. The dominion was not given to woman, not to man and woman conjointly, but to man."[74] Fuller's sin, in the eyes of Briggs and Brownson, is that she gives woman an independent spiritual agency beyond the control of man. By locating the "idea of woman" in women's souls, in an independent spiritual authority symbolized by the goddess Minerva, she suggests that they have the power to determine their own lives. Even Emerson, we have seen, was not completely willing to relinquish spiritual autonomy to women.

Once made aware of the spiritual agency within herself, nineteenth-century woman would be much less likely to imitate uncritically the familiar role of "model-woman of bride-like beauty and gentleness" (WNC, 20). Other roles, beyond the scope of male authority, would also be available. "Union," Fuller observes, "is only possible to those who are units" (106). Therefore, she advocates a stage of female separatism that might allow woman to "establish the legitimacy of freedom, the power of self-poise the perfection of motion" (106). "I would have her," Fuller continues, "like the Indian girl, dedicate herself to the Sun, the Sun of Truth, and go no where if his beams did not make clear the path. . . . Men, as at present instructed, will not help this work, because . . . they are under the slavery of habit" (107). By advocating female self-reliance outside of male-female relations, Fuller strikes directly at nineteenth-century faith in motherhood as the ideal of female being.

In addition, Fuller goes on to challenge the popular nineteenth-century view that spirit, reflecting the form of God the Father, is masculine. It "was a frequent belief among the ancients," she notes, "that the *body* was inherited from the mother, the *soul* from the father" (41). Fuller saw examples of a similar view in her own age, for Brownson's assertion that male dominion reflects the "Holy Ghost" exemplifies this sexual hierarchy. Mary Daly explains the implications of such a position: "If God in 'his' heaven is a father ruling 'his' people, then it is in the 'nature' of things and according to divine plan and the order of the universe that society be male-dominated."[75]

But the consequences of such male domination, Fuller saw, were even more insidious. The Roman definition of woman as body "permitted a man to lend his wife to a friend, as if she were a chattel" (*WNC*, 42). Throughout *Woman in the Nineteenth Century* Fuller complains that women have been treated as "bond-maids" (147); their nature has been defined in physical, rather than spiritual, terms. In "slavery," she argues, woman "is a work-tool, an article of property" (51). Wives who exist only to bear children or to labor in the house fare little better in her eyes. The cause of such objectification, she insists, lies with men who refuse to recognize woman "as soul" with "a destiny of its own" (100). Fuller's goal, in opposition, is to establish woman "in the rights of an immortal being" (58), a being whose body is not seen "as the tool of servile labor, or the object of voluptuous indulgence" (150). As a result, her lengthy discussion of prostitution, which shocked nearly all of her readers, merely works out the implications of viewing all women in spiritual terms. Fuller rejects the view that certain women—for example, the ten thousand prostitutes that New York legislators found "a fair proportion to one city" (134)—are soulless and hence beyond redemption. Only if the spiritual authority of all women is recognized can such beings be seen as corrupted, rather than as evil others.

By asserting that the spiritual essence is female, as well as male, Fuller attempts to remove woman from the position of "the Other." She shares with Hélène Cixous the goal of helping woman "return to the body which has been more than confiscated from her, which has been turned into the uncanny stranger on display."[76] This reversal is effected in several ways. For example, Fuller's assertion of androgynous being exorcises what Mary Daly calls "the internalized patriarchal presence," "a demonic power within the psyche—the masculine subject . . . within—that reduces the self to an object."[77] At the same time Fuller attacks prevailing sexual attitudes by reversing the prevailing stereotype that spirit is masculine and body or nature female. Instead, she sees man as a being who all too often fails to control his "brute nature" (*WNC*, 122), a creature who sometimes acts like a "Satyr" (122). Fuller's comments on the "virgin" nature of the female soul counterbalance this image of male physicality. In addition, Fuller exploits the popular stereotype of woman's otherness by arguing that women embody an "electricity," a pool of volatile psychic energy that many men find unsettling. If fallen women manifest an uncanny physical quality, she suggests that woman's imaginative power, her "Muse" aspect, is equally upsetting: "Those, who seem overladen with electricity frighten those around them" (91). According to Fuller, such is the effect of Cassandra (94) and of her own alter-ego, Miranda (28).

One of the most effective means that Fuller uses to clarify the social and psychological position of women is the dramatization of dialogues between feminine and patriarchal consciousness. Bell Gale Chevigny has suggested that the dialogue between "Free Hope" and "Self-Poise" in *Summer on the Lakes* represents a fictionalized encounter between Fuller and Emerson.[78] But similar moments occur in "The Magnolia of Lake Pontchartrain," "Festus," Fuller's translation of "Marie van Oosterwich," and "Dialogue," all of which stage verbal confrontations between generalized male and female characters. By the opening pages of "The Great Lawsuit" (later to become *Woman in the Nineteenth Century*), Fuller has perfected the form as a tool of analysis:

> "Is it not enough," cries the sorrowful trader, "that you have done all you could to break up the national Union, and thus destroy the prosperity of our country, but now you must be trying to break up the family union, to take my wife away from the cradle, and the kitchen hearth, to vote at polls, and preach from a pulpit? Of course, if she does such things, she cannot attend to those of her own sphere. She is happy enough as she is. She has more leisure than I have, every means of improvement, every indulgence."
> "Have you asked her whether she was satisfied with these indulgences?"
> "No, but I know she is. She is too amiable to wish what would make me unhappy, and too judicious to wish to step beyond the sphere of her sex. I will never consent to have our peace disturbed by any such discussions."
> "'Consent'—you? it is not consent from you that is in question, it is assent from your wife."
> "Am I not the head of my house?"
> "You are not the head of your wife. God has given her a mind of her own."
> [*D*, 4:10]

When she came to write *Woman and Nature*, Susan Griffin records, she found that she could only contend with "patriarchal thought" by establishing a "dialogue" between female consciousness and "the parody of a voice" with patriarchal assumptions.[79] Throughout *Woman in the Nineteenth Century* Margaret Fuller uses the same rhetorical strategy.

A second device, the fictionalized representation of herself as an exemplary persona, is evident in Fuller's account of "Miranda" (*WNC*, 27–29). Like Emerson, Thoreau, and Whitman, Fuller presents a version of herself as a model of being. Unlike most women in nineteenth-century America, Miranda was educated as "a living mind," a "temple of immortal intellect" (27). The result was a woman able to take "a course of her own," a woman exemplifying the self-culture that Fuller hopes to instill in her female readers. Lest we miss the pointed reference to Emerson, she has Miranda argue that "the position I early was enabled to take was one of *self-reliance*. And were all women as sure of their wants as I was, the result would be the same" (29, italics mine). Unfortunately, Miranda continues, most women are "so overloaded with precepts by guardians" that "their minds are impeded by doubts." Fuller's portrait of Miranda provides a counterexample, demonstrating the benefits of a less restricted education that develops women's minds. As Marie Urbanski notes, Fuller argues that "all women need and, in fact should aspire to the same self-culture and fulfillment that she herself had desired."[80]

Fuller's numerous portraits of great women and of powerful female characters serve a similar function. They demonstrate that energy and creativity are not only masculine attributes. In this regard, Fuller anticipates Emerson's *Representative Men* by providing a gallery of "representative women" who embody "the idea of woman." These figures, according to Urbanski, "serve as models of conduct to inspire or instruct women."[81] Each of Fuller's many examples counteracts the assumption that women are unable to be self-reliant and exercise power. Her portraits of Mary Wollstonecraft and of George Sand function somewhat differently. At the same time that they exemplify female genius, they represent women who challenge conventional sexual attitudes. "Such beings as these," Fuller asserts, "ought not to find themselves, by birth, in a place so narrow, that, in breaking bonds, they become outlaws" (*WNC*, 62). By supporting Wollstonecraft and Sand, Fuller turns this process of outlawing back on itself; she willfully transgresses the sexual norms of her own society. "Within the systems of discourse and representation which repress the feminine," Mary Jacobus argues, "woman can only resubmit herself to them; but by refusing to be reduced to them, she points to the place and manner of her exploitation."[82] In this fashion Fuller's deliberate transgression of restrictive sexual norms shocks her audience into awareness of their existence.

Ultimately, Margaret Fuller's social analysis depends upon a redefinition of human psychology. Like Emerson and his followers, she engages in psychological mythmaking. According to Fuller, poets are "led and fashioned by a divine instinct . . . to develope [*sic*] and interpret the open secret of love passing into life, energy creating for the purpose of happiness" (*WNC*, 7). The artist, "drawn by a pre-existent harmony," both "moulds" energy "to forms of life" and "reveals her meaning to those who are not yet wise enough to divine it" (7). Fuller's model of artistic creation parallels Emerson's, since she also sees creation as a dual process of expression and interpretation. As Friedrich Schlegel taught the Romantic age, creation involves both the liberation of deeply buried energies and a process of critical control.[83] The literary work, as a result, is not a formless effusion, pure organic growth. Rather, it involves the release of power within an interpretive context that focuses its impact.

Fuller's depictions of the self exhibit just such control. Miranda, for example, is portrayed critically as a possible model of being. Similarly, Fuller articulates her vision of psychology by means of mythical figures framed within commentaries designed to shape her reader's response. Thus her psychological mythmaking, like Emerson's, involves the self-conscious interpretation of models of potential being.

Early on in *Woman in the Nineteenth Century* Fuller establishes that "the idea of woman was nobly manifested" by the ancients "in their mythologies and poems"—that is, through figures such as Sita, Isis, the Sphinx, Ceres, Proserpine, Diana, and Minerva (39). At this point in her argument, such myths function as ideals of being, equivalent to Emerson's "exemplary ideal man behind or within every individual."[84] But as Fuller's discussion progresses, her mythical figures become what Robert D. Richardson calls "archetypes of human character."[85] Just as Carl Jung later compares the psyche's archetypes to "the invisible presence of the crystal lattice in a saturated solution," Fuller describes the archetype as an appearing crystal.[86] At the moment that "every arbitrary barrier" inhibiting woman is "thrown down," she writes, "we should see crystallizations more pure" of "the divine energy" (*WNC*, 26).

One of Fuller's favorite archetypes in *Woman in the Nineteenth Century* is the popular Romantic "myth of the Androgyne."[87] According to Henri Ellenberger in *The Discovery of the Unconscious*, this myth "was well suited to express the Romantic idea of the fundamental bisexuality of the human being, and it was elaborated in many ways by the Romantics." Although Fuller's myth of androgyny seems a genuine contribution to American culture, it was familiar to her from such continental and British sources as Swedenborg and Thomas Taylor. In addition, Fuller points out "the feminine development" of Shelley (*WNC*, 101) and spends some time discussing the ambiguous female characters of Goethe's *Wilhelm Meister*. Similarly, Fuller presents George Sand, who "smokes, wears male attire, wishes to be addressed as 'Mon frere,'" as a woman embodying male and female traits (63).

Ultimately, Fuller's mythological framework in *Woman in the Nineteenth Century* derives from the commentaries of the Platonist Thomas Taylor. The "twelve powers," according to Taylor (whom Fuller adopts without attribution), are first the *"demiurgic or fabricative,* i.e., Jupiter, Neptune, Vulcan; the second, *defensive,* Vesta, Minerva, Mars; the third, *vivific,* Ceres, Juno, Diana; and fourth, Mercury, Venus, Apollo, *elevating and harmonic"* (*WNC*, 105). Fuller greatly streamlines this scheme by making the fabricative and defensive powers "masculine" and the vivific and harmonic "feminine." While the "two aspects of woman's nature" were "represented by the ancients as Muse and Minerva" (102), the two aspects of male nature are Apollo and Vulcan (106). "Man partakes of the feminine in the Apollo," Fuller explains, "woman of the masculine as Minerva" (104).

As David Robinson points out, the danger of referring to masculine and feminine traits is that it is too easy to slip into sexual cliches.[88] This is the response of Chevigny, who argues that Fuller's discussion "strikes contemporary feminists as surrendering to oppressive stereotypes."[89] But we have to remember that Fuller is writing for a culture that largely considered male and female to be mutually exclusive categories. "The only way in which any good can be rendered to society," Charles Briggs wrote in his review, "is by making woman more womanly and man more manly."[90] Although they may seem tame to twentieth-century readers, Fuller's assertions that male and female qualities "have not been given pure" either to men or women (*WNC*, 155) and that "they are perpetually passing into one another" (103) are quite radical for her age, for they directly challenge the prevailing sexual mythology.

Even more striking is Fuller's repeated insistence that the purest form of woman is not the wife and mother, but the virgin. Fuller's use of the virgin as a symbol of self-reliance, reflecting the ancient idea of virginity, is an aspect of her thought that many readers have downplayed or tried to ignore. Yet the most dominant motif of *Woman in the Nineteenth Century* is the composite image of the Madonna (44), "the betrothed of heaven" (45), the woman of "vestal loveliness" (48–49), the "vestal solitude" of Iphigenia in Aulis (88), the woman "betrothed to the Sun" (89), "Minerva" (106), all of whom exhibit "the force of woman's nature, virgin and unbiassed" (185). Woman's innate power, Fuller insists, needs to be developed in solitude beyond the interference of men whose own "energies are repressed and distorted" (37) and who oppress women in return. "Grant her, then, for a while," Fuller pleads, "the armor and the javelin. Let her put from her the press of other minds and meditate in virgin loneliness" (108). Only in twentieth-century feminist discourse does this theme, challenging the very foundations of patriarchal assumptions, reach a widespread acceptance. In the eyes of Fuller's contemporaries, the idea that an unmarried woman could be powerful was merely perverse.

Finally, Margaret Fuller symbolizes the psychological and spiritual re-birth of woman with an image that dates back to her study of Isis, whose "hovering in the form of a swallow" was interpreted by Fuller in 1841 as an emblem of "divine force" (Dall, 54–55). The image of "birds," Fuller asserts, is "chosen always by the feminine poet as the symbol of his fairest thoughts" (*WNC*, 43). Accordingly, at the climax of *Woman in the Nineteenth Century* she portrays the emerging idea of woman as the goddess "Iduna" who "strives to return among us, light and small as a swallow. We must welcome her form as the speck on the sky that assures the glad blue of Summer" (143). Whenever "religion had its course," she asserts a few pages later, "the dove presaged sweetly from Dodona's oak" (157). Fuller amplifies her use of bird as symbol by defending her own unique position among American women in the following way: there is "no need to clip the wings of any bird that wants to soar and sing, or finds in itself the strength of pinion for a migratory flight unusual to its kind" (160).

Like the Sun worshiped by Fuller's Indian girl, swallow and dove symbolize a spirituality freed from the constraints of a sex-bound age. Through such figures Fuller celebrates a female ideal of wisdom, Sophia, which has frequently been associated with the flight of birds. "Over the figure of the spirit with its outspread arms," Erich Neumann comments, "flies the upper bird of the Great Mother, the dove of the Holy Ghost."[91] Fuller's accomplishment in *Woman in the Nineteenth Century* is to suggest that this spiritual principle is not solely male in essence, that women as well as men can manifest that ideal. Attacking the idols of her age, she walked alone through a landscape littered with broken "effigies that once stood for symbols of human destiny" (163). Defining a new myth of the mind, Margaret Fuller presented nineteenth-century America with a powerful vision of the Goddess within, one of the "tides that betoken a waxing moon" (95).

Materializing the Psyche: The Counterexample of Poe, Hawthorne, and Melville

TRANSPARENCY OR MASQUERADE

It makes a great deal of difference whether or not the self is seen as incarnating transcendent spiritual power. If God—as Emerson believed—is found at the root of the psyche, one's attitude toward psychic phenomena such as intuitive promptings can be one of faith, of subordination to a "higher" power. In Emerson's view the language of the self needs to be made "transparent" in order to reveal the presence of the transcendental signified that he locates in the unconscious. But even though Emerson dreamed of subordinating language to "the unveiling of an unambiguous spiritual or moral truth," he encountered in his literary practice the intractability of words that could not be entirely shaped to the contours of transcendent power.[1] While the new American scholar is to embody in his language "the sacred germ of his instinct" (*CW*, 1:61), "the pure efflux of the Deity" (57), Emerson still recognized that the "distillation" of "life into truth" (55) could never be made perfect. The "conventional, the local, the perishable" (55) always would linger in his words, for no signifier could be made totally transparent.

In various ways the writings of Thoreau, Whitman, and Fuller suggest a similar semantic slippage. Although both Thoreau and Whitman anchored their writing in their intuition of the self's divine potential, both also included in their works a centrifugal impulse that rooted language in the manifold attractions of the sensuous world. Although this play of attention frequently reminded them of the "correspondence" between a universal spiritual power and natural phenomena, one finds at times in their works an opposing tendency to celebrate the unique and idiosyncratic life experiences of the individual. Similarly, when Fuller turns from her feminine archetypes to a consideration of the specific social injustices hindering women's self-development, she also contributes to a "diffusion" of "the center of meaning" that Emerson had so triumphantly located within the self.[2]

Despite the tensions in Emerson's works between mythic images of power and a potentially decentering skepticism, between what Evan Carton describes as his "creative claims" and "critical counterclaims" that undercut his affirmations, the force of his rhetoric is toward the assertion of belief.[3] As a result, Emerson's "self-parody" (as Carton terms the process) sharpens the reader's awareness of the hermeneutic aspect of any language of the self. The distance between Emerson's symbols of regenerated being and the self-critical awareness that frames them measures the existential and spiritual distance to be crossed before one can become regenerated. In similar ways Thoreau, Whitman, and Fuller use a controlling Romantic irony in order to highlight the dependence of self-awareness upon the preconceptions embodied in any psychological terminology. In order to become aware of the "dawn," the "procreant urge," or the "Minerva" within, one must lend each psychological myth the hermeneutic faith that simultaneously constitutes and "reveals" hitherto unseen powers within the self. As we have seen, this process of self-discovery essentially parallels the dynamic of religious conversion.

As Poe, Hawthorne, and Melville cultivated in their works what might appear to be a similar language of self-parody, they moved toward a totally different conception of the self and its interpretation. Losing faith in the authority of a divine unconscious, they developed a secularized vision of the relation between conscious and unconscious, signifier and signified. Philip Gura characterizes this shift as the discovery of "a rhetoric of ambiguity, a mode of expression suitable to a world which had no final center of linguistic or semantic authority."[4] In the arena of psychological meaning this new "rhetoric of ambiguity" manifested itself through a greater attentiveness to the varieties of individual self-interpretation and a corresponding attentiveness to the play of psychological signifiers.[5] As we shall see, Poe undermines the "transparency" of Emersonian psychological allegory, and Hawthorne attends to the uncanny discrepancies between forms of social signification and individual psychological needs. Even more ruthlessly, Melville casts us afloat in "a universe whose center of meaning seem[s] indeterminate," a voyage into ambiguity that leads both author and reader into a "labyrinth of semantic madness."[6]

We can clarify the distance between Transcendentalist "rhetorics of regeneration" and this new "rhetoric of ambiguity" by contrasting Samuel Taylor Coleridge's model of signification with that of Friedrich Nietzsche. Coleridge, as well as American popularizers of his thought like James Marsh and Emerson, emphasized the ways in which symbolic language could evoke the transcendent center of the self.[7] Although this

center could never be fully known, it could be suggested—Coleridge
believed—through language that revealed "the translucence of the eternal through and in the temporal."[8] Although Coleridge, like Emerson,
paid great attention to the forms of words, his ultimate emphasis lay
upon the divine meaning that symbolic language unveiled. His theory of
representation (in contradistinction to his literary practice) imagined the
symbol as a "centered structure . . . beyond the reach of play."[9] The
idiosyncratic play of the signifier, like disparate moments of a person's
life, was to be animated and controlled by a central, divine meaning.

In contrast to the centered texts and psyches imagined by Coleridge
and Emerson, other nineteenth-century writers began to view language
as "a self-reflexive linguistic web which has displaced man's special relationship to both word and things."[10] Philip Gura, for example, finds in
Horace Bushnell's theories of language an emphasis upon the "freeplay"
of the signifier that anticipates the "deconstructive" theories of Jacques
Derrida.[11] For our purposes, Nietzsche's view of language in *The Birth of
Tragedy* provides an analogous model of words distanced from meaning.
Nietzsche's formulations are especially relevant to our understanding of
the psychological transformation taking place during the American Renaissance because they suggest that psychic surface and psychic depth, as
well as signifier and signified, participate in different levels of being. As
a result, the language of the self exists on a plane discontinuous with
that which it attempts to evoke—an alien unconscious. Rather than finding, like Coleridge or Emerson, a continuity between the "divine"
depths of the unconscious and consciously held religious ideals, Nietzsche argues that the unconscious and consciousness are radically dissimilar. The corollary of this view is a "darkening" of the unconscious, which
is defined as a natural force instead of as a divine power. In other words,
the proto-Freudian definition of the unconscious in terms of physical
or sexual impulse necessitates a model of psychological signification in
which manifest and latent contents, surface and depth, are carefully distinguished. The effective result of such distinctions is a de-idealization of
the psyche and its language.

In *The Birth of Tragedy* Nietzsche sees individuated "Apollonian" consciousness as "a veil" hiding the "Dionysian world" of the unconscious
from man's vision.[12] This unconscious energy, initially nonverbal and
nonvisual, is seen to project itself into bright images of order, such as
"the Olympian world which the Hellenic 'will' made use of as a transfigured mirror."[13] Artistic genius, Nietzsche argues, involves more than this
bright consciousness of spiritual order, for the artist must transform
primitive psychic energies into spiritualized images. From this perspec-

tive, the "mistake" of earlier thinkers (such as Coleridge and Emerson) is their confusion of projected ideals for the darker forces motivating them. They accept at face value "the Apollonian appearances in which Dionysius objectifies himself"; while Nietzsche sees these bright images—for example, "the bright image projections of the Sophoclean hero"—as compensations, "necessary effects of a glance into the inside and terrors of nature."[14] They are "luminous spots to cure eyes damaged by gruesome night," a "bright image which healing nature projects before us after a glance into the abyss."[15] Viewing the psychological signifier as a mask disguising deeper, nonverbal forces, Nietzsche articulates a theory of language and mind that necessitates the demystification of rhetorics of regeneration. From this angle Emerson's evocations of the "sun" within are revealed as psychological myths, rather than as accurate depictions of the depths of the mind. Indeed, Nietzsche shows us that any theory of the unconscious is a myth, for each psychological terminology translates nonverbal phenomena into a recognizable language.

At the same time, however, we need to measure the spiritual expense of this shift in perspective. Nietzsche's formulations enable us to define more clearly the spiritual and psychological crisis confronting Emerson's age. Is the "unconscious" a "heart of light" or a "heart of darkness"? Is it the locus of rational spirit or irrational passion? The problem for Emerson, as well as for the other major writers of the period, is that neither light nor darkness exists in a pure form. Especially during the American Renaissance, we observe a darkening of languages of the self as the irrational and the physical take on an increasingly important role in visions of the psyche. There is a general movement from pantheistic visions of the world, "shining and awake with a life of mind or spirit," toward an acceptance of Dionysian urges.[16] Through this darkening, the body reenters the mind, while the mind is placed again back in the body. In the process, the rationalism inherited from the eighteenth century starts to give way to biologically oriented models of the psyche.

At this point we can see the spiritual crisis that impended throughout Emerson's lifetime not merely as the decline of religion or the loss of contact with unconscious forces of inspiration. A more useful scheme is to view both spiritual and psychological losses as symptomatic of a dissociation that threatened to fragment the self into extremes of bodiless spirit and spiritless body, into an inhuman "light" or a savage "darkness." In America the lines of cleavage were there, waiting for sufficient force to divide the mind against the body. Many among the clergy were growing increasingly abstract and immaterial in their speculations, while much of the populace succumbed to the lure of materialistic gain. On the one hand, there was the threat of losing the "sense of solidity and substantiality of existence"; for as Hegel had seen, the desiccated fruit of self-consciousness was a state of mind that had moved beyond even the "extreme of insubstantial reflection of self into self."[17] From this pole, one desperately sought to regain "the substantial fullness of life" and to "restore the feeling of existence"[18]—motives that prompted Emerson's evocation of his growth "in the warm day like corn and melons" (*CW*, 1:35). But on the other hand, there was the threat of a materialism so complete that one becomes "sunken in what is sensuous, vulgar, and of fleeting importance"—the "mind and interest . . . so deeply rooted in the earthly that we require a . . . power to have them raised above that level."[19] Bodiless religion or atheistic materialism (Barzilli Frost, Emerson's "spectral" preacher, or State Street, Boston's financial district) were the Scylla and Charybdis that confronted the age of Emerson.

Attempts to steer between these two poles led to the development of two rival psychological traditions in the nineteenth century—traditions distinguished by whether one found God or physical nature at the bottom of the psyche. On the one hand, there was the tradition of psychological discourse stretching from the German Idealists through Coleridge and Carlyle to Emerson. This view subordinated Nature to Spirit, by envisioning a divine "unconscious" that manifests itself as a force embodied through natural forms. Such forms could be read as transparent "signs" of Spirit. But in contrast, there was a countertradition, implicit in Poe, Hawthorne, and Melville, and emerging fully in Nietzsche. This view subordinated Spirit to Nature, viewing the "unconscious" as a "dark" physical energy that sublimates and disguises itself in ambiguous signifiers.

The conflict between these two languages of the self resulted from internal contradictions within Romantic organicism and its vision of psychic energy. Attempting to maintain the "correspondence" of Spirit and Nature, Emerson and his age confronted the unsettling truth that the fusion of theological ends with biological metaphors formed an unstable compound, for concepts of psychic energy lay open to increasingly materialistic interpretations. Although Emerson began to describe psychic energy as an abstract "power" instead of as a quasi-theological "spirit," contemporaries such as Poe, Hawthorne, and Melville found beneath the masks of consciousness potentially violent natural energies. As many critics have noted, it is but a short step from their disturbing images to the sexual libido of Freudian psychology. It was one thing to identify with Coleridge the force driving the psyche as "spirit" expressing itself through natural forms. But what about the disturbing sugges-

tion that this polarity might be reversed, that "spirit" might be a function of natural energy—one of the disguises of the body's power?

So long as psychic energy was viewed as spirit, there was little difficulty in associating intuited depths of the mind with moral order. If God
resides within, in the "unconscious," our most spontaneous impulses
receive a divine sanction. But within the context of nineteenth-century
intellectual history, such idealism runs counter to a general movement
toward materialistic conceptions of psychic energy. Inner contradictions
in the psychological terminology of Romantic organicism contributed
to this advancing materialism; for the organic view of the mind, with
its analogy between psychic dynamics and physical growth, contained
within its assumptions the unsettling suggestion that psychic energy
might be entirely physical in its provenance. This possibility was there
from the earliest comparisons of the unfolding mind to a growing plant.
Thus when writers such as Emerson or Melville describe the mind's
"current," one wonders how literally to read such an image.

Returning to Emerson, we note that he combines physical metaphors
of psychic energy with spiritual aims in different proportions at different
stages of his career. From the beginning, one suspects, Emerson sensed
the natural origin of spirit in the body's physical energy. But in his early
works this physical aspect is lost in the glare of spiritual illumination.
But as Emerson's thought developed, the physical took on more and
more importance. Thus, in "The Method of Nature" (1841) his characterization of the mind hovers ambiguously close to later, more materialistic, descriptions: "Do what you know, and perception is converted into
character, as islands and continents were built by invisible infusories, or
as these forest leaves absorb light, electricity, and volatile gases" (*CW*,
1:136). "Light," "electricity," "gases"—we see Emerson groping for terms
to express his sense of what Freud calls "libido."

Brooding from the beginning of his career upon the problem of individual creative growth, Emerson came to see that growth as the expression of a quasi-physical "power." This development is typical of a growing materialization of Romantic thought in general. By the 1850s, when
Hawthorne and Melville were writing their major romances and Emerson was composing *The Conduct of Life*, the sexual aspects of libido had
become much more apparent. Indeed, Joel Porte has documented instances of the "spermatic economy" throughout the 1830s and 1840s.[20]
Such observations link the sexual themes of Hawthorne's *The Scarlet
Letter* and of Melville's *Pierre* to a growing cultural awareness of sexual
energy and its vicissitudes. In *Pierre* especially, Melville openly examines
the self-delusion of a character who mistakes sexual attraction for spiri-

tual illumination. The commentary upon Transcendentalist intuition is clear, as Melville ruthlessly questions the sincerity of a philosophy founded upon spontaneous impulse. Late in the romance, for example, Pierre's quasi-Transcendentalist "enthusiasm" transforms itself into a "sudden storm of nature in his soul" (*P*, 289). How does one know, Melville asks in such a passage, what forces are being released by faith in the unconscious? Is it not all too easy to mistake the tempestuous message of instinct for that of "Reason"? Freud's position is adumbrated here—the view that faith in a spiritual energy motivating the psyche is an illusion masking more primitive urges.

Rather than viewing natural process as metaphor or symbol of spiritual unfolding, Freud deemphasized spirit in favor of the analysis of physical energy and its "vicissitudes." Conceiving the mind to be the product of a physical energy, libido, that is derived from the body and is transformed or "sublimated" into ideas, Freud thus views the religious impulse as one of the manifold "disguises" or "masks" of instinct. *The Future of an Illusion* culminates this line of thought. After suggesting that religion and idealism in general have served the important function of taming our instincts, Freud goes on to characterize religion as "a system of wishful illusions together with a disavowal of reality."[21] From the perspective of instinct, idealism will always seem an illusion. But if this is so, one wonders about the ultimate applicability of Freudian viewpoints to the writings of Emerson, Thoreau, Whitman, and Fuller. For does not this perspective obscure the spiritual impact of their idealizing rhetorics of regeneration?

Completing the process of interiorization established years before by German Romantic philosophers, Freud envisions a universe in which the dynamic principle of causality has shrunk entirely to the human sphere. Impulses once found in a spiritualized nature now exist entirely within the person, who maintains an uneasy relationship with the body's volatile, physical energies. This "dehumanization" effectively alienates us from Nature without and Nature within, from both the world and the "unconscious." The only option open is an adversarial relationship; we must try to dominate Nature or be dominated in return. We must subordinate natural resources, including the "natural resources" of the mind, to imperialistic directives. Accordingly, Freud imagines the end of psychoanalysis as the advance of the ego's circle of domination: "Psychoanalysis is an instrument to enable the ego to achieve a progressive conquest of the id."[22] Though there are moments—for example, in "Circles"—when Emerson speaks in similar, imperialistic tones, his "psychic imperialism" is tempered by a reverence totally absent in Freud. Ultimately, Emerson and his circle admit into their definitions of the psyche the recognition of a divine power that inspires both creativity and faith.

In contrast, the unconscious for Poe, Hawthorne, and Melville largely lacks that aspect of "light" and religious illumination. Instead, it stands behind cognition as a dark, impenetrable horizon. As a result, the plane of consciousness pulls away—into a "mask" disguising half-seen motives. We read of Melville's Pierre, for example, that "his very soul was forced to wear a mask" (P, 183). This sense of the language of the self as mask (instead of as transparent field of illumination) reflects the biological premises underlying Melville's depiction of the psyche and its energy. Given the necessary distance between the physical roots of libido and the conscious reasons cherished by the "I," the self must be seen to embody deception as an integral consequence of its structure. When consciousness, Ludwig Binswanger observes, is viewed as the product of the body and its drives, then it becomes "a mere 'superstructure'—a 'fabrication' (Nietzsche) . . . an illusion (Freud)."[23] In other words, the demystification of consciousness is a necessary consequence of any psychological myth that measures the self in terms of its physical archeology.

POE AND THE LIMITS OF PSYCHOLOGICAL ALLEGORY

Emerson offers his age the hope that the "truth" of both psyche and nature could be unveiled. Casting himself and his reader in the midst of "transparent" narratives, he imagines a universe susceptible to interpretation. Shining through phenomena, he assumes, would be the power of divinity. Although he attends to the variety of the "substantive" world, it seems at times as though daily complexities fade before the presence of that in-streaming glory. In the effort to inculcate faith in that "God within," Emerson diminishes the importance of individual moments in the face of transcendent meaning. Imagining a condition of pure "presence," he looks toward that transfigured state in which the psyche's signifiers might vanish in the face of pure power.[24] At such moments he places his reader in the midst of a divine allegory in which thought and action perfectly reveal "the workings of the Original Cause through the instruments he has already made" (CW, 1:21).

In contrast to Emerson's dream of uncovering "the hidden relationship between shape and inner meaning," Poe depicts "the problematic disrelation of form and impulse, mask and motive."[25] In his writing the signifiers of self and nature have pulled away into an indeterminate and ambiguous surface that threatens to generate an autonomous, "arabesque" purity.[26] Instead of connecting this surface to a transcendent source that might illuminate its details, Poe emphasizes the impossibility of translating the signifier into a totally accessible meaning. Like Freud, Poe rejects a vision of the psyche as "a system of signifiers" with "'a permanent code' that would allow 'a substitution or transformation of signifiers while retaining the same signified.'"[27] In his works "truth" is a function of the "veil"; the signifier suggests meaning indirectly through "a rhetoric of signifying effects."[28]

As a result, we must resist the temptation to turn Poe's dreamlike figures and settings into signs hiding a latent content. Whether we identify that center of meaning as being the unconscious, the anima, or the id, the result is roughly the same so long as we replace the fictional surface with a critically determined meaning. To read Poe in this way is to view his writing as psychological allegory. Like Emerson and his circle, we tend to view the self and its works as emblems that can be made transparent when embedded within our own rational discourse.[29] But Poe vehemently resists allegory as a proper mode of writing or reading. "Pure allegory," he comments, "is at all times an abomination— a remnant of antique barbarism—appealing only to our faculties of comparison, without even a remote interest for our reason, or for our fancy" (*ER*, 159). "The fallacy of the idea that allegory, in any of its moods, can be made to enforce a truth," he observes elsewhere, ". . . could be promptly demonstrated" (582). Not only do Poe's arguments challenge those critics who read his works for their hidden meaning, they throw down the gauntlet before his Transcendentalist contemporaries. Neither text nor psyche, he argues, can be made transparent. If Poe views writing as necessarily opaque, he also sees the "soul" as "a cypher, in the sense of a cryptograph" (1178).[30] Rather than openly revealing a level of ideas within, both literary and psychic texts can only express meaning indirectly through techniques of suggestiveness.

Rather than contributing to one idea, the mysterious details of "The Fall of the House of Usher," for example, build up a unified but elusive emotional effect. From the very first sentence, phrases start to cohere into a harmony of resonant echoes. We encounter "a dull, dark, and soundless day," "clouds [which] hung oppressively low," "a singularly dreary tract of country," "the shades of evening," "vacant eye-like windows," "a black and lucid tarn" (*T*, 397–98). The gaps between these images are punctuated by moments of self-reflection in which the narrator attempts to gauge, not their meaning, but their effect upon his feelings. The narrator's response illustrates the value that Poe places upon the "under-current," the "glimpse," the "echo" over the open revelation of meaning.

Unable to understand the depths of his mind, the narrator is plagued by "shadowy fancies" (*T*, 397) whose "power" lies beyond the limits of "analysis" (398). Filled with "vague sentiments" (400), he becomes more and more infected by the "atmosphere of sorrow" and "gloom" (401). Early on, he obtains a "glimpse" of Madeline Usher, but nothing more. Within this setting, redolent with hints of promised meaning, "the wild improvisations" of Usher's "speaking guitar" (404), as well as his "phantasmagoric" paintings, seem highly expressive. But if the narrator shudders "thrillingly" at such "vaguenesses," he shrinks from the open attribution of their significance: "from these paintings (vivid as their images now are before me) I would in vain endeavor to educe more than a small portion which should lie within the compass of merely written words" (405). Instead of focusing upon the meaning of such artistic productions, erasing Usher's signifiers in favor of some privileged signified, the narrator concentrates upon their play and effect. Like Freud, he maintains a distance between the play of language and the hidden meaning that it attempts to convey.

Poe resists the reduction of character, setting, and event to idea. He similarly rejects the Emersonian drive toward a "transparency" that would turn both self and literary text into allegorical works limiting the play of the signifier by reducing signs to determinate meanings. Instead, it is exactly the play of the signifier, cut loose from determinate meaning, that Poe emphasizes both in his reviews and tales. In the poetry of Thomas Moore he hears "a ghostly, and not always a distinct, but an august and soul-exalting *echo*" (*ER*, 337). Elsewhere, he argues that "a didactic moral might be happily made the *under-current* of a poetical theme" (691). In similar terms Poe argues that "the imagination" often brings "the imaginative man . . . to a glimpse of things supernal and eternal—to the very verge of the *great secrets*" (1293). This repeated emphasis upon echo, undercurrent, glimpse, and secret measures Poe's distance from allegory and from methods of reading that would attribute fixed textual or psychological meanings.

Instead of identifying, like Emerson, the nature of the psyche's center, Poe self-consciously analyzes the ways human beings confront an irrationality found both in nature and within themselves. Many of his tales portray inconclusive acts of self-interpretation that result from the need his characters feel to confront and make sense of their own subjective experiences. On two different levels (that of character and reader), such scenes of interpretation present a "phenomenology of power-relations" by analyzing the appearance, metamorphosis, and effect of the Other within the field of reflection.[31] The appearance of both the character's

and the reader's phenomenological fields depends initially upon a suspension of disbelief. Confronted with the mysterious House of Usher,
both narrator and reader eventually "bracket" their skepticism as to the
reality of the events they encounter.[32] Unless the narrator and reader
provisionally believe in what is happening, those events lose all impact.
Instead of disbelieving their experiences, they are caught up in Usher's
world, carried along on a current of feeling.

But in order for that current of feeling to have psychological meaning,
the play of subjectivity must be framed through maneuvers that enable
both Poe's narrator and the reader to step back and interpret what is
happening to them. In "The Fall of the House of Usher" (as well as in a
number of other tales) this process of self-interpretation is facilitated by
the presence of a character who becomes the object of psychological
reflection. Roderick Usher, for instance, provides a mirror for the narrator's and the reader's reactions. Observing Roderick, the narrator reflects:

> There were times, indeed, when I thought his unceasingly agitated mind was
> laboring with some oppressive secret, to divulge which he struggled for the
> necessary courage. At times, again, I was obliged to resolve all into the mere
> inexplicable vagaries of madness, for I beheld him gazing upon vacancy for
> long hours, in an attitude of the profoundest attention, as if listening to some
> imaginary sound. It was no wonder that his condition terrified—that it in-
> fected me. I felt creeping upon me, by slow yet uncertain degrees, the wild
> influences of his own fantastic yet impressive superstitions. [*T*, 411]

Both narrator and reader are pulled toward a superstitious terror defined
by Roderick Usher's agitated state. But they never reach that limit of
terror; instead, Roderick's subjectivity becomes the focus of their psychological reflection, a reflection that is facilitated by the ironic distance
maintained between Roderick and both narrator and reader. In other
words, the reader's and narrator's perception of a gap between their
reflection and Roderick's terror establishes the psychological meaning of
Poe's tale.

In stories like "The Black Cat" and "The Tell-Tale Heart," Poe uses a
second method of setting up the distance necessary for psychological
reflection. In those works this gap is provided by temporal delay. Rather
than observing the psychological reactions of another person who becomes more and more like oneself, the narrators of those tales present
their own past selves as objects available for analysis. "TRUE!—nervous—
very, very nervous I had been and am; but why *will* you say that I am
mad?" (*T*, 792)—"The Tell-Tale Heart" opens with a movement of self-
objectification. Taking his own terrified reactions as the object of analy-

sis, the narrator attempts to explain himself and to comprehend his own motivation. Once again, psychological reflection is generated by a reciprocal movement of involvement and detachment, emotional engagement and distance. Following the curve of Roderick Usher's subjectivity, we pulled back at critical moments to analyze his mental state and its relationship to our own. In these second instances Poe's characters perform such analysis upon themselves, describing their own psychological development with clinical precision: "The fury of a demon instantly possessed me. I knew myself no longer. My original soul seemed, at once, to take its flight from my body; and a more than fiendish malevolence, gin-nurtured, thrilled every fibre of my frame" (851). The speaker of this passage is able to see his own past self as an actor motivated by uncontrollable impulses. In the words of Jacques Lacan, his "discourse is played out . . . on a stage implying the presence not only of the chorus, but also of the spectators."[33]

By emphasizing the dynamic, theatrical quality of self-reflection, Poe develops a model of psychology that differs significantly from Emersonian "correspondence."[34] At least in theory, Emerson's model of psychological understanding depends upon a one-to-one, allegorical relationship between spirit and nature. Behind this approach is the faith that the right key properly applied might unlock the secrets of the psyche. Poe undermines this myth of correspondence through his portrayal of characters who exist in an essentially unknowable world that thwarts easy equations between motive and observed phenomena. Instead of finding themselves in nature, they confront the specter of an alien and threatening power that at first seems to have no relationship to their being. Rather than expanding their "dominion" over successively humanized fields of endeavor, Poe's characters face a world that threatens to overwhelm them. Ultimately, Emerson's myth of a collective Oversoul finds its negative image in Poe's portrait of a universe in which metaphysical and psychological unity has been diffused into myriad, imperfect fragments that cannot be reunited in moments of transcendent awareness, but only in death.

As a result, the act of self-interpretation runs against the possibility of nonmeaning. Or rather, in Poe's writing psychological meaning cannot be defined in rational terms, as ideas, but only as effects of power. Consequently, Poe's scenes of psychological interpretation fail to domesticate being to understanding; instead, they portray the emotional reactions of characters who attempt to free themselves from the Other. If Emerson's personae resemble the literary critic who looks for themes and ideas, Poe's characters focus instead upon the rhetorical impact, the dynamics of power. Thus it makes less sense to discuss the ideas lying "behind" Poe's writing than to analyze his presentation of power-relationships. Psychological understanding, in his fictional world, proceeds through the recognition of the power of the Other.

In chapter 1, we had occasion to consider Wolfgang Iser's analysis of the duality of the reading process, how it oscillates between identification with the voice presented in a text and then critical detachment from that process of identification. As we read the works of Emerson and his circle, we stressed the first half of Iser's model, arguing that Transcendentalist "rhetorics of regeneration" emphasized the reader's participation in dramatized models of being that idealized human potential. Such an approach assumed that we need to lend the Transcendentalist voice enough faith to allow it to function rhetorically. But now, as we turn to Poe and other writers shaped by the Gothic tradition, our critical emphasis must alter. In Poe's works, for example, we find a demystification of the Transcendentalist self informed throughout by a skeptical detachment from any voice or rhetoric that might compel identification. Because the effect of eloquence is not always self-enlargement but sometimes possession by an overpowering Other, wariness toward the dominating voice of the Other is the position taken by Poe's self-conscious narrators. As the Other's voice spreads its dominion into the avenues of their being, they feel invaded by a threatening power.

The most extreme cases, of course, involve those situations where the Other's voice is belatedly recognized as one's own. The narrators of both "The Fall of the House of Usher" and "Ligeia," for example, finally realize that the Other's presence stirs to consciousness an alien side of themselves that had lain dormant. Unable to assimilate to any model of rationality the voice that they hear themselves begin speaking, they observe with fascinated horror the invasion of their personalities by uncanny and undomesticated forces. Their only options are to succumb to psychic invasion or, in Freud's words, to safeguard "the frontiers of the ego" by giving the "ego back its mastery over lost provinces of . . . mental life."[35] This effort to regain psychic mastery depends upon the achievement of a critical distance sufficient to see one's own gestures as a role scripted by irrational powers.

But as Poe's characters come to recognize the theatricality of the possessed "I," his readers go through an analogous process. Like the narrator of "The Fall of the House of Usher," they are possessed and transfixed by the emotional energies released by Poe's fiction until they, too, demystify that obsession through the achievement of critical distance. Perhaps the clearest example of this tension between possession and analysis occurs near the end of "The Fall of the House of Usher." As he interprets the tale that he reads to Roderick Usher, the narrator sets the model for the reader's own response to Poe's narrative: "Here again I paused abruptly, and now with a feeling of wild amazement—for there could be no doubt whatever that, in this instance, I did actually hear (although from what direction it proceeded I found it impossible to say) a low and apparently distant, but harsh, protracted, and most unusual screaming or grating sound—the exact counterpart of what my fancy had already conjured up for the dragon's unnatural shriek as described by the romancer" (*T*, 414). Analyzing his own psychological reactions to a fictional work that parallels his situation, the narrator initiates a process of reflection that culminates in the reader's own examination of Poe's tale and the emotional depths that it stirs in his or her own being. By thematizing the process of reading, Poe makes us aware of the analogy between the narrator's possession by Roderick Usher's terror and our own possession by Poe's terrifying fiction. Indeed, he dramatizes the narrator's emotions as a literary response, thereby suggesting that psychological analysis and literary analysis are paired constructions.

As a model of reading, the narrator's response measures fiction in terms of its emotional effect. Poe's comments upon his literary intentions make it clear that his writing was not designed like Emerson's to educate, but rather to concentrate, "to arrest" (*ER*, 1322), the reader's attention. "In the brief tale," Poe asserts in his review of Hawthorne's fiction, "the author is enabled to carry out his full design without interruption. During the hour of perusal, the soul of the reader is at the writer's control" (586). In other words, Poe's model of literary response emphasizes the emotional power of the author's text over the reader. Unlike Emerson, Poe does not view his writing as the presentation of exemplary personae as ethical ideals. While Emerson's concern was with influencing and transforming the psychic being of his audience, Poe utilizes a different kind of rhetorical power. Rather than inspiring or transforming his audience, Poe's fiction possesses it in a fashion similar to the possession of the "I" by the Other in his tales. He exposes the reader to the power of terror and, according to the efficacy of the ironic frames in play, places him or her at a rationalizing distance that initiates reflection. This model is based upon a pattern of exposure and defense, not upon openness and apotheosis. The power that Poe unleashes can amuse or terrify, but not metamorphose, the self.

The Other in Poe's tales achieves a power over his characters analogous to that generated by his text over the reader. Just as Poe's reader learns to rationalize and analyze the sources of terror, his characters must find ways to defend themselves against potentially overpowering forces. The act of interpretation for both character and reader involves the attempt to exercise control over the mobility of the Other. Confronted with the reemergence of his dead wife, the narrator of "Ligeia" reflects upon his possession: "I had long ceased to struggle or to move, and remained sitting rigidly upon the ottoman, a helpless prey to a whirl of violent emotions, of which extreme awe was perhaps the least terrible, the least consuming" (*T*, 329). In contrast to such fixation, the old mariner in "A Descent Into the Maelstrom" learns to escape from "the influence" of the whirlpool's "deadly attraction" (582). In both tales the play of Otherness inscribes the track of an unknown power across the "I." That power appears to reflection in manifestations that display a "phenomenology of power-relations." By analyzing the power-relations portrayed in Poe's fiction, we can thus follow the effects of the Other's power—its range of surface disturbances transforming the plane of attention, creating bulges or gaps, indentations or rifts.

Power in Poe's world is determined by the Other, by the difference between self-determination and direction by the Other. Instead of measuring the self's imperialistic will-to-power, this difference marks the valence of alien energies that threaten to invade the borders of awareness. From a psychoanalytical perspective, the power of the Other reveals the force of psychic energies projected unconsciously into objects that confront the "I" as alien beings disguising the self's hidden face. In Poe's theater of desire, the dramatization of these power-relations displays the gap between consciousness and a truly alien unconscious.

Rather than attempting like Emerson to give the unconscious a name, the best Poe's characters and readers can do is to analyze the surface effects of its power, effects that lead to an increasing disruption of the plane of attention. In "Berenice," for example, the narrator's "monomania" leads eventually to the "terrible ascendency" (*T*, 216) of his fixation. In general, the progression of attention in Poe's fiction begins with interest; but interest can quickly metamorphose into attraction and then fascination, finally giving way to possession and engulfment.[36]

It is striking that Poe's scale of power-relations represents an absolute antithesis to the range of attention portrayed by Emerson, Thoreau, Whitman, and Fuller. Attention in their work involves the extension of libido, the laying down of new psychic pathways, the tending of psychic energy to an expanding field of dominion. In contrast, libido in Poe's works does not find new areas in which to expand, but rather falls back into a well-worn track that has been forgotten or repressed. Poe's characters are "haunted" by forces that have been cut away and expelled from self-awareness. Thus when Ligeia returns to "the pathway she had abandoned" (*T*, 323), she comes back with all the force of a fresh discovery. But the narrator of "Ligeia" discovers nothing new; he merely recognizes at last the terrifying force of his desire, which, as Lacan shows us, is mediated through the desire of the Other. According to Freud, this "uncanny" return of the repressed manifests itself as a "compulsion to repeat," a process of "involuntary repetition."[37] Replaying its fixation upon a power that cannot be recognized as its own, the self remains stuck in the groove of an alien energy.

In Poe's writing psychological meaning arises from the portrayal of Otherness as it affects self-conscious characters who attempt to understand and defuse its power. The Other, in his tales, gains significance as it forms the nucleus of his characters' reflection. By themselves, Poe's fantastic figures—his demonic women, his maelstroms, his mysterious animals—have no psychological meaning. Only to the extent that they elicit a character's (and ultimately, the reader's) response do they become signifiers in an ongoing psychological discourse. Without this interpretive frame, they remain at the level of pure fable. Madeline Usher, in other words, becomes psychologically significant because the narrator (paralleling the reader's response) is forced to confront his reactions to her mysterious being. Poe emphasizes over and over in his tales that such logical reflection must contend with moods and feelings that lie outside the province of reason. "A feeling, for which I have no name, has taken possession of my soul," one narrator observes (*T*, 141). Another focuses his attention upon the profundity of "*moods* of mind exalted at the expense of the general intellect" (638). Finding himself "upon the verge of some great secret," he moves beyond the Emersonian "dominion" of expansive consciousness.

In Poe's Gothic universe it is the Other and not the conscious self that gains dominion. "My evil destiny pursued me as if in exultation," the narrator of "William Wilson" laments, "and proved, indeed, that the exercise of its mysterious dominion had as yet only begun" (*T*, 444–45). In similar fashion Roderick Usher's poem "The Haunted Palace" dramatizes the collapse of "the monarch thought's dominion" (Emerson's dream) and its replacement by a divided and haunted sensibility punctuated by the fantastic movement of "vast forms" (406–7). As the narrator of "The Fall of the House of Usher" unwittingly shows us, this shift from reason to unreason necessitates a new model of interpretation; for Poe is dealing with emotional processes that lie outside of reason and that become apparent only in their effects—for example, in the rapid acceleration of terror.

Rather than resting "embosomed . . . in nature" like Emerson's secure personae, Poe's characters are instead haunted minds existing on "the brink of a precipice": "Our first impulse is to shrink from the danger. Unaccountably we remain. By slow degrees our sickness, and dizziness, and horror, become merged in a cloud of unnameable feeling. By gradations, still more imperceptible, this cloud assumes shape" (*T*, 1222). Poe's genius was to give that cloud a name—"perverseness." In contrast to the "intellectual or logical man" (1219) who constructs for himself a rational and allegorical model of the universe (one thinks here of Emerson), Poe attends to the irrational impulses that undermine the quest for identity. As a result his characters remind one of the narrator of Dostoevsky's *Notes from Underground*—that man of "caprice" who asserts that "suffering is the sole origin of consciousness."[38] From this perspective human beings cannot be measured against the horizon of projected ideals; rather, the self is split in two by a mobile and uncanny energy found within. Poe's inscription of this "imp of the perverse" effectively de-idealizes the psyche.

According to Poe, "inductive" examination of the psyche reveals the existence of "a primitive impulse" lying outside any scheme of the mind based upon prior understanding (*T*, 1221). Any intellectualized model of the psyche, as well as any psychology such as Emerson's in which "Reason" is the ultimate term, will not see this impulse; it occupies their blind spot. Poe's subject, in contrast, is the impulse to be irrational, "to do wrong for the wrong's sake" (1221), to be caught up by "uncontrollable longing" (1222). He analyzes moments of lost self-control, moments in which the creative expansiveness of Emerson and Whitman runs aground against a dark substratum only dimly imagined in their psychologies.

As a result, consciousness in Poe's fiction is punctuated by absence and discontinuity. Rather than existing unbroken, awareness is marked by gaps that can only be reconstructed retroactively. "Arousing from the most profound of slumbers, we break the gossamer web of *some* dream. Yet in a second afterward, (so frail may that web have been) we remember not that we have dreamed" (*T*, 682). The narrator of "The Pit and the Pendulum" awakens from such a slumber and then attempts to reconstruct what transpired during "the state of seeming nothingness into which my soul had lapsed," the "condition of seeming unconsciousness" (683). His intense awareness is forced to define itself in terms of periods of oblivion. Instead of seeing his existence as an unbroken continuity, he finds it marked with alternating light and darkness. Similarly, in "Berenice" reawakening becomes the occasion for horror as Egaeus slowly realizes that his obsession with Berenice's teeth has caused him to maim her unconsciously. "As fast as you conform your life to the pure idea in your mind," Emerson wrote at the end of *Nature*, "that will unfold its great proportions" (*CW*, 1:45). Existence, in Poe's fiction, lacks such conscious intentionality. His characters find themselves unable to construct their own worlds or to shape the course of their motivation.

Poe's writing suggests that the "I" is inscribed by unmanageable and only partially knowable powers. In place of the image of a unified being in charge of his destiny, Poe finds duality and duplicity, what he calls "the Infernal Twoness" (*T*, 342). Instead of Emersonian "transparency" revealing a divine "Reason" within, Poe portrays the self as opaque and essentially bewildering in its irrational motivation. Rather than an inherently knowable cosmos mapped by the "correspondence" between Spirit and Nature, Poe finds a world in which all correspondence lapses into indeterminacy. Unable to write Emersonian scripts of mastery, Poe's characters act out roles written by the Other. Poe's examinations of the "nightmare of the soul" (1225) thus destroy the illusion that the human mind can be adequately defined in terms of conscious intentions or reasons; for at any moment, the consciousness of a Poe character can swerve away from control toward a "maelstrom" of self-destructive impulse. In place of self-certitude, Poe imagines a self split in two by an Otherness that always speaks from elsewhere. Compulsion and repetition reveal the power of unconscious forces that shake all faith in the self-sufficiency of conscious intentions. Poe's characters are incapable of seeing expansive projects to the end; for them, self-mastery is a mirage. Rather than aiming successfully toward the future, they are pulled back inexorably into half-seen and uncanny scenarios. Unlike Emerson and his circle, Poe finally compels us to recognize the power of his demonic and dreamlike figures to generate reflection but not necessarily explanation; for in his writing, the "heart of light" has been replaced by a "heart of darkness."

HAWTHORNE AND THE PSYCHOLOGY OF OPPRESSION

In contrast to Emerson's quest for sincerity, Hawthorne details the psychological duplicity necessitated by existence in social relation. The decentering pressures of society did not escape Emerson. "It is with Society that Seeming comes in," he asserts in an early lecture. "The child is sincere, and the man when he is alone; but on the entrance of the second person hypocrisy begins" (*EL*, 2:296). But rather than leading Emerson, like Hawthorne, toward greater understanding of the necessary forms of hypocrisy, this insight into social masquerade merely intensifies his emphasis of expressive character. "Human character," he insists, "does evermore publish itself. It will not be concealed. It hates darkness. It rushes into light" (129). Asserted in a public lecture in 1837, two years after the appearance of Hawthorne's "Young Goodman Brown," Emerson's bold affirmation depicts a bright world totally at odds with Hawthorne's shadowy realm of secret sin and duplicity. Goodman Brown returns from the forest a "bewildered man" (*CE*, 10:88) totally unsure of his perception of character, doomed to live in a world in which social appearance and intuited depths can never again coincide. In contrast, Emerson cheerily tells his audience that the "form," the "face," and the "gesture" of another become "transparent with the light of his mind" (*EL*, 2:130), for the "soul . . . will not be hidden but evermore publishes its nature through action, word, countenance" (149).

Even later in his career, despite his growing recognition of physical necessity, Emerson argues against the possibility of psychological concealment. Because of the transparency of the self, he maintains that the character of another person is accessible. "Wise men," Emerson observes, "read very sharply all your private history in your look and gait and behavior" (*W*, 6:177). "We look into the eyes to know if this other form is another self," he comments later in the same essay, "and the eyes will not lie, but make a faithful confession what inhabitant is there" (179). The clue to Emerson's maintenance of psychological transparency, despite the daily counterexample of intractable friends and elusive motives, lies in his theory of expression. "The core will come to the surface," he affirms over and over (187).

Given his stress upon the unfolding of spiritual impulses found deep within the self, Emerson finds it difficult to appreciate the psychological impact of social pressure. Social norms, according to his theory of the mind, have no positive function; they are merely obstacles to authentic self-development. What distinguishes Hawthorne's psychological perspective, in contrast, is his growing awareness that the psyche is shaped as much by external social demands as it is by inner forces. Those characters, such as Wakefield or Ethan Brand, who attempt to assert an individual destiny outside of social relation pay a high price. In Hawthorne's world, the self is shaped by the needs, desires, and affections of others.

In order to clarify the contrast with Emerson, we might say that Hawthorne socializes the Transcendentalist psyche. One of the most striking examples of Hawthorne's socialization of the psyche is his analysis of the psychology of victimization. Over and over again he illustrates the human expense of attitudes that diminish the ontological status of proscribed individuals. Whether religious criminals or sexually threatening women, such marginal characters usually return to haunt the collective mind. By dramatizing this "return of the repressed," Hawthorne indicates the fault lines that ratify identity through what they exclude. Weak points in the individual and collective psyches (which validate each other's exclusions), these faults mark the site of psychological and political repression. By eliminating or victimizing the individuals who embody qualities removed from their own psyches, Hawthorne's Puritans, Aylmer, Giovanni, and the Pyncheons all achieve self-definition through repression. They eliminate or victimize individuals who embody qualities removed from their selves. Hawthorne reveals these lines of repression by allowing the repressed to return and become "uncanny"; for the appearance of uncanny figures in his fiction indicates the fault lines—the unconscious barriers—that divide awareness into the acceptable and the unacceptable, the normal and the abnormal. During those moments when such fault lines are depicted, crazing the mirror of the psyche, the reader becomes aware that in Hawthorne's world repression constitutes public identity.

   Given Hawthorne's vision of the mind's clouding, such repression is inevitable. Unable to depend self-reliantly upon the authority of "unconscious Reason," his characters come to awareness in a world that is masked. Reflecting the realization that the mind lacks the transparency that Emerson had dreamed of, Hawthorne's fiction thus complicates self-reliance by dramatizing the inaccessibility of one's own inner depths and, hence, of other persons who are equally clouded. Taking us into the world that Nietzsche was later to analyze—the world of "simulation," "deception," "posing," and "being masked"—his tales demonstrate the failure of regenerative rhetorics based upon consensus and participation in collective personae.[39] Turning instead upon moments of concealment and disclosure, they portray the complications, and even the tragedy, that occurs when others' motives are hidden and when even an individual's own impulses undercut avowed aims.

   The presence of the other, within and without, constrains individual expression. Hawthorne's characters do not exist alone like Emerson's or Whitman's Adamic figures molding the world to the contours of their irrepressible energies. Instead, they exist within complicated networks of interest, desire, and ambition—forces that shape who they become. Stained by what Reverend Hooper calls the "mortal veil" (CE, 9:47), they are limited by their bodily urges, by their feelings, by their transgressions against each other. Their stains—Georgiana's birthmark, Hester's scarlet letter, Jaffrey Pyncheon's necklace of blood—mark their human imperfection, their fallibility, and their mortality. Hawthorne's exploration of fault lines frequently turns upon the analysis of characters who resist such human limitation by erecting psychological and social orders that repress substantive being as an index of fault. The Puritans of Hester's Boston and Jaffrey Pyncheon both monopolize substantiality; those with less rigid psychic and sexual economies are deprived of physical expression. Manifesting an imbalance between the spirit and the flesh, the intellect and the body, such characters attempt to impose a rigid control upon the impulses of others who remind them of their own weakness and physical limitation. In Jungian terms, their victims become their "shadows"—figures seen as "other" because they embody qualities "that the subject refuses to acknowledge about himself."[40] In some cases, Jung reminds us, entire societies cast a shadow—witness the persecution of Quakers by the Puritans, Indians by nineteenth-century Americans, Jews by German Nazis.

As Freud later observed in *Civilization and Its Discontents*, "It is always possible to bind together a considerable number of people in love, so long as there are other people left over to receive the manifestations of their aggressiveness."[41] By showing us what communities fear and cast out, Hawthorne helps us to understand the psychological stratagems that remove certain individuals from ordinary categories of being, transforming their ontological status into "alien" or "other." For the Puritans in "The Gentle Boy," Quakers take on this quality of otherness. For Aylmer in "The Birth-mark" and Giovanni in "Rappaccini's Daughter," the place of the other is occupied by women whose physical presence disrupts these men's intellectualized conceptions of being. Hester Prynne is branded as a criminal and cast out from an offended polity that cannot countenance her "licentious" being. The Pyncheons in *The House of the Seven Gables* see Maules as uncanny others.

In a number of Hawthorne's works the feminine, the body, and unrestrained libido ("sunshine") are depicted as being repressed by a masculine, intellectual, "iron-hearted" sensibility. Refusing to accept the interdependence of spirit and body, Hawthorne's Puritans, for example, attempt to "transcend an intrinsically divided human situation" by turning division into hierarchy.[42] What ensues is the assertion of masculinity over femininity, the mind over the body, psychological restraint over expressive freedom. As the popular literary archetype of the "Dark Lady" makes clear, all three hierarchies are interrelated. The image of the sexually uninhibited woman merges easily, in the nineteenth-century imagination, into images of physicality, natural luxuriance, and unchained libido. Looking momentarily only at the physical plane, we can relate the repression of the body to the uneasy detente that existed, in mid-nineteenth-century America, between idealism and physical urges. We saw this in Emerson's *Nature*, with its fragile compromise between idealism and "substantive being." Emerson skirted a mind-body dualism that he was not ultimately able to reconcile; many of Hawthorne's characters demonstrate an even more radical divorce of reason from the body, spirit from the flesh.

Despite the efforts of individuals like Lorenzo and Orson Fowler—the American popularizers of phrenology who promoted the benefits of healthy diet, physical exercise, and sex education—many nineteenth-century persons were incapable of Whitman's enthusiastic acceptance of physicality.[43] Instead, their emerging physical awareness tended to undercut public ideals and etherealized aims. Hawthorne explores the psychological implications of such contradiction as he portrays repressive characters who attempt to banish the physical aspects of being from their self-definitions. In the words of Sharon Cameron, such characters "try to create a division between their own corporeal essence and the meaning of that corporeality."[44] This pursuit of meaning at the expense of the body gives physicality the uncanniness that disturbs so many of Hawthorne's male characters.

A similar point can be made about Hawthorne's portrayal of the feminine and its repression. In works such as "The Birth-mark," "Rappaccini's Daughter," and *The Blithedale Romance*, intellectual young men are forced to confront within themselves a fallibility and a desire initially repressed from their self-images. The agent of such confrontation is a familiar character-type: the "Dark Lady" whose sexuality and passion disrupt the male world around her. Such figures exude a physical presence that obsesses, even spellbinds, men: "The instant that [Giovanni] was aware of the possibility of approaching Beatrice, it seemed an absolute necessity of his existence to do so. It mattered not whether she were angel or demon; he was irrevocably within her sphere, and must obey the law that whirled him onward, in ever lessening circles, towards a result which he did not attempt to foreshadow" (*CE*, 10:109). As Perry Miller noticed long ago, the typical nineteenth-century literary response to such uncanny attractiveness is hostility. The Dark Lady, as a result of her deviance from sexually repressive norms, is "beyond the pale," outside of "respectable society." One of the conventions of the romance is that this figure be eliminated, "disruptive passion in the female . . . thus . . . conveniently disposed of."[45] Georgiana, Beatrice Rappaccini, Hester Prynne, and Zenobia all exhibit the literary fate reserved for the overly attractive woman. Because they threaten the male fiction that socialized woman is "an ethereal, aphysical being," such women are ostracized and often destroyed.[46] Such fictions, Barbara Berg reminds us, structured nineteenth-century social behavior, as well as the careers of literary characters.

At this point we have moved beyond Eric Sundquist's discussion of uncanniness in *Home as Found*. The strange atmosphere of Hawthorne's fiction, Sundquist argues, reveals the return of repressed forces, of "a throng of ancestral fathers, all waving their paternity before his susceptible imagination like faces in a mirror."[47] Using Freud's essay on "The Uncanny" to analyze this haunting, Sundquist identifies it with Oedipal anxieties lying behind Hawthorne's work, with Hawthorne's "inability to dodge the issue of ancestry and the peculiar history of his 'fatherland.'" While often provocative and illuminating, Sundquist's discussion obfuscates the possibility that feminine, as well as masculine, forces might be repressed. The difficulty stems from his analysis of Hawthorne's psychology, rather than of Hawthorne's portrayal of repression within his characters and their societies. For our purposes, Hawthorne's Oedipal anxieties are of less interest than the fact that his paternal figures are frequently portrayed as repressing both physical impulses and the feminine. Such repression leads to the victimization of an otherness that such male characters cannot tolerate within themselves. As a result Hawthorne's fiction presents a searching critique of the relationship between patriarchal psychology and attitudes toward both Woman and Nature.

What gives Hawthorne's depiction of repression a special interest is that he shows how shadow figures become uncanny as they draw attention to their exclusion. In a political sense the repressed returns as she openly resists identification as a victim. Let us retain the feminine pronoun, since Hawthorne's analysis of repression frequently turns on issues of sexual politics. In his fiction the feminine and the weak are cast out as they threaten dominant male ideologies. In a real sense Hawthorne's Quakers and Maules are portrayed as being "feminine." Tracing through "The Birth-mark," "Rappaccini's Daughter," *The Scarlet Letter*, and *The Blithedale Romance*, we can see how Hawthorne's portrayal of the return of the repressed gives the victim of repression greater and greater license to speak and, hence, to draw attention to the fault lines of repression.

In both "The Birth-mark" and "Rappaccini's Daughter" female figures become uncanny because they embody physical qualities that the men around them cannot consciously acknowledge. The plots of both works reveal the fault lines leading to the victimization of women as cleavages existing in the minds of the men who destroy them. Aylmer's flaw in "The Birth-mark" is that he is unable to realize that being stained is an ineradicable sign of the human condition. Ignoring the body with its emotional and sexual demands, he attempts to eliminate the "ineludible gripe" of "mortality" (CE, 10:39). Georgiana is at fault in her husband's eyes because of his repression of the body, especially the female body, that "earthly part" that thwarts his "higher nature" (49). Aylmer's attempt to erase his wife's birthmark, the sign of her corporeality, reveals the fault lines that divide his psyche into two regions: acceptable intellection and unacceptable physical urges. As she dies, Georgiana draws attention to the repression that motivated her destruction. "My poor Aylmer!" she tells her husband, "You have aimed loftily!—you have done nobly! Do not repent, that, with so high and pure a feeling, you have rejected the best that earth could offer" (55). Within the context of Hawthorne's story as a whole, these words are bitterly ironic. By explicitly refusing to call into question the purity of motives that have just led to her death, Georgiana forces the reader to consider that Aylmer's repression of the body has led to the victimization of his wife.

In "Rappaccini's Daughter" Giovanni suffers from a similar conflict over Beatrice Rappaccini's luxuriant physicality, a quality that makes her "poisonous." Giovanni's idealism—his impulse to see in Beatrice a "transparent soul" (CE, 10:112) in which "sunlight" and "diamonds" sparkle (113)—runs aground against his eventual recognition of her corporeality. The mind, Hawthorne suggests in contrast to Emerson, is clouded by the body, which contributes the intoxicating but dangerous lure of sexuality. Existing in a world not just of vision but also of desire, Giovanni belatedly comes to realize that the soul's "sunlight" and the body's rich "perfume" might destroy each other. Attempting to erase Beatrice's body by giving her an antidote that would cancel its "poison," Giovanni succumbs to a physical definition of the self that eradicates the very spirit that he might have cherished. Beatrice Rappaccini's dying words, like Georgiana's, draw attention to this act of repression: "Farewell, Giovanni! Thy words of hatred are like lead in my heart but they, too, will fall away as I ascend. Oh, was there not, from the first, more poison in thy nature than in mine?" (127). As in "The Birth-mark," the victim of oppression explicitly reminds her victimizer of the unconscious motives that led to the exorcism of the body.

In similar fashion Hester Prynne overtly "comments" upon her social position by embroidering her scarlet letter. Resisting her preordained role as sexual criminal, a "general symbol . . . of woman's frailty and sinful passion" (CE, 1:79), she transgresses against the sign of her ostracism by bringing that signification itself to the center of attention. As a result Hester's ornate embroidery disturbs the populace, throwing "a lurid gleam along the passage-way of the interior" (69), because it brings toward public recognition the repression of physicality that her behavior threatened. At the same time that Hester's badge of shame satisfies a collective ritual of punishment, it also represents a "return of the repressed," as the otherness erased from the public's heart stands visibly before them. In Hester Prynne the "stern and tempered" Puritan fathers are faced with their uncanny other. The reverse of Governor Bellingham's armored existence, she forces us to see, is a magnified scarlet letter, standing for the impulses that are excluded from his rigid psychic and political economy. By focusing upon the effect of Hester's presence in this community, Hawthorne thus analyzes the fault lines cleaving its being.

What distinguishes Hawthorne's writing is the extent to which he analyzes the political and psychological operation of such stereotypes, instead of using them solely to determine his plots. By giving his Dark Ladies the opportunity to draw attention to their social uncanniness, he compels us to recognize the fault lines that exile the body, especially the feminine body, into a region of repression. In this way, he brings to light the psychological dynamics underlying the victimization of femininity and the exploitation of corporeality in general. Aylmer's envy of nature's fecundity reflects a masculine worldview set off from and opposed to feminine materiality. Privileging "pure" thought and spirit, Aylmer replicates the sin of Hawthorne's Puritans, who also believe that one can distance oneself from the body and its urges. But Georgiana, Beatrice Rappaccini, and Hester Prynne all compel the men around them to recognize the demands of the physique as well as the spirit. By confronting the male exclusion of physicality, such characters reveal the social dimensions of unconscious lines of force that initially defined their bodies as being "at fault."

Perhaps Coverdale's final impression of Zenobia most poignantly stresses both Hawthorne's social awareness and his sensitivity to the uncanniness of the sexual victim. Brooding upon the after-image that she left behind her when she departed for the last time, Coverdale reflects that "I was affected with a fantasy that Zenobia had not actually gone, but was still hovering about the spot, and haunting it. I seemed to feel her eyes upon me. It was as if the vivid coloring of her character had left a brilliant stain upon the air" (*CE*, 3:228). Even after her departure, the memory of Zenobia remains, "haunting" Coverdale. She has become part of his history, never to be forgotten, wound into the fabric of his being in a way in which other people never seem to touch our Transcendentalist writers. "I seemed to feel her eyes upon me": Coverdale the "detached" observer here acknowledges his social involvement with Zenobia, signifying his involvement with her through what Jean-Paul Sartre calls the "gaze of the other."[48] We are not detached, Coverdale finally learns. There is always that answering and questioning stare, carrying us into the circle of relationship, making demands upon us, involving us in social responsibilities. But it is that final sentence which lingers: "It was as if the vivid coloring of her character had left a brilliant stain upon the air." Zenobia stains the air, coloring it to the hue of her character. Each one of us, Hawthorne suggests, stains the setting in which we find ourselves. We do not exist in a vacuum as independent, self-reliant individuals. Instead, we make up part of a social fabric—clothed, whether we like it or not, by our being for and with others.

MELVILLE'S *PIERRE* AND THE ABYSS WITHIN

Reading Emerson and his sources, Melville found a vision of psychological dynamics at odds with his own understanding of human nature. Like Hawthorne, he shared with Emerson a Romantic model of creative expression, but that model began to break down for Melville precisely at the points where Emerson demanded faith in the divinity of the mind and in its correspondence to an analogous spirit found in Nature. Melville's mature works offer what begins as an "implicit criticism of self-reliance" but which turns into an explicit critique of idealized myths of the psyche.[49] Melville's "critique of idealistic assumptions," according to Michael Kearns, extended to all those who perceived a "divinely designed 'primary harmony' between soul and universe."[50] The target includes both Emerson's vision of "correspondence" and popular psychologies—such as those of Dugald Stewart and Thomas Upham—that Kearns sees as "committed to a belief in a divine ordering of the universe and in the God-given ability of human beings to discover this ordering." By insisting upon the idiosyncratic, personal sources of thought and motivation, Melville threatens both the Transcendentalist faith that divinity can be perceived within and the more conservative faith that the mind is structured so as to harmonize with a divinity without. "In general," Kearns remarks, "characters who subscribe to an idealistic psychology of perception . . . fail to see their own minds as the source of many of their sensations." The tragic error of both Ahab and Pierre is that each, in the words of Richard Chase, is "victimized by a disturbed 'self-reliance'" that leads him to mistake inner impulse for divine truth.[51]

Taking Emerson and Melville as touchstones of a cultural crisis that was widening during the 1850s, we can see that the difference between their views of the mind measures what Lionel Trilling aptly calls "the moral life in process of revising itself."[52] The dramatic tension between Emerson's dominant assertion of self-faith and Melville's persistent skepticism foreshadows the impending collapse of psychological idealism in America. Less than fifty years later William James would be able to write that "An acquired habit, from the physiological point of view, is nothing but a new pathway of discharge formed in the brain, by which certain incoming currents ever after tend to escape."[53] Although he maintains a veneer of Romantic idealism, Melville's description of the "lightning" that has scorched Ahab's mind inclines in this direction. It sacrifices Emerson's and Whitman's vision of libido as divine force in favor of the recognition of personal psychic energy. This difference enables Michael Davitt Bell to observe that Melville, along with Hawthorne, "registered . . . not the twilight of romance but the twilight of Romanticism."[54] In Melville's writing, Emerson's merger of metaphysics and psychology comes to an abrupt end, for Melville is a master at unveiling the contradictions that accrue when one theologizes the psyche.

As we have seen, Emerson's assertion of the ultimate divinity of the mind reflected a larger godhead that he saw about him in Nature. His benign assurance that the mind's most secret promptings must lead to good depended upon his sense that these impulses reflected a moral power innate to the very structure of the universe. Attempting to justify faith in an age of increasingly self-conscious skepticism, a period marked by "Ennui" and by persons who had become "too intellectual" (CW, 1:180), Emerson consistently subordinated natural force to spiritual aspiration. Thus, instead of seeing the mind as physical in provenance, he read back into the psyche his sublimation of physical energy into idealized motives that "proved" that introspection could be a return to God. The paradox of Emerson's position was that for the moral man, securely in control of his desires and socialized by the religious values of his culture, self-reliance provided the strongest possible support for individual assertion. But it offered no means of control upon the will or wishes of the immoral man, unready or perhaps unable to recognize the true source of his actions.

Much of the enduring appeal of Emerson's thought was that it validated the motives of essentially good people, at the same time that it provided a genteel secularization of Christian imperatives. Coming to serve for many the same function that Norman Vincent Peale played for a later generation, Emerson's self-reliance was easily reduced to a "power of positive thinking" that confirmed both a general democratic faith and a nebulous religiosity freed from restrictive creeds. In contrast to Emerson's popular appeal, Melville's critique of psychological idealism placed him outside the dominant moral and religious assumptions of his culture. One is startled even today by the virulence and hostility exhibited by contemporary reviewers of *Pierre*, who found the work "a torrent rhapsody uttered in defiance of taste and sense" (*P*, 382), an example of "disgusting" characterization (387), and a story that seemed to teach "the impracticability of virtue" (390). Such reactions demonstrate the sense, common among Melville's first readers, that his later works threatened their deepest convictions. We can see from the reception of Melville's work by his contemporaries that his dilemma as a writer was one later shared by Friedrich Nietzsche and Sigmund Freud in different circumstances. In order to illustrate the dangers that result from idealizations of the psyche, each had to become an "immoralist," committing himself to topics considered shocking and even objectionable.

By writing about the demonism of Ahab, the incestuous desire of Pierre, and the religious fraudulence of his Confidence Man, Melville demanded that his audience take seriously literary figures and situations that had been reserved for Gothic entertainment. It was one thing to titillate one's readers with mad priests and necromancers; it was quite another to suggest that such individuals might embody universal truths of human psychology. In order to read *Moby-Dick*, for example, one had to extend a degree of sympathy to Captain Ahab; for unless one accepted the connection that Melville provided between Ahab's malevolence and his personal psychology, this figure lost all tragic stature. He ceased to be a doomed individual, blinded by his impulses, and became a raging madman. Melville, in other words, required that his readers comprehend the psychological causes of Ahab's monomania, that they accept the link between his unorthodox religious convictions and his unconscious motivation. A similar problem was presented in *Pierre*, as Melville anatomized the hidden desires motivating his hero's "idealistic" espousal of his attractive half-sister's cause. By connecting ideal with sexual impulse, conscious aim with unconscious force, Melville offended all those who wished to view ideals and conscious directives as sacred objects beyond question and analysis. The personal expense of ruthlessly anatomizing nineteenth-century ideals became increasingly clear to Melville: "all the world does never gregariously advance to Truth," he writes in *Pierre*, "but only here and there some of its individuals do; and by advancing, leave the rest behind; cutting themselves forever adrift from their sympathy, and making themselves always liable to be regarded with distrust, dislike, and often, downright—though ofttimes, concealed—fear and hate" (166).

In particular, *Pierre* teaches us to view with suspicion all idealizations of self-development based upon the recovery of creative forces discovered in the unconscious. Subverting the scheme of self-reliance, it posits in its stead a model based upon a radical discontinuity between conscious intention and unconscious desire. In Newton Arvin's words, Melville reveals the "abysmal contrast" between the "conscious, rational, social surface and the wild irrationality of what lies out of sight below."[55] In *Pierre* the unconscious is not a benign creative force but keeps knocking at the gate of consciousness, threatening like Madeline Usher to unleash a maelstrom of self-destructive power.

More than the tale of a young man's disillusionment, *Pierre* becomes a scathing critique of all psychological visions predicated upon the self-sufficiency and transparency of motive. Pierre's journey into ambiguity directly contradicts the faith exhibited by Emerson and his followers, for it suggests that the depths of the self can neither be recovered nor reconciled to a model that excludes sexual desire. Ultimately, Melville presents a portrait of the mind so disturbing in its implications that narrative duplicity seems the only method that its author can follow. But such duplicity, he shows us, merely replicates the subterfuges and unconscious maneuvers of each person's mind. *Pierre*, like all the works we have been considering, functions as a mirror held up to the reader, but the reflection that it presents of the mind's depths is so horrifying that no member of Melville's generation could fully confront it. As radical as any of Nietzsche's works, this book undercuts faith in all idealism by demonstrating that every ideal is a mask disguising hidden motives and desires.

Before he is awakened to the titanic depths of his heart, Pierre exists in a world in which transparency of motive is the norm. Both Pierre's mother and his fiancée Lucy Tartan believe that a perfect openness exists between them and Pierre. "Thou must be a wholly disclosed secret to me," Lucy exclaims (*P*, 37), and Mrs. Glendinning is alarmed at the idea that there might be "some region of thought" in her son "wholly unshared by herself" (47). Linked to this belief in transparency is an idealized vision of Nature, human relationships, and experience itself. Lacking the least obscurity, all entities in the pastoral world of Saddle Meadows display an "ideality" that facilitates the translation of all human situations into heavenly analogues. Pierre's mother interprets his love as a "heavenly evanescence" (16); Lucy appears to Pierre as a "visible semblance of the heavens" (24); Pierre sees his grandfather as "a noble, godlike being" (30). Supported by the complacent faith of its inhabitants,

Saddle Meadows itself extends under a "starry vault" that corresponds to the "soul's arches" within (51).

The self-certitude of this world is shaken by the awakening of unconscious forces within Pierre. Once he has glimpsed Isabel Banford, the "secret chambers of his unsuspecting soul" (*P*, 105) become realigned to a power emerging from "the deepest and subtlest fibres of his being" (48). Significantly, the stirring of Pierre's unconscious completely destroys the transparency that had characterized his existence. Newly aware of desires and urges falling outside of socially sanctioned patterns of motivation, Pierre resorts to subterfuge in order to hide his "haunted spirit" (50) from both his fiancée and his mother. As new "half-crazy" impulses make themselves "legible in his soul" (62), he finds within a turbulent depth of self-awareness that contrasts with the calm social exteriors around him. In contrast to Emerson's optimistic vision of self-disclosure, Pierre's self-awareness leads to masquerade, for Melville recognizes the existence of inner forces that threaten to violate social bonds. Ultimately, only Lucy Tartan is able to remain "transparently immaculate, without shadow of flaw or vein" (317). But such virginity of soul, a reflection of the nineteenth century's idealization of women, is a standard that few other characters can maintain.

In contrast to the Apollonian control over unconscious content imagined by Emerson, the powerful unconscious forces imagined by Melville exhibit the capacity to warp self-awareness to their "magnetic" core (*P*, 151). Possessed by what Henry Murray, following Jung, calls "the aroused soul-image, or anima," Pierre realigns his being "in favor of the unconscious as a directing influence in his life."[56] Like Hawthorne, Melville uses the psychological vocabulary of Gothic romance to describe this inner development. Pierre is "enchanted" by Isabel and "sat motionless and bending over as a tree-transformed and mystery-laden visitant, caught and fast-bound in some necromancer's garden" (128). As in the case of Giovanni in "Rappaccini's Daughter," his thoughts collapse into a spiral of obsession: they "wheeled around Isabel as their center" (14) until he is almost "deprived of consciousness" (150).

If consciousness, as Melville imagines, is subject to powerful attraction, it is also distorted by the existence of unconscious motives that cannot be admitted to awareness. Rather than containing benevolent energies promoting his self-development, Pierre's unconscious harbors a medley of incompatible urges. This is especially evident in Melville's portrayal of Pierre's complex emotional involvement with Isabel. On the one hand, Pierre is motivated by the highest idealism. His determination to embrace his sister's cause partakes of a high-mindedness verging on the heroic, a sense of duty that leads him to sacrifice both reputation and inheritance in order to assist her. But, much to the horror of Melville's nineteenth-century audience, Pierre's idealism is presented as a disguise covering a much less noble set of motives. Although these ideals enable Pierre, in Henry Murray's words, "to defend his resolution before the high court of conscience," Melville calls that "high court" into question by suggesting that Pierre's position is a psychological defense.[57] From the beginning, Pierre finds Isabel "bewilderingly alluring" (*P*, 107). Betrayed at moments into the half-recognition of his "overardent and incautious warmth" toward her (112), he retreats from the open confrontation of his desire by sublimating his image of Isabel into "the highest heaven of uncorrupted love" (142). But Pierre's "sacred cause" is undermined by the pressure of his desire. While at first, the thought of embracing Isabel "never *consciously* intruded" into his "uncontaminated soul" (142, italics mine), eventually a "terrible self-revelation" pierces Pierre as he starts to recognize his duplicitous interest in Isabel.

This lack of coincidence between intuition and ideals of self-perfection measures Melville's distance from Emerson, who had been able to make his map of individual self-fulfillment coincide with society's expectations of moral behavior. Ultimately, Melville's novel destroys that edifice of respectability by suggesting that the deepest levels of the psyche manifest a power that is not inherently moral, a power that threatens to erode the masks of selfhood worshiped by civilized men and women. As in the case of many of Mark Twain's or Theodore Dreiser's characters, this liberation of impulse undermines society by eroding the resolve necessary to sustain individual moral perfection. Instead, Melville confronts disturbing questions of the physical, even sexual, origin of psychic energy. Allowing his hero to succumb to the seductive lure of his half-sister Isabel, a physical attractiveness that he initially disguises from himself, Melville has Pierre face the "fascination of the terrible," a phrase anticipating the "fascination of the abomination" in Conrad's *Heart of Darkness*. Set afloat upon "appalling" depths of soul (*P*, 327), Pierre fails to discover within the "correspondence" longed for by Emerson, but finds instead an unbearable moral ambiguity that registers the gap between the ego's Apollonian aspirations toward transcendence and the Dionysian violence of unconscious forces.

Pierre's dream, like Emerson's, was that he might escape the artificial entanglements of social relation into a self-created realm of authentic being. By responding to the call of his half-sister Isabel, an individual who teaches him to equate divinity with "impulse," he aspires to a psychological position outside of his family identity.[58] He will live from within, following a vein of duty that gives him spiritual independence. But Pierre never escapes filial relation, for his leap into freedom is propelled by the decision to sacrifice his own happiness in order to preserve his father's reputation. But by assuming the fictitious role of Isabel's husband, Pierre imitates his father, taking on a role that is further complicated by his sexual feelings toward his half-sister. Ultimately, Michael Rogin argues, "the sacrifice of the son to preserve the father is contaminated by the desire to destroy the father and take his place."[59] The impulse to be original and self-reliant is complicated by the belatedness and secondariness of all self-representations, which are entangled within a network of inherited patterns. Instead of exhibiting an Emersonian freedom, Pierre's career demonstrates "that every individual act derives its meaning or significance from an earlier one that it displaces and repeats (often unconsciously) in much the same way that the son displaces and repeats the father in the genealogical chain."[60] Emerson's dream of escaping all homage to "the sepulchres of the fathers" (*CW*, 1:7) thus finds its ironic echo in Pierre's self-defeating repetition of his father's desire.

Pierre's secondary, preinscribed existence arises from the nature of the "unconscious" that he discovers when he decides to follow Isabel along the road of impulse. Whereas Emerson's dream of spiritual freedom had been supported by a divine power intuited within the mind, Pierre's quest is fueled by a psychic energy that disguises itself in the forms of duty. Beneath his heroic and Christlike renunciation, Pierre slowly discovers, lies an inescapable sexuality. Isabel's cause, he half admits to himself, is reinforced by her physical attractiveness. Pierre's involvement with Isabel demonstrates the failure of "sublimation," as Emerson understood the term. Discovering a "sublime" (i.e., divine) power within the self, Emerson had been able to promote intuition as the means of spiritual ascent. The individual aspires toward the sublime by casting off the artificial impediments of external restraints, thus freeing the spiritual power latent within. Melville's sense of sublimation, in contrast, is much closer to Freud's portrayal of the translation of sexual energy into social forms. As Freud details in *Civilization and Its Discontents*, this process involves the sacrifice of individual pleasure for overriding social goals. But at the same time, the discontinuity between private impulse and social form leads inevitably to the conclusion that the process of civilization frequently inhibits and distorts individual psychic energies that are forced to conform to public values.

Although most of Melville's nineteenth-century readers were incapable of seeing beyond their outrage at his hero's incestuous involvement

with his sister, some sensed that Melville's depiction of Pierre's mixed
motives threatened faith in idealized patterns of social relationship dear
to the age. Not only idealized womanhood but idealized paternity falls
victim to Melville's pen. The most devastating recognition of all for
Pierre was that his father, whose image "tyrannized over his imagination" (P, 104), was not the pure, godlike being that he had imagined but
had consummated an illicit affair that led to the birth of Isabel Banford.

This recognition is so horrifying for Pierre that, once he has weath-
ered the first throes of disillusionment, he decides to offer himself "a
victim to the gods of woe" rather than publicly expose his father. "Thus,
many years before Freud," Murray observes, "Melville, opening his mind
to undercurrents of feeling and imagery, discovered the Oedipus Complex and unashamedly represented it with colorful embellishments, as it
would flower in the wishful fantasy of a victimized adolescent."[61] Identifying with the father's authority, Pierre (mirroring Melville's disillusionment with his own father) is deeply wounded by the revelation of his
wrongdoing. "Ay, Pierre," Melville poignantly laments, "now indeed art
thou hurt with a wound, never to be completely healed but in heaven;
for thee, the before undistrusted moral beauty of the world is forever
fled; for thee, thy sacred father is no more a saint; all brightness hath
gone from thy hills, and all peace from thy plains; and now, now, for the
first time, Pierre, Truth rolls a black billow through thy soul!" (P, 65).
But Pierre is incapable of remaining in such disillusionment; he restores
the sacred image of his father by splitting himself in two. He consciously
imitates an intensified version of his former ideal of paternal behavior by
nobly defending his half sister, while he unconsciously repeats a pattern
of desire and deception analogous to his father's earlier duplicity.

Once Pierre determines to aid Isabel by masquerading as her husband,
he loses forever the possibility of existing in a transparent world. Having
learned already, because of his deep interior development, to wear a
"face" before his mother and Lucy Tartan (P, 94), he permanently enters
a masked realm in which motive and appearance are dissociated from
each other. Beneath "our garbs of commonplaceness," Pierre dimly realizes, lie "enigmas" that no one is able to "resolve" (139). If the reader is
meant to see, by the climax of Pierre's emotional crisis, that the complacent pastoral realm of Saddle Meadows has been a fiction obscuring the
depths of the self, this sense of masquerade is firmly driven home as
Pierre journeys to New York. Plinlimmon's pamphlet, which Pierre finds
on the coach, turns the discrepancy between the ideal and the real into
an absolute principle.

Since Pierre lacks the purity of the "chronometrical" soul, his assumption of "abstract heavenly righteousness" (P, 213) will prove a disastrous

self-deception. According to Plinlimmon, the inspired soul (presumably an idealized version of Melville) "will but array all men's earthly time-keepers against him" (212), while "inferior beings" who attempt "to live in this world according to the strict letter of the chronometricals" (Pierre's class) will become involved "in strange, *unique* follies and sins" (213). The fate of both sets of individuals inverts Emerson's contention that a divine core of virtue can be revealed and disseminated through action in the world. In contrast to Emerson's idealism, Pierre's self-destructive rush toward disaster reiterates the duplicity that Melville found in human motivation. Those who act, he suggests, will not realize an internal godhead, but instead will subject themselves to the pressure of ambiguous inner forces and relentless social demands.

In a sense, the second half of *Pierre*, set in New York, dramatizes the Plinlimmonian doctrine that the ideal and the real have become completely divorced from each other. As a result of this dissociation, human character permanently loses the clarity and transparency imagined by Emerson, for ideality no longer resides as an attribute of the unconscious. In the fallen world of New York, a world antithetical to Emerson's Nature, human beings are guilty of "locking, and bolting, and barring" their hearts as well as their windows and doors (P, 230). No one is as he or she seems to be, for sincerity is an impossibility.

Melville's extended portrait of Pierre's cousin, Glen Stanly, drives home the point that we have entered a masked world. The narrator asks us "to quit the mere surface of the deportment of Glen, and penetrate beneath its brocaded vesture" to "the long-lurking and yet unhealed wound of all a rejected lover's most rankling detestation of a supplanting rival" (P, 224). "For the deeper that some men feel a secret and poignant feeling," he generalizes, "the higher they pile the belying surfaces" (224). As in Hawthorne's fiction, the discovery of subjectivity leads to masquerade; the inner self threatens, rather than reinforces, social values.

As *Pierre* draws to a conclusion, this sense of masquerade is intensified. When Lucy Tartan joins Pierre's involuted domestic establishment in New York, Pierre must hide his true feelings toward Lucy from Isabel, while Isabel half-disguises her growing jealousy. When Pierre and Isabel visit a New York gallery, they view the "double-hooded" visage of the beautiful Cenci in a portrait—her beauty hiding feelings of "incest and parricide" (P, 351) roughly analogous to Pierre's deepest impulses. Ultimately, the world itself assumes a mask. In Pierre's penultimate daydream of Enceladus, the natural landscape presents a benign appearance but, like the deceptive sea surface in *Moby-Dick*, hides a titanic wildness beneath.

Within the context of the American Renaissance, with its dominant

Emersonian strain, Melville's portrayal of the spirit's masks has momentous literary implications. It suggests that a writing based upon the liberation of unconscious impulse, a writing following the path laid down by Emerson or Thoreau or Whitman, will not lead to the liberation of a universal spiritual energy but rather to the celebration of private desire. Attempting to plumb the depths of his soul as a writer in New York, Pierre finds that he is unable to locate the firm bedrock of illumination that had sustained Melville's Transcendentalist contemporaries. The inevitable result is the transformation of literary form from paradigmatic and prophetic utterance into a private and ambiguous act of self-reflection.

Unlike Emerson's or Whitman's personae, Pierre cannot escape vertiginous slippage into self-mirroring because he fails to find within a power that transcends personal drives. His writing, like that of later French Symbolists and post-Structuralist theorists, displays "an infinite regress" that mirrors the potentially endless progression of Pierre's own psychological interpretation.[62] Pierre, unlike Emerson, is unable to escape from vertigo by positing a "First Cause" within. "If I have described life as a flux of moods," Emerson finally asserts in "Experience" after a horrifying slide toward a disillusionment similar to Pierre's, "I must now add that there is that in us which changes not and which ranks all sensations and states of mind" (W, 3:72). Once again secure in his intuition of an "unbounded substance" within (72), Emerson affirms even more triumphantly his quest toward the ever elusive "Ideal" that "journeys" constantly "before us" (75).

But Melville stands at the threshold of momentous change in the imagination of the psyche and its buried power. By turning away from idealizations of the unconscious toward the recognition of the mind's physical basis, he anticipates all those later writers—ranging from Nietzsche to Derrida—who see self-representation as a fictional activity rather than as a Neoplatonic memory of essential truth. The only self that we can know, Melville reluctantly apprehends in *Pierre*, is the self that we construct. Instead of finding a living myth in the unconscious, he comes to see that our vision of the unconscious is a fiction that gives shape to our understanding of motivation and belief. From one perspective, this redefinition of the mind displays a loss of faith, for it relinquishes the age-old longing to find the human form magnified and perfected in the lineaments of a god perceived within. From another perspective, Melville's vision of the mind reveals a realistic movement from an untenable glorification of the psyche and its origins. Either way, Melville intimates the human expense of this new psychological direction. Cast entirely upon his own resources, with no internal or external standards to prop him up, Pierre finds himself in a world that he has not made and in a consciousness that he can never entirely control. The best he can do is to join the masquerade, fictionalizing the self.

As he wakens to the unconscious depths of his psyche, Pierre is cast adrift upon an endless voyage of self-discovery. The mining of the self, he finds, is an interminable activity leading to nothing but "surface stratified on surface" (*P*, 285) and not to the central power imagined by Emerson, Whitman, Thoreau, and Fuller. Determined to locate the heart's secret and to "lift the veil" (41), Pierre attempts to follow the vein of insight "to the latent gold in his mind" (258). But there is no pure lode of spirit; the work of excavation extends the deeper he probes. "Deep, deep, and still deep and deeper must we go," Melville writes, "if we would find out the heart of a man; descending into which is as descending a spiral stair in a shaft, without any end, and where that endlessness is only concealed by the spiralness of the stair, and the blackness of the shaft" (288–89). In this remarkable image, Melville projects the depths of the mind as a heart of darkness, a vision that directly counters the Transcendentalist vocabulary of illumination. Sharing Coleridge's perception that "the lowest depth that the light of our consciousness can visit even with a doubtful glimmering is still at an unknown distance from the ground," Melville refuses to step with Coleridge from ambiguity into the intuition of a "universal light" that is "the power of universal and necessary convictions."[63]

Ultimately, Melville's portrait of the mind in *Pierre* undermines Romantic theories of expression predicated upon the recovery of some psychological essence. Writing, in Melville's hands, begins to free itself "from the necessity of 'expression'" and to consider instead what Michel Foucault calls the "gaps and fault lines" found within any representation of the self.[64] Attempting to recover the book "writ down in his soul" (*P*, 304), Pierre discovers an increasing disparity between his conscious motives and his impulses. The deeper he probes, the less sure he becomes of himself and his decisions. Like Nietzsche's genealogy of morals, Melville's writing at this point "seeks to make visible all those discontinuities that cross us."[65] Self-awareness, Melville shows us, is discontinuous with unconscious forces that cannot be "thoroughly comprehended" and that are "kept a secret" (294) from the probing "I." Unlike Whitman's or Emerson's personae, Pierre is unable to possess "that enchanter's wand of the soul" (284) that casts his inner regions into light. Such enchantments, Melville suggests, are illusions.

Throughout *Pierre* Melville stresses the obscurity of human motivation. "In their precise tracings-out and subtile causations," he observes, "the strongest and fiercest emotions of life defy all analytical insight" (*P*, 67). "Yet so strange and complicate is the human soul," he argues later, ". . . that the wisest man were rash, positively to assign the precise and incipient origination of his final thoughts and acts" (176). Such comments signal the death-knell to any idea of a rhetoric of regeneration based upon Transcendentalist principles. In contrast to those fictions that "unravel" and "spread out" the "profounder emanations of the human mind," Melville documents the unresolvable opacity and intricacy of the psyche (141).

Knowing that the deepest impulses cannot be translated but only ambiguously suggested, he refuses to give a "definite form or feeling" (*P*, 82) to his portrait of the mind. Doubting that the writer can ever fully recover the unconscious and knowing that the mind contains profane impulses that contradict the highest ideals, Melville loses faith in writing as an act of original expression. He observes, in contrast to Emerson's enthusiastic discovery of the "God within," that "our God is a jealous God; He wills not that any man should permanently possess the least shadow of His own self-sufficient attributes" (261). The unconscious, in these terms, is not a divine power amenable to the needs of the spirit, but instead a dark alien force that decenters the subject. Early on, Pierre suspects that "not always in our actions, are we our own factors" (51). Pierre's sense that his unconscious is a "Fate" (276), a force beyond conscious control, unmistakably decenters the self-reliant subject.

In Melville's view, the individual who attempts to achieve self-reliance by living solely from within suffers a complete isolation from society's values. Another "Ishmael" (*P*, 89), Pierre "was solitary as at the Pole" (338). Relying on his inner impulses, he comes to exist in a world in which "all the surfaces of visible time and space" cease to reflect collective values, but manifest in their place "one infinite dumb, beseeching countenance of mystery" (52). Gone forever is Emerson's vision of a pastoral realm that reveals a divine power animating all souls. "Say what some poets will," Melville writes, "Nature is not so much her own eversweet interpreter, as the mere supplier of that cunning alphabet, whereby selecting and combining as he pleases, each man reads his own peculiar lesson according to his own peculiar mind and mood" (342). Existence, in other words, becomes an endless act of interpretation, a process of reflection that stops only with the annihilation of consciousness or death. At this point, one senses the great resonance of Emerson's later complaint that the "young men" around him "were born with knives in their brain, a tendency to introversion, self-dissection, anatomizing of motives" (*W*, 10:329). Without Emerson's leap from an abyss of personal reflection into faith in a transcendent source found within the mind, self-awareness leads to vertigo.

Pierre's fate, his slip from ontological security into bewilderment and despair, stands as a warning to the age. Unable to keep his "firm footing" (*P*, 12) in the substantial world of everyday reality, he sets out on his "own secret voyage of discovery" (53), a voyage sustained by an "ether of visions" (85). Like Ahab, Pierre loses contact with a stable ground transcending the self. Emerson had located that ground within by translating theological imperatives into psychological truths; Melville, at the other extreme, ultimately refused to mythologize the unconscious into a transpersonal ground of being. Although he uses symbol and myth to intimate the alien forces found within, he draws back before the affirmation of a collective unconscious or Oversoul. Recording that refusal, *Pierre* thus stands as the fullest critique of the psychological mythmaking engaged in by Transcendentalist writers. But even as Melville dismantles that psychological idealism piece by piece, he must resort to Transcendentalist psychology for the very terms that he uses. Behind his novel stands the shadowy image of Emerson, an antagonist whose doctrines were internalized by the age and became part of the very fabric of its self-reflection. Unable to escape fully from the pervasive spirit of self-reliance, Melville offers in *Pierre* its anatomy. The new religion of the individual, he suggests, has been founded upon bad faith; the human soul is entirely other than what Emerson had imagined.

SEVEN

The Question of the Subject

The nineteenth-century American vision of the self, we can conclude, oscillates between Emersonian "self-reliance" and Melville's suspicious disruption of "confidence." Patterns of faith and participation are cast into doubt by Melville—as well as by Poe and Hawthorne—who express a "principled antagonism to sincerity," speaking "in praise of what they call the mask."[1] By revising Emerson's idealization of the unconscious, all three writers develop conceptions of the self that question the benignity of intuitive models of being. Melville's Ahab and Pierre disastrously complicate their existences by trusting the promptings of inner "spirit"; Hawthorne's characters live in worlds marked by subterfuge and masquerade, not by the revelation of divine power within. Similarly, Poe portrays a violent universe marked by power-relations, not the beneficent assimilation of productive energies. Their characters fail to recognize themselves or others, suggesting that neither self nor others are as accessible or trustworthy as Emerson assumes.

The conflict between rhetorics of regeneration and the psychological vision of Poe, Hawthorne, and Melville establishes a debate over the nature of the self. Is it transparent or opaque, motivated by divine or sexual energies? This debate has not yet been resolved. As a result, the psychological examinations of the American Renaissance have direct relevance to today's critical discussions. In order to understand the dimensions of this issue for nineteenth-century American writers, this study has engaged in a polar movement. On the one hand, it utilizes critical strategies that promote imaginative participation in the psychological myths of Emerson, Thoreau, Whitman, and Fuller. These methods are borrowed from the fields of reader-response aesthetics, hermeneutic theory, phenomenology, and Jungian psychology. On the other hand, the fields of deconstructive criticism and Freudian psychology provide critical models needed to analyze Poe's, Hawthorne's, and Melville's demystifications of Transcendentalist patterns of identification. Recent critical debates over the autonomy of self-consciousness—over the "presence" or "absence" of the Cartesian *cogito*—recapitulate the tension between these two opposed methods of reading. As a result, we are able to mediate the psychological myths of Transcendentalist writers and their more skeptical contemporaries by positioning their viewpoints within the disagreement between phenomenological and deconstructive theorists over the "question of the subject." Indeed, one might question whether the nineteenth-century debate over the nature of the self is reenacted by the later controversy in philosophy and literary theory. If this is so, then the literary and theoretical dialogues should be mutually illuminating.

Recent Structuralist and post-Structuralist theorists have challenged the unified subject assumed by earlier critics—a subject seen to be "present" to itself, consciously in charge of its intentions and motives. Such presence is assumed by phenomenological critics who attend to the manifestations of subjective phenomena within the field of reflection. Suspending disbelief as to the reality of perceived phenomena (Husserl's "epoche" or "bracketing"), these writers posit a provisional faith in the phenomena that they are examining. In similar fashion, Transcendentalist "rhetorics of regeneration" encourage belief in the benign power of intuited psychic energies. Articulating this energy in expanded fields of reflection, such rhetorics encourage their readers to accept the transformative power of language; they assume that unconscious "spirit" can be incarnated and made present in their texts. Learning to reconnect consciousness with this divine unconscious, the reader regains a psychic presence that parallels the power present in the text he is reading. In other words, the gap between psychological signifiers and psychic signified (unconscious power) is believed to be erasable both on the page and in the mind of the reader. Participation lies at the center of this process. Rhetorics of regeneration work if readers participate in them as models of potential being.

In opposition, those who raise the question of the subject (whether Melville or Freud) attend to the forces underlying consciousness and whatever meanings appear within it. From this viewpoint, both textual and psychic surfaces depend upon unseen operations that shape their contours. As a result, models of the psyche are seen as fictions that conceal (if not repress) the energies that constitute identity. The importance of this second viewpoint becomes apparent when we realize that our own critical understanding of Emerson's writing, of its self-dramatizing power, depends in large part upon our being able to view his literary personae as compelling fictions offered as paradigms of being. If a phenomenology of participation reveals the rhetorical power of this literary performance, a concomitant critical skepticism is needed to reveal its fictionality. In this regard, Poe, Hawthorne, and Melville—by raising the question of the subject for the American Renaissance—teach us how to read Emerson without becoming a predicate of his psychological mythmaking. By placing us outside the stage of his imperialistic rhetoric, they help us to cultivate what Hans Robert Jauss describes as "the distancing act in which consciousness measures itself against the object of its astonishment." Only in this way can the danger of "unfree imitation" be replaced by "free emulation."[2]

Our goal has been to understand how Transcendentalist rhetorics of regeneration transform their readers, without our being spellbound by their rhetorics. At this point, we can more fully appreciate Poe's, Hawthorne's, and Melville's dramatizations of the power-relationships latent in any form of discourse based upon participation and identification; for the contrast between the two poles of "admiring identification" and "fascination" returns us to the question of the subject. Each model of interaction implicates a different vision of the self and the unconscious. Emerson, Thoreau, Whitman, and Fuller base their rhetorical practices upon faith in a collective ideality located in the depths of both author and reader; their more skeptical contemporaries view the psyche's interior as the locus of an irrational power, which manifests itself in compulsive power-relationships.

A convenient way to amplify this aspect of the question of the subject is to contrast Carl Jung's and Sigmund Freud's visions of the self. Jung (like Emerson) recapitulates an essentially Romantic vision of the self as longed-for presence, but Freud details the gaps and absences underlying such idealism. This is especially clear in the contrasting ways in which Jung and Freud use the term the *unconscious*. For Jung, the unconscious is akin to what the nineteenth century frequently called "spirit." Freud, on the other hand, sees the unconscious not as spirit, but in terms of irrational force. In his economy of the psyche, unconscious energy undergoes a series of transformations or "vicissitudes" that ultimately result in conscious phenomena. Whereas Jung's unconscious manifests itself in imagistic terms continuous with the plane of conscious cognition, Freud's unconscious is wholly disparate from consciousness, undercutting conscious intention through slips of the tongue and neurotic symptoms. In other words, Freud's subject (the "I") is structured by unseeable forces lying "behind" it. The attempt to study those forces raises the question of the subject.

We can recognize an essential kinship between Jung's vision of consciousness and the unified subject of phenomenology. Both Jungian psychology and phenomenology attend to the unfolding of phenomena within the field of reflection, and not to the half-visible forces lying behind that field. The point is to study what appears on this side of the "horizon," on the "stage" of reflection, not what lies on the other side. As Jung himself emphasizes, his own researches constitute a phenomenology. "I trust I have given no cause for the misunderstanding that I know anything about the nature of the 'centre,'" he writes, "—for it is simply unknowable and can only be expressed symbolically through its own phenomenology."[3] Jung studies the conscious manifestations, the symbolical unfolding, of unconscious energy. His studies thus constitute what can be described as a phenomenology of fantasy.

To borrow a phrase from Paul Ricoeur, Jung focuses upon "the process of 'becoming conscious.'"[4] This process is facilitated through symbols of the mind or the self. "The subject must mediate self-consciousness through spirit or mind," Ricoeur observes, "that is, through the figures that give a telos to this 'becoming conscious.'" Such figures define the endpoint of consciousness, a goal that is articulated by means of mythical images. In the terms of this study, the mediation of self-consciousness through figures that project the ultimate transfiguration of the mind constitutes a process of psychological mythmaking. Emerson's Oversoul, Thoreau's "dawn," Whitman's "procreant urge," Fuller's "idea of woman," all posit the telos of consciousness through figures that merge the self with a transpersonal, sublimating energy.

We might amplify Jung's psychological perspective by comparing it briefly with the phenomenological perspective of the literary critic Gaston Bachelard. Like Jung, Bachelard focuses upon the manifestation of unconscious energies within consciousness, upon what Bachelard describes as "the *onset of the image* in an individual consciousness."[5] Instead of viewing the unconscious as an antagonistic force below consciousness, Bachelard examines unconscious motivation as an inextricable part of consciousness. Accordingly, he describes the poetic image as "a sudden salience on the surface of the psyche," a view that parallels Jung's phenomenological description of dream-images appearing within consciousness.[6] Rejecting the analysis of "psychological antecedents" behind consciousness in favor of exploring the unique demands of the image before him, Bachelard—like Jung—attends to the imaginative foundation of dwelling. This emphasis upon the appearance of images within the field of consciousness essentially coincides with Emerson's portrait of his own creative process: "A man conversing in earnest, if he watch his intellectual processes, will find that always a material image, more or less luminous, arises in his mind, cotemporaneous with every thought, which furnishes the vestment of the thought. Hence, good writing and brilliant discourse are perpetual allegories" (*CW*, 1:20).

In contrast, those who announce the question of the subject turn away from the phenomenal manifestations of different "powers" within consciousness. Bracketing "the existential and thinking subject," these writers dispossess the subject's self-certitude—its faith in allegory—by "a decentering of the home of significations, a displacement of the birthplace of meaning."[7] In their view, "the subject is never the subject one thinks it is."[8] In contrast to such self-certitude, they establish "an anti-phenomenology. . . dispossessing me of the illusory Cogito which at the outset occupies the place of the founding act, *I think, I am.*"[9] Viewing the subject as "written" by unconscious forces exceeding cognition, Poe, Hawthorne, and especially Melville demonstrate such a skepticism as to the self-sufficiency of the individual. Engaging Emersonian self-reliance in a dialogue, they anticipate many of the points made by twentieth-century writers who "question" the subject. The target is the same for both groups—the idealized image of a self-aware individual imagined as being in control of his or her destiny.

Jacques Lacan gives us one of the fullest critiques of the self-sufficient individual. "The question that the unconscious raises," Lacan writes, "is the question of the subject. The subject cannot simply be identified with the speaker of the personal pronoun in a sentence. . . . It is as if a demon plays a game with your watchfulness. The question is to find a precise status for this subject which is exactly the sort of subject that we can determine taking our point of departure in language."[10] With this passage, we move completely from Emerson's or Jung's "metaphysics of presence" to a theoretical position that challenges their idealization of human potential. In contrast to their faith in the recoverability of unconscious energy, Lacan argues that unconscious forces defer consciousness and are never fully recoverable by the conscious mind.

Focusing upon the "inmixing of otherness" in conscious states, Lacan shows us how conscious intentions and attitudes are displaced by messages that come "from the Other," from alien forces within the psyche.[11] This vision of the mind coincides with that found in the following passage: "What is it, what nameless, inscrutable, unearthly thing is it; what cozening, hidden lord and master, and cruel, remorseless emperor commands me; that against all natural lovings and longings, I so keep pushing, and crowding, and jamming myself on all the time; recklessly making me ready to do what in my own proper, natural heart, I durst not so much as dare? Is Ahab, Ahab? Is it I, God, or who, that lifts this arm?" (*MD*, 444–45). Lacan would understand the motivation of Captain Ahab very well; for Ahab is driven by an otherness he cannot control, an otherness that manifests itself in disturbances of the psychic surface.

The play of otherness, Lacan asserts, leads to a radical "splitting" that cleaves the subject into conscious illusion and unconscious force.[12] The subject is no longer Emerson's unified and stable observer, potentially present to itself, but seen as "intermittent."[13] Accordingly, Lacan argues that assertions of the unity of the mind are fictions. Against "the idea of unity as the most important and characteristic trait" of the mind, he asserts that "the mind is not a totality in itself."[14] Recognition of this radical split in the psyche undermines unitary psychological assumptions, replacing the unified fields of reflection cherished by Emerson and Jung with a radical alterity located at the heart of the psyche.[15]

This view of the mind was elaborated by Friedrich Nietzsche, the thinker along with Freud who has most profoundly influenced current demystifications of the self. "What indeed," Nietzsche asked, "does man know of himself! Can he even once perceive himself completely, laid out as if in an illuminated glass case? Does not nature keep much the most from him, even about his body, to spellbind and confine him in a proud, deceptive consciousness, far from the coils of the intestines, the quick current of the blood stream, and the involved tremors of the fibers?"[16] This passage introduces a theme that takes on increasing importance for nineteenth-century psychological reflection—the desire to place the mind back into the body, to reconnect cognition to its "natural" roots. If we find this aim at the end of the century in Freud's conception of libido, it crops up much earlier in the attention that Hawthorne and Melville give to sexual impulses as the ultimate source of conscious motivation. Commenting on this development, Northrop Frye observes that "from Rousseau's time on" the human being "is thought of as a product of the energy of physical nature."[17]

Whether or not this origin is seen as "demonic" (as Frye goes on to assert) depends upon one's vision of "Nature." To the extent that its energies are seen as physical rather than as divine or spiritual, idealized versions of the self are threatened, for conscious motives are interpreted in terms of prior causes that come from a lower level of being. For those (like Emerson and his contemporaries) trained to associate mental and spiritual phenomena, the subject is seen as out of control, because its ideals become the mask or disguise of deeper-lying forces, rather than the imitation of a superior power. Within the prevailing Christian mindset of the nineteenth century, the unconscious could *only* be divine or demonic. The development of metaphysically neutral evaluations of the psyche had to await the shift from theological typologies of the self to paradigms borrowed from the fields of economics and biology.

Elsewhere in "On Truth and Lie in an Extra-Moral Sense," Nietzsche develops the metaphor that has facilitated our understanding of the demystification of rhetorics of regeneration. He describes consciousness as a mask:

> The intellect, as a means for the preservation of the individual, unfolds its chief powers in a simulation. . . . In man this art of simulation reaches its peak: here deception, flattery, lying and cheating, talking behind the back, posing, living in borrowed splendor, being masked, the disguise of convention, acting a role before others and before oneself—in short, the constant fluttering around the single flame of vanity is so much the rule and the law that almost nothing is more incomprehensible than how an honest and pure urge for truth could make its appearance among men.[18]

Evoking the masked worlds of Poe, Hawthorne, and Melville, this passage undermines Emerson's vision of intuited truth.

Decentering faith in the "I," Melville demonstrates the dependence of self-awareness upon hidden impulses. Reading Melville's fiction in conjunction with Nietzsche's philosophy, we come to see that it "psychoanalyzes" idealized models of the mind best represented by Emerson's psychological mythmaking. Implicit in this approach to Melville is the assumption that his works are fundamentally "dialogic," in M. M. Bakhtin's sense of the term.[19] Taking Transcendentalist psychology as an internal antagonist, they dramatize and caricature intellectual positions that are easily identifiable as simplified versions of those held by Emerson.

Again, the analogy with Nietzsche is useful, for Nietzsche's writings also work out their own implicit dialogue with Emerson, the author—according to Nietzsche—"who had been richest in ideas in this century."[20] Not only was Nietzsche reputed to have carried a copy of Emerson's essays with him everywhere, he used a quotation from Emerson's essay "History" as an epigraph to *The Gay Science* and reread and annotated Emerson just before he wrote *Zarathustra*.[21] One of the results of this familiarity, Walter Kaufmann suggests, was Nietzsche's concept of the *Übermensch*, the "over-man," which seems to echo Emerson's Oversoul.[22]

But ultimately, the differences between Emerson and Nietzsche are much more apparent than the similarities. It is these differences that we want to stress, for the connection between Melville and Nietzsche would seem merely gratuitous if each writer's admiration and suspicion of nineteenth-century idealism had not led him to find in Emerson's writing one of the most striking examples of idealism's strengths and weaknesses. Although Emerson is present in the foreground of Melville's writing, in

Nietzsche's work he stands further back, part of a medley of voices that are better represented for Nietzsche by Emerson's antecedents among the German Idealist philosophers.

Perhaps the most striking similarity between Melville's and Nietzsche's demystifications of Emersonian self-faith involves their shared interest in masks and masquerades as the antithesis of sincerity and transparent expression. As a literary or a philosophical theme, the concept of mask effectively short-circuits demonstrations of the individual's sincerity. Commenting upon Emerson's *Essays* in 1841, Thomas Carlyle had praised its truthfulness: "I love Emerson's book . . . simply because it is his own book; because there is a tone of veracity, an unmistakable air of its being *his* . . . and a real utterance of a human soul, not a mere echo of such. . . ."[23] Cherished by both Carlyle and Emerson, sincerity was a popular nineteenth-century ideal that imagined "a congruence between avowal and actual feeling," a continuity between persona and inner self.[24] Connecting inner and outer selves, Emerson's vision of self-reliance takes sincerity as one of its basic conditions. Only with the recognition of insincerity, a theme beyond Transcendentalist myths of the psyche, does one need a concept of persona, of personality as impersonation of social values rather than the unimpeded expression of character.

But Nietzsche goes far beyond observing that the insincere individual wears a mask; he questions whether sincerity itself is even possible. Part of the problem, Nietzsche suggests, resides in the very terms that are being used. Our "entire science," he complains, "still lies under the misleading influence of language and has not disposed of that little changeling, the 'subject.'"[25] Elsewhere, he asserts that the ego is "a fiction" that takes one into "a realm of crude fetishism" where "one projects this faith in the ego-substance upon all things."[26] "There exists neither 'spirit,' nor reason, nor thinking, nor consciousness, nor soul, nor will, nor truth," Nietzsche asserts even more vehemently; "all are fictions that are of no use."[27] Disposing of the ego and the subject as suspect psychological myths, Nietzsche must reject sincerity or divinely sanctioned self-reliance as ideals; for such concepts tend to hypostatize a divine psychological essence, which is used as an index of behavior. This essence exhibits the quasi-theological "need . . . to develop unconditional self-confidence on the basis of some ultimate and indisputable commandment that is inherently sublime."[28] By rejecting the divine basis of human motivation, Nietzsche disposes of all ideals that calibrate thought and motivation against a supernatural standard. By deifying their motives, Nietzsche insists, human beings have sought to disguise and thus legitimate their desires.

Nietzsche's method of demystifying the psyche foreshadows the techniques of psychoanalysis. He searches out "all the hideouts where the ideal is at home—where it has its secret dungeons and, as it were, its ultimate safety."[29] Throwing "an incisive light into this *underworld* of the ideal," he comes to see consciously held ideals as stoppers used to plug "gaps" in the "spirit."[30] Freud found similar "gaps" in Dora's memory, gaps that revealed her repressions. Similarly, French psychoanalysts elaborate the idea that repression creates a "rip" or "rent" in the psyche, an absence that is "darned" or "rewoven."[31] Recognizing that the conscious self masks deeper and more primitive forces, Nietzsche adumbrates the observations of twentieth-century analysts by concluding that "most of the conscious thinking of a philosopher is secretly guided and forced into certain channels by his instincts," by "impetuous torrents of the soul."[32] A generation earlier, Melville's mature works reflect a similar recognition that irrational force, and not spirit, lies at the heart of the psyche. Ahab's vengeful quest is driven by "the innermost necessities" of his being, not by motives that he can consciously control (*MD*, 145); similarly, Pierre's "conscious judgment" disguises "the more secret chambers of his unsuspecting soul" (*P*, 105). Melville's recognition of the unconscious leads him like Nietzsche toward the realization that idealism is frequently a subterfuge covering over less noble impulses.

Disguising the unconscious, consciousness becomes a mask. As he confronted both himself and others, Ahab "did long dissemble" (*MD*, 161). Similarly, Pierre's "soul was forced to wear a mask" (*P*, 183), for "the deeper that some men feel a secret and poignant feeling, the higher they pile the belying surfaces" (224). We see from these examples that Melville's unconscious, like Nietzsche's and Freud's, is discontinuous from conscious intentions. It is something other, not a benign spirit that elides easily into recognizable motives. Instead, such motives cover up and disguise deeper forces that can only be dimly and indirectly perceived. The great nineteenth-century delusion, both Melville and Nietzsche suggest, has been to mistake the mask of consciousness for the whole truth of human being. "As they attain a more advanced age," Nietzsche complains, "almost all Europeans confound themselves with their role. . . . the role has actually *become* character."[33] However, this recognition of the psyche's masquerades does not lead easily to the spiritual conversion of character; for the "spirit," all psychic explorers have learned to their profound uneasiness, "enjoys the multiplicity and craftiness of its masks."[34] Confronted with such "resistance" (to use Freud's term), Melville and Nietzsche attempted to convince their respective cultures that smug self-confidence was a sham and a fiction.

The only antidote to such self-deception, Nietzsche argues, is "a critique of moral values"; indeed, *"the value of these values themselves must first be called into question."*[35] By revealing morality "as symptom, as mask," Nietzsche makes us aware both of the depth and the obscurity of the psyche.[36] "I am a *Doppelganger*," he remarks in a voice that sounds remarkably like that of Poe or Melville, "I have a 'second' face in addition to the first. *And* perhaps also a third."[37] Melville's major works perform a similar demystification of consciousness. Behind Ahab's and Pierre's avowals of purpose, he shows us a demonic "second face" that manifests the ambiguous shadings of an alien unconscious. "Gnawed within and scorched without, with the infixed, unrelenting fangs of some incurable idea" (*MD*, 162), Ahab reveals the dangerous potential of total self-determination. Spellbound by the "sparkling electricity" (*P*, 151) of his half-sister Isabel, Pierre becomes possessed by "a usurper mood" that leads him to destroy even "the most intense beloved bond, as a hindrance to the attainment of whatever transcendental object that usurper mood so tyrannically suggests" (180).

Bound for New York after he sacrifices the feelings of his fiancée, his own mother, even his own respectability, to the cause that has seized control of him, Pierre like Ahab thus becomes a caricature of Transcendentalist independence. "Henceforth," Melville ironically observes, "cast-out Pierre hath no paternity, and no past; and since the Future is one blank to all; therefore, twice-disinherited Pierre stands untrammeledly his ever-present self!—free to do his own self-will and present fancy to whatever end!" (*P*, 199). "Nothing is at last sacred but the integrity of your own mind," Emerson had told his age; "I shun father and mother and wife and brother, when my genius calls me" (*CW*, 2:30). In a sense, both Ahab and Pierre represent the consequences of accepting such dictums at face value, for the "integrity" of the mind, Melville shows a horrified age, may be totally unreliable.

"I remove the veil," Whitman's poet boldly asserts in "Song of Myself" (l. 519), as he celebrates the expressive embrace of attention fondling a malleable world. In this view, the self's development follows an ascending curve of expression. Enacted through a poetics of participation and identification, this release blurs difference in favor of merger. Both poet and reader, we are meant to see, share a collective energy found in the soul. In contrast, the veiled psyches portrayed by Poe, Hawthorne, and Melville presuppose a different model of object-relations. Divided from the depths of themselves, their characters find that a translucent (but not transparent) veil separates them from each other. Just as elements within the psyche resist reflection, the faces that others present disguise their true motives. As a result, patterns of identification are impossible. Whereas speakers and auditors blend together in Emerson's and Whitman's writing, individuals tend to pull apart in the fiction of Poe, Hawthorne, and Melville. The relationships between their characters, as well as the relationship between implied author and reader, follow a dynamics of power-relations marked by duplicity and not union.

Part of this difference results from the fact that in a fictional work human motivation cannot be discussed in ideal terms; rather, it must be measured in terms of practical consequences. Thus, at least part of Poe's, Hawthorne's, and Melville's disagreement with Emerson results from the fact that they work in a different genre, Gothic romance, a genre influenced in part by a Calvinist awareness of the heart's opacity and of the often disturbing gaps between spiritual aspiration and desire.[38] Instead of participating in the "voices" constituted within their texts, we must attend to the ironic tensions between voice and event, between consciousness and drama. Their portrayal of the self's masks entails a consideration of the social dimensions of personality, as well as of its theatricality.

Kenneth Burke's distinction between dialectic and drama helps to clarify the psychological differences between rhetorics of regeneration and the romances of Poe, Hawthorne, and Melville:

> Both drama and dialectic treat of persons and their characteristic thoughts. But whereas drama stresses the *persons* who have the thoughts, and the dialectic of a Platonic dialogue stresses the *thoughts* held by the persons, in both forms the element of personality figures.
>
> However, dialectic can dispense with the formal division into cooperatively competing voices. The thoughts or ideas can still be vibrant with personality, as they so obviously are in the essays of Emerson. Yet we think of them as various aspects of the same but somewhat inconsistent personality, rather than as distinct *characters* in various degrees of agreement and disagreement, like in a Platonic dialogue.[39]

As we have seen, thoughts for Emerson can be "vibrant with personality," generating a corresponding persona that becomes a role-model for his auditors. But turning to the fiction of Poe, Hawthorne, and Melville, we find a necessary emphasis upon persons and social exchange. Instead of representing eloquent personae as role models, all three writers engage Emerson's personae in a constructive dialogue by showing how such personages subvert normal temporal, physical, and social relations.

Burke's comments suggest that eloquence in the arena of thought means one thing, whereas eloquence as the basis of relationship between persons means quite another. In the former case, the eloquent personality aims to become the vehicle of an ongoing illumination. But in the latter case, the eloquent personality often causes social effects that impede, rather than enhance, communication. Dwelling in their works upon the "spell" cast by the persuasive orator, Poe, Hawthorne, and Melville demonstrate that this power, based upon an emotional rather than an intellectual response, simulates the kind of rhetorical relationship utilized by Emerson. But such simulation turns into parody, as they construct "scenes of rhetorical power" that lead to reflection upon the social efficacy and moral legitimacy of relationships based upon one person's superior persuasive abilities. Eloquence, all three suggest, can be a dangerous tool. Only if the unconscious contains the benign energies that Emerson finds there can eloquence fully serve the cause of individual perfection. Otherwise, the eloquent speaker stirs depths of passion or desire as a means of subordinating others to his or her own fantasy or ideology.

Poe, Hawthorne, and Melville comment upon Transcendentalist persuasion as they demonstrate the personal expense of being trapped within overpowering rhetorics. All three suggest that eloquence can be made to serve the desire for mastery over others, who become infected and contaminated by images that may be alien to their being. If this domination is momentarily the fate of Poe's narrator in "The Fall of the House of Usher," it is also the position occupied by the female characters in Hawthorne's *Blithedale Romance* and the crew in Melville's *Moby-Dick*. All these characters are victimized as they are forced to act out roles they did not write and to exist on stages constructed by eloquent ideologues. Representing "scenes of rhetorical power," Poe, Hawthorne, and Melville suggest that the self is a dramatic function of scripts written by individuals who are willing to subordinate others to their quests for meaning. As Poe, Hawthorne, and Melville demonstrate how the self is enacted by dominant ideologies, they move us outside the stage into the position of the spectator. No longer on the inside, instigated to act out a role whose theatricality has been mystified, the reader of their works is positioned so as to see how the persona of any individual—once he or she enters into a rhetorical relationship—is a theatrical presentation. Each individual has no choice but to play a role, to wear a mask; for each one of us exists on multiple stages imagined by ourselves and others.

In Transcendentalist rhetorics of regeneration, self-present "voice" takes precedence. Like Husserl's philosophy, they valorize "an immediate and self-present intuition."[40] Implicit in Hawthorne's and Melville's critiques of Transcendentalism is the awareness that such privileging of voice threatens the more realistic demands of fiction writing. In the words of Jacques Derrida, "everything that escapes the pure spiritual intention, the pure animation by *Geist*, that is, the will, is excluded from meaning . . . and thus from expression. What is excluded is, for example, facial expressions, gestures, the whole of the body and the mundane register, in a word, the whole of the visible and spatial as such."[41] Although this overstates the case for Transcendentalist writers, it does clarify the tendency of their writing to include "visible and spatial" phenomena *only so far as they can be made a function of the writer's will.* Whitman's catalogues represent the literary limit of this will-to-power over nature, the ultimate hyperextension of a poetics of voice.

Ultimately, what Emerson, Thoreau, Whitman, and Fuller cannot fully include in their writing is the reciprocal impingement of another's will. There is no effective social pressure limiting the expansion of the "self-evolving circle, which, from a ring imperceptibly small, rushes on all sides outwards to new and larger circles, and that without end" (*CW*, 2:180). Missing from Emerson's and Whitman's early work is any fully realized sense of centripetal force, pushing inward, restraining the onrush of power. This omission of the other results from the Transcendentalists' model of human nature. By stressing the spiritual identity of mankind, they are forced to bracket human difference. But to the extent that the reader participates in a common paradigm of being, he or she loses the possibility of actually affecting a writer who has subsumed the reader's being under a controlling ideology. If an author subordinates all aspects of existence to the "power which resides in him," then—as Emerson asserts—"father and mother and wife and brother" (*CW*, 2:28, 30) really are not necessary. "None knows better than I," Emerson lamented in a letter to Fuller, "the gloomy inhospitality of the man, the want of power to meet and unite with even those whom he loves in his 'flinty way'" (*L*, 2:350–51). Rather than attributing this social isolation solely to a defect in Emerson's temperament, we can see that it results from his vision of the mind.

As his early enthusiasm waned, Emerson gave greater weight to physical necessity. But an even more effective response is found in the works of Poe, Hawthorne, and Melville. All undermine self-reliance by inverting the Transcendentalist rhetoric of regeneration. Emerson's exemplary persona, exhibiting processes of sublimation and idealization, turns into a Roderick Usher, a Hollingsworth, an Ahab. Rather than using the speaker-auditor relationship to project images of an idealized unconscious located within the ideal reader, each uses it to examine issues of personal domination, the will-to-power over others. In their scenes of fascination and mesmerism, all three writers stage an interpersonal dynamic opposed to Emerson's model of rhetorical exchange.

Although this is a book about reading Emerson and the Emersonian tradition, it begins to focus upon a larger concern—upon the questioning of psychologies of "presence" at three historical moments. One finds the nineteenth-century debate over the nature of the self recapitulated in the later disagreements of Jung and Freud, and then again in the conflicting views of phenomenological writers and Lacan. These three moments define a problematic of selfhood that has not been resolved, which indeed probably has no final resolution. In following the debate between Emerson, his imitators, and their more skeptical contemporaries, we finally approach an intellectual limit. Attempting to examine some of the strategies that constitute the psyche as we know it, we find staring back at us our own psychological reflection.

Ultimately, a study like this one begins to alter one's vision of American literary scholarship, for the recent competition between humanistic and deconstructive readings of our classic writers is seen as a necessary consequence of their literary complexity. In other words, deconstructive readings of Emerson, Hawthorne, Melville, and others reenact a critical skepticism already present in their works—an intellectual discipline that gives shape to their distinctive dramatizations of the self. But conversely, we find in all three (as well as in Poe, Thoreau, Whitman, and Fuller) an imaginative power, an authority, that seems to contradict such skepticism. These two sides are not antagonists, but rather are hermeneutically paired. The skepticism of the age depends upon previous affirmations in order to appear, and vice versa. Deconstruction and construction, rhetorics of regeneration and demystification, are intertwined in an endless dance. Thus, in order to understand the spectacle of self-representation during the American Renaissance, we need to act a while upon the stages that its best writers constructed, but we also must stand back and examine the dimensions of each role. Only in this way can we begin to appreciate both the rhetorical power and the existential compulsion of their psychological myths.

Notes

CHAPTER I

1. F. O. Matthiessen, *American Renaissance: Art and Expression in the Age of Emerson and Whitman* (New York: Oxford University Press, 1941), p. 7.

2. All references to works written by Emerson, Thoreau, Whitman, Fuller, Poe, Hawthorne, and Melville will be made parenthetically in the text. For full bibliographic information, see the list of abbreviations.

3. Harold Bloom, *Agon: Towards a Theory of Revisionism* (New York: Oxford University Press, 1982), p. 166.

4. Lawrence Buell, *Literary Transcendentalism: Style and Vision in the American Renaissance* (Ithaca, N.Y.: Cornell University Press, 1973), p. 105.

5. Matthiessen, *American Renaissance*, p. 17.

6. Marshall W. Alcorn, Jr., and Mark Bracher, "Literature, Psychoanalysis, and the Re-Formation of the Self: A New Direction for Reader-Response Theory," *PMLA* 100 (1985): 348.

7. Barbara Packer, *Emerson's Fall: A New Interpretation of the Major Essays* (New York: Continuum, 1982), p. 8.

8. Hans Robert Jauss, *Toward an Aesthetic of Reception*, trans. Timothy Bahti (Minneapolis: University of Minnesota Press, 1982), p. 21.

9. Ibid., p. 23.

10. William Ellery Channing, *The Works of William E. Channing* (Boston: American Unitarian Association, 1899), p. 507. I am indebted to Kevin Van Anglen for drawing my attention to this passage.

11. Thomas DeQuincey, "Literature of Knowledge and Literature of Power," rpt. in *English Romantic Writers*, ed. David Perkins (New York: Harcourt, Brace & World, 1967), p. 743.

12. For a discussion of the ways a literary work alters an audience's "horizon of expectations," see Jauss, *Toward an Aesthetic of Reception*, pp. 24–25. Alcorn and Bracher develop a similar idea when they suggest that literature alters the reader's "cognitive map" ("Literature, Psychoanalysis, and the Re-Formation of the Self," p. 344).

13. Henry Nash Smith, "Emerson's Problem of Vocation," in Milton R. Konvitz and Stephen E. Whicher, eds., *Emerson: A Collection of Critical Essays* (Englewood Cliffs, N.J.: Prentice-Hall, 1962), pp. 64–65.

14. Buell, *Literary Transcendentalism*, pp. 287–88, 289.

15. Alcorn and Bracher, "Literature, Psychoanalysis, and the Re-Formation of the Self," p. 348.

16. Walker Gibson, "Authors, Speakers, Readers, and Mock Readers," in Jane Tompkins, ed., *Reader-Response Criticism* (Baltimore: Johns Hopkins University Press, 1980), p. 5.

17. Andrews Norton, "A Discourse on the Latest Form of Infidelity," in Perry Miller, ed., *The Transcendentalists: An Anthology* (Cambridge, Mass.: Harvard University Press, 1950), pp. 211–12.

18. Rudolf Bultmann, *Essays: Philosophical and Theological*, trans. James C. G. Greig (New York: Macmillan, 1950), p. 261.

19. Ibid., p. 239.

20. Ibid., p. 253.

21. Ibid., p. 242.

22. Sigmund Freud, "Constructions in Analysis" in *The Standard Edition of the Complete Psychological Works*, ed. James Strachey, 24 vols. (London: Hogarth Press, 1953–74), 23: 266.

23. A useful discussion of critical and psychoanalytic frames of reference is provided by Barbara Johnson in "The Frame of Reference: Poe, Lacan, Derrida," *Yale French Studies* 55/56 (1977): 457–505.

24. Hans Robert Jauss, *Aesthetic Experience and Literary Hermeneutics*, trans. Michael Shaw (Minneapolis: University of Minnesota Press, 1982), p. 93.

25. Ernest G. Bormann, *The Force of Fantasy: Restoring the American Dream* (Carbondale, Ill.: Southern Illinois University Press, 1985), p. 97.

26. Gibson, "Authors, Speakers, Readers, and Mock Readers," p. 2.

27. Georges Poulet, "Criticism and the Experience of Interiority," in *Reader-Response Criticism*, p. 44.

28. Alcorn and Bracher, "Literature, Psychoanalysis, and the Re-Formation of the Self," p. 349.

29. Wolfgang Iser, "The Reading Process: A Phenomenological Approach," in *Reader-Response Criticism*, p. 67.

30. Paul Ricoeur, *Hermeneutics and the Human Sciences*, trans. John B. Thompson (Cambridge, England: Cambridge University Press, 1981), p. 142.

31. Ibid., p. 94.

32. Ibid., p. 141.

33. Alcorn and Bracher, "Literature, Psychoanalysis, and the Re-Formation of the Self," pp. 349–50, analyze this regenerated self as an expanded "ego ideal." This is an attractive line of argument, but it is difficult to reconcile with the claims of Transcendentalist writers that they are transcending egotism. Jung's conception of the self (which includes the unconscious along with the ego) becomes a more useful paradigm at this point.

34. Iser, "The Reading Process," p. 64.

35. Ibid., p. 61.

36. Ibid., p. 64.

37. Paul Ricoeur, *Freud and Philosophy: An Essay on Interpretation*, trans. Denis Savage (New Haven: Yale University Press, 1970), p. 33. Alcorn and Bracher make a similar point when they argue that "literature works most effectively to promote a re-formation of the self" as it "integrate(s) narcissistic aspiration with superego restraints" ("Literature, Psychoanalysis, and the Re-Formation of the Self," p. 350).

38. See Jauss, *Aesthetic Experience and Literary Hermeneutics*, p. 160: "For neither mere absorption in an emotion, nor the wholly detached reflection about it, but only the to-and-fro movement, the ever renewed disengagement of the self from a fictional experience, the testing of oneself against the portrayed fate of another, makes up the distinctive pleasure in the state of suspension of aesthetic identification."

39. Georges Poulet, quoted by Sarah Lawall, *Critics of Consciousness: The Existential Structures of Literature* (Cambridge, Mass.: Harvard University Press, 1968), p. 2.

40. Lawall, *Critics of Consciousness*, p. 7.

41. Iser, "The Reading Process," p. 67.

42. Ibid., p. 64.

43. Jacques Derrida, *Writing and Difference*, trans. Alan Bass (Chicago: University of Chicago Press, 1978), p. 203.

44. Roland Barthes, *Mythologies*, trans. Annette Lauers (New York: Hill & Wang, 1972), p. 131.

CHAPTER 2

1. Octavius Brooks Frothingham, *Transcendentalism in New England: A History* (1876; rpt. Philadelphia: University of Pennsylvania Press, 1972), p. 136.

2. Francis Bowen, *Christian Examiner* 21 (Jan. 1837): 377–78. Rpt. in Merton M. Sealts, Jr., and Alfred R. Ferguson, eds., *Emerson's Nature: Origin, Growth, Meaning* (Carbondale, Ill.: Southern Illinois University Press, 1979), p. 84.

3. Gay Wilson Allen, "Emerson and the Unconscious," *American Transcendental Quarterly* 19 (Summer 1973): 27.

4. Martin Bickman, *The Unsounded Centre: Jungian Studies in American Romanticism* (Chapel Hill, N.C.: University of North Carolina Press, 1980), p. 13.

5. M. H. Abrams, *The Mirror and the Lamp: Romantic Theory and the Critical Tradition* (New York: W. W. Norton & Co., 1958), pp. 184–225.

6. Stephen E. Whicher, *Freedom and Fate: An Inner Life of Ralph Waldo Emerson* (Philadelphia: University of Pennsylvania Press, 1953), p. 23.

7. Carl Gustav Jung, *The Portable Jung*, ed. Joseph Campbell (New York: Viking Press, 1971), p. 479. The succeeding quotation is from p. 470.

8. Bickman, *The Unsounded Centre*, p. 81.

9. Dieter Wys, *Depth Psychology: A Critical History*, trans. Gerald Onn (New York: W. W. Norton & Co., 1966), p. 355.

10. *The Portable Jung*, p. 167.

11. Ibid.

12. Ibid., p. 122.

13. Ibid., pp. 121–22.

14. Ibid., pp. 423, 420.

15. Paul Ricoeur, *Freud and Philosophy: An Essay on Interpretation*, trans. Denis Savage (New Haven: Yale University Press, 1970), p. 459.

16. Paul Ricoeur, *The Philosophy of Paul Ricoeur: An Anthology of His Work*, ed. Charles E. Reagan and David Stewart (Boston: Beacon Press, 1978), p. 225.

17. Ricoeur, *Freud and Philosophy*, p. 31.

18. Lawrence Buell, *Literary Transcendentalism: Style and Vision in the American Renaissance* (Ithaca, N.Y.: Cornell University Press, 1973), p. 103.

19. Ibid., p. 105.

20. Arthur Cushman McGiffert, "Introduction" to *Young Emerson Speaks: Unpublished Discourses on Many Subjects* (Boston: Houghton Mifflin Co., 1938), pp. xxiv–xxv.

21. Ibid., p. xviii.

22. Ibid., p. xx.

23. Jacques Derrida, *Of Grammatology*, trans. Gayatri Chakrovorty Spivak (Baltimore: Johns Hopkins University Press, 1976), pp. 7, 12.

24. Jacques Derrida, *Positions*, trans. Alan Bass (Chicago: University of Chicago Press, 1981), p. 22.

25. Jacques Derrida, *Speech and Phenomena and Other Essays on Husserl's Theory of Signs*, trans. Newton Garver (Evanston, Ill.: Northwestern University Press, 1973), p. 35.

26. R. A. Yoder, *Emerson and the Orphic Poet in America* (Berkeley: University of California Press, 1978), p. 11.

27. M. H. Abrams, *Natural Supernaturalism: Tradition and Revolution in Romantic Literature* (New York: W. W. Norton & Co., 1971), pp. 193, 255. The passages in the next sentence are from pp. 28, 47.

28. Michel Foucault, *The Order of Things: An Archeology of the Human Sciences* (New York: Random House, 1973), pp. 231, 239, 251.

29. Hans-Georg Gadamer, *Truth and Method* (New York: Crossroad, 1975), p. 164.

30. Ibid., p. 168.

31. Thomas Carlyle, "Characteristics," *Critical and Miscellaneous Essays*, 5 vols. (New York: Charles Scribner's Sons, 1899), 3: 4.

32. Geoffrey H. Hartman, "Romanticism and Anti-Self-Consciousness," *Beyond Formalism: Literary Essays 1958–1970* (New Haven: Yale University Press, 1970), pp. 298–99.

33. Edward Edinger, *Ego and Archetype: Individuation and the Religious Function of the Psyche* (Baltimore: Penguin Books, 1973), p. 48.

34. Bickman, *The Unsounded Centre*, p. 8.

35. Foucault, *The Order of Things*, p. 326.

36. Ibid., p. 327.

37. Harold Bloom, *Poetry and Repression: Revisionism from Blake to Stevens* (New Haven: Yale University Press, 1976), p. 239; subsequent quotations are from Harold Bloom, *Wallace Stevens: The Poems of Our Climate* (New Haven: Yale University Press, 1976), pp. 239, 375.

38. Carolyn Porter, *Seeing and Being: The Plight of the Participant Observer in Emerson, James, Adams, and Faulkner* (Middletown, Conn.: Wesleyan University Press, 1981), p. 107.

39. Ibid., p. 106.

40. Sigmund Freud, *The Standard Edition of the Complete Psychological Works*, ed. James Strachey, 24 vols. (London: Hogarth Press, 1953–74), 19: 151. Cited by Anthony Wilden, trans. of Jacques Lacan, *The Language of the Self: The Function of Language in Psychoanalysis* (New York: Dell Publishing Co., 1968), p. 98.

41. Whicher, *Freedom and Fate*, pp. 13, 12.

42. F. O. Matthiessen, *American Renaissance: Art and Expression in the Age of Emerson and Whitman* (New York: Oxford University Press, 1941), p. 48.

43. Roland Barthes, *The Pleasure of the Text*, trans. Richard Miller (New York: Hill & Wang, 1975), pp. 6–9.

44. Samuel Taylor Coleridge, *The Complete Works of Samuel Taylor Coleridge*, ed. W. G. T. Shedd, 7 vols. (New York: Harper & Bros., 1884), 1: 129.

45. Martin Heidegger, *Basic Writings*, ed. David Krell (New York: Harper & Row, 1977), p. 332.

46. Sacvan Bercovitch, *The Puritan Origins of the American Self* (New Haven: Yale University Press, 1975), p. 177.

47. Sampson Reed, *Observations on the Growth of the Mind* (1826; rpt. New York: Arno Press, 1972), pp. 14, 35.

48. Ibid., p. 11.

49. Abrams, *Natural Supernaturalism*, p. 230.

50. Reed, *Observations*, p. 28.

51. Ezra Pound, *The Literary Essays of Ezra Pound*, ed. T. S. Eliot (New York: New Directions, 1968), p. 115.

52. Stanley Cavell, "Thinking of Emerson," *New Literary History* 11 (1979): 174.

53. Martin Heidegger, *Being and Time*, trans. John Macquarrie and Edward Robinson (New York: Harper & Row, 1962), p. 98.

54. Rollo May, "Contributions of Existential Psychotherapy," in *Existence: A New Dimension in Psychiatry and Psychology*, ed. Rollo May, Ernest Angel, Henri Ellenberger (New York: Basic Books, 1958), p. 60.

55. Porter, *Seeing and Being*, p. 105.

CHAPTER 3

1. Joel Porte, *Emerson and Thoreau: Transcendentalists in Conflict* (Middletown, Conn.: Wesleyan University Press, 1965), p. 195.

2. For a discussion of Emerson's dualistic terminology, see Charles Feidelson, Jr., *Symbolism and American Literature* (Chicago: University of Chicago Press, 1953), p. 126.

192
Notes to Pages 42–52

3. Maurice Merleau-Ponty, *Sense and Non-Sense*, trans. Herbert L. Dreyfus and Patricia Allen Dreyfus (Evanston, Ill.: Northwestern University Press, 1964), p. 130.

4. Karl Marx, *Early Writings*, trans. and ed. T. B. Bottomore (New York: McGraw-Hill, 1964), pp. 206–7.

5. Ibid., p. 214.

6. Ibid., p. 215.

7. Ibid., p. 217.

8. Ibid., p. 201.

9. Ibid., pp. 161, 163.

10. Ibid., p. 171.

11. Ibid., p. 159.

12. Fredric Jameson, *The Political Unconscious: Narrative as a Socially Symbolic Act* (Ithaca, N.Y.: Cornell University Press, 1981), p. 62.

13. Hans Robert Jauss, *Toward an Aesthetic of Reception*, trans. Timothy Bahti (Minneapolis: University of Minnesota Press, 1982), p. 16.

14. See Stanley Cavell, *The Senses of Walden* (New York: Viking Press, 1972), p. 8. Cavell defines Thoreau's concern as "building new structures and forming new human beings with new minds to inhabit them."

15. Medard Boss, *Psychoanalysis and Daseinsanalysis*, trans. Ludwig B. Lefebre (New York: Basic Books, 1963), p. 30.

16. Ibid., p. 34.

17. Ibid., p. 43.

18. Cavell, *The Senses of Walden*, p. 52.

19. Ibid., pp. 9, 80.

20. Ibid., p. 72.

21. Ibid., p. 79.

22. Martin Heidegger, *Being and Time*, trans. John Macquarrie and Edward Robinson (New York: Harper & Row, 1962), p. 191.

23. Ibid., pp. 190–91.

24. Marx, *Early Writings*, p. 121.

25. Wolfgang Iser, *The Act of Reading: A Theory of Aesthetic Response* (Baltimore: Johns Hopkins University Press, 1978), p. 79.

26. Samuel Taylor Coleridge, *Biographia Literaria*, ed. George Watson (London: Dent, 1956), p. 169.

27. Friedrich von Schiller, *Naive and Sentimental Poetry and On the Sublime*, trans. Julius A. Elias (New York: Frederick Ungar, 1966), pp. 116, 154.

28. Iser, *The Act of Reading*, pp. 34–35, 58.

29. Ibid., pp. 120, 128.

30. Perry Miller, "Thoreau in the Context of International Romanticism," *Nature's Nation* (Cambridge, Mass.: Harvard University Press, 1967), p. 176.

31. Lawrence Buell, *Literary Transcendentalism: Style and Vision in the American Renaissance* (Ithaca, N.Y.: Cornell University Press, 1973), p. 188.

32. Georges Poulet, *The Interior Distance*, trans. Elliott Coleman (Ann Arbor: University of Michigan Press, 1964), p. vii.

33. The phrase is from Buell, *Literary Transcendentalism*, p. 211.

34. Samuel Taylor Coleridge, *The Complete Works of Samuel Taylor Coleridge*, ed. W. G. T. Shedd, 7 vols. (New York: Harper & Bros., 1884), 1: 119.

35. Harold Bloom, *Poetry and Repression: Revisionism from Blake to Stevens* (New Haven: Yale University Press, 1976), p. 287. This passage is cited by John Carlos Rowe, *Through the Custom-House: Nineteenth-Century American Fiction and Modern Theory* (Baltimore: Johns Hopkins University Press, 1982), p. 22.

36. Sigmund Freud, *Dora: An Analysis of a Case of Hysteria*, intro. Philip Rieff (New York: Collier, 1963), p. 30.

37. Sigmund Freud, *The Standard Edition of the Complete Psychological Works*, ed. James Strachey, 24 vols. (London: Hogarth Press, 1953–74), 15: 138.

38. Carl Gustav Jung, "On Psychic Energy," in *Collected Works of C. G. Jung*, trans. R. F. C. Hull, 20 vols. (Princeton, N.J.: Princeton University Press, 1957–79), 8: par. 55.

39. Ibid., par. 56.

40. Ibid., par. 72; Sigmund Freud, "On the Mechanism of Paranoia," *General Psychological Theory: Papers on Metapsychology* (New York: Macmillan, 1963), p. 32.

41. Jung, *Collected Works*, 8: par. 87.

42. Jacques Derrida, *Speech and Phenomena and Other Essays on Husserl's Theory of Signs*, trans. Newton Garver (Evanston, Ill.: Northwestern University Press, 1973), p. 136.

43. Porte, *Emerson and Thoreau*, p. 152.

44. Gaston Bachelard, *The Poetics of Reverie: Childhood, Language, and the Cosmos*, trans. Daniel Russell (Boston: Beacon Press, 1971), p. 14.

45. Rowe, *Through the Custom-House*, p. 33.

46. Buell, *Literary Transcendentalism*, p. 165.

47. Ibid., p. 181.

48. Cited by Raymond J. McCall, *Phenomenological Psychology: An Introduction* (Madison: University of Wisconsin Press, 1983), p. 75.

49. Porte, *Emerson and Thoreau*, p. 168.

50. Derrida, *Speech and Phenomena*, p. 142.

51. Edmund Husserl, *Ideas: General Introduction to Pure Phenomenology*, trans. W. R. Boyce Gibson (New York: Collier, 1962), p. 108.

52. Wolfgang Iser, "The Reading Process: A Phenomenological Approach," in Jane Tompkins, ed., *Reader-Response Criticism* (Baltimore: Johns Hopkins University Press, 1980), p. 67.

53. Paul Ricoeur, *Hermeneutics and the Human Sciences*, trans. John B. Thompson (Cambridge, England: Cambridge University Press, 1981), p. 144.

54. Ibid., p. 143.

55. Marx, *Early Writings*, p. 160.

56. Martin Heidegger, *Basic Writings*, ed. David Farrell Krell (New York: Harper & Row, 1977), p. 322.

57. Boss, *Psychoanalysis and Daseinsanalysis*, p. 38.

58. Ibid., p. 39.

59. Coleridge, *Works*, 1: 131.

60. Jacques Derrida, *Writing and Difference*, trans. Alan Bass (Chicago: University of Chicago Press, 1978), p. 42.

61. Rowe, *Through the Custom-House*, p. 29.

62. Robert D. Richardson, Jr., *Myth and Literature in the American Renaissance* (Bloomington: Indiana University Press, 1978), p. 122.

63. Ibid., pp. 95, 106.

64. Sherman Paul, *The Shores of America: Thoreau's Inward Exploration* (Urbana, Ill.: University of Illinois Press, 1958), p. 9.

65. Ernst Cassirer, *The Philosophy of Symbolic Forms*, trans. Ralph Manheim, 3 vols. (New Haven: Yale University Press, 1955–57), 3: 71.

66. Ricoeur, *Hermeneutics and the Human Sciences*, p. 142.

CHAPTER 4

1. Albert Gelpi, *The Tenth Muse: The Psyche of the American Poet* (Cambridge, Mass.: Harvard University Press, 1975), p. 157.

2. Robert D. Richardson, Jr., *Myth and Literature in the American Renaissance* (Bloomington: Indiana University Press, 1978), p. 138.

3. Perry Miller, *The Life of the Mind in America: From the Revolution to the Civil War* (New York: Harcourt, Brace & World, 1965), p. 318.

4. Gay Wilson Allen, *Waldo Emerson* (New York: Penguin Books, 1982), p. 580.

5. D. H. Lawrence, *Studies in Classic American Literature* (New York: Viking Press, 1964), p. 171.

6. Justin Kaplan, *Walt Whitman: A Life* (New York: Simon and Schuster, 1980), p. 147.

7. G. W. F. Hegel, *The Phenomenology of Mind*, trans. J. B. Baillie (New York: Harper & Row, 1967), p. 72.

8. Edwin Haviland Miller, *Walt Whitman's Poetry: A Psychological Journey* (New York: New York University Press, 1968), p. 97.

9. The first phrase is from Kaplan, *Walt Whitman: A Life*, p. 193. For an analysis of the image of the body in the works of Melville and Hawthorne, see Sharon Cameron, *The Corporeal Self: Allegories of the Body in Melville and Hawthorne* (Baltimore: Johns Hopkins University Press, 1981).

10. Friedrich Nietzsche, *The Will to Power*, trans. Walter Kaufmann and R. J. Hollingdale (New York: Random House, 1968), p. 72.

11. Ibid., p. 358.

12. Friedrich Nietzsche, *Thus Spoke Zarathustra*, in *The Portable Nietzsche*, ed. and trans. Walter Kaufmann (New York: Viking Press, 1954), p. 146.

13. Arthur Wrobel, "Whitman and the Phrenologists: The Divine Body and the Sensuous Soul," *PMLA* 79 (1974): 20.

14. Ibid., p. 17.

15. Ibid., p. 19.

16. Ibid., p. 21; F. O. Matthiessen, *American Renaissance: Art and Expression in*

the Age of Emerson and Whitman (New York: Oxford University Press, 1941), p. 525.

17. Edmund Reiss, "Whitman's Debt to Animal Magnetism," *PMLA* 78 (March 1963): 81.

18. John T. Irwin, *American Hieroglyphics: The Symbol of the Egyptian Hieroglyphics in the American Renaissance* (New Haven: Yale University Press, 1980), p. 99.

19. Ibid., p. 111.

20. Ibid., p. 101.

21. Ibid., p. 106.

22. Matthiessen, *American Renaissance*, p. 600.

23. Ibid., p. 518.

24. Ibid., p. 569.

25. Ibid., p. 622.

26. Rollo May, "Contributions of Existential Psychotherapy," *Existence: A New Dimension in Psychiatry and Psychology*, ed. Rollo May, Ernest Angel, Henri Ellenberger (New York: Basic Books, 1958), p. 61.

27. The phrase is from Charles Feidelson, Jr., *Symbolism and American Literature* (Chicago: University of Chicago Press, 1953), p. 18.

28. Roy Harvey Pearce, *The Continuity of American Poetry* (Princeton, N.J.: Princeton University Press, 1961), p. 75.

29. Jacques Derrida, *Writing and Difference*, trans. Alan Bass (Chicago: University of Chicago Press, 1978), p. 5.

30. James E. Miller, Jr., *A Critical Guide to Leaves of Grass* (Chicago: University of Chicago Press, 1957), pp. 6–7.

31. Paul Bové, *Destructive Poetics: Heidegger and Modern American Poetry* (New York: Columbia University Press, 1980), pp. 134–35.

32. Edwin H. Miller, *Walt Whitman's Poetry*, p. 101.

33. Gay Wilson Allen, *The New Walt Whitman Handbook* (New York: New York University Press, 1975), p. 212.

34. Kaplan, *Walt Whitman: A Life*, p. 128.

35. Charles Olson, "Projective Verse," in *The New American Poetry*, ed. Donald M. Allen (New York: Grove Press, 1960), p. 387.

36. James E. Miller, *Critical Guide to Leaves of Grass*, pp. 6–35.

37. Ibid., p. 25.

38. Ibid., pp. 25–26.

39. Edwin H. Miller, *Walt Whitman's Poetry*, p. 106.

40. Gelpi, *Tenth Muse*, p. 172.

41. Ibid., p. 167.

42. Ibid., p. 206.

43. See ibid., p. 197: "Throughout 28 and early 29, there are suggestions of unusual and particular anxiety, fear, even shame and guilt, which raise inescapable questions concerning Whitman's sexuality in the middle of a poem proclaiming his newfound sexual self."

44. Kaplan, *Walt Whitman: A Life*, p. 143.

45. Victor Turner, *Dramas, Fields, and Metaphors: Symbolic Action in Human Society* (Ithaca, N.Y.: Cornell University Press, 1974), pp. 231–32. I must thank my colleague William L. Andrews for drawing my attention to the psychological significance of Turner's work.

46. Victor Turner, *The Forest of Symbols: Aspects of Ndembu Ritual* (Ithaca, N.Y.: Cornell University Press, 1967), p. 95.

47. Bové, *Destructive Poetics*, p. 149.

48. Turner, *Dramas, Fields, and Metaphors*, p. 238.

49. Paul Ricoeur, *Hermeneutics and the Human Sciences*, trans. John B. Thompson (Cambridge, England: Cambridge University Press, 1981), p. 144. I have slightly rephrased Ricoeur's wording.

50. Arthur O. Lovejoy, *The Great Chain of Being: A Study of the History of an Idea* (1933; rpt. Cambridge, Mass.: Harvard University Press, 1976), p. 300.

51. Sigmund Freud, *The Standard Edition of the Complete Psychological Works*, ed. James Strachey, 24 vols. (London: Hogarth Press, 1953–74), 21: 15.

52. Ibid., 11.

53. Friedrich Nietzsche, *Beyond Good and Evil*, trans. Walter Kaufmann (New York: Random House, 1966), p. 24.

54. Ibid., p. 100.

55. See Norman O. Brown, *Life Against Death: The Psychoanalytic Meaning of History* (Middletown, Conn.: Wesleyan University Press, 1959), p. 148: "The aim of psychoanalysis—still unfulfilled, and still only half-conscious—is to return our souls to our bodies, to return ourselves to ourselves, and thus to overcome the human state of self-alienation."

56. Roy Harvey Pearce, in *The Continuity of American Poetry*, p. 76, argues that the poet here "is witness to the marriage of his own two minds." James E. Miller, Jr., suggests that it dramatizes the "marriage of body and soul" (*Critical Guide to Leaves of Grass*, p. 10); and Albert Gelpi reads it as "the identification of spiritual energy with sexuality" (*Tenth Muse*, p. 182).

57. Carl Gustav Jung, *Symbols of Transformation*, vol. 5 of the *Collected Works of C. G. Jung*, trans. R. F. C. Hull, 20 vols. (Princeton, N.J.: Princeton University Press, 1957–79), passim.

58. Erich Neumann, *The Origins and History of Consciousness*, trans. R. F. C. Hull (Princeton, N.J.: Princeton University Press, Bollingen Series 42, 1970), p. 344.

59. For an excellent discussion of Melville's use of this theme, see Warwick Wadlington, *The Confidence Game in American Literature* (Princeton, N.J.: Princeton University Press, 1975).

60. Quentin Anderson, *The Imperial Self* (New York: Alfred A. Knopf, 1971), pp. 122, 142.

61. See ibid., p. 153.

62. Ibid., p. 145.

63. Ibid., p. 148.

SPAIN COLUMBIA LITERATURE 29 (SUMMER 1978) (LITERATURE

FORUM ISSUE. # 7790-3271

WRIGHT, WILLIAM, William Greenleaf; THE FARGO AND THE MENLO

109 [DENVER] : D's - SECONDARY INDUSTRIES : CF FULL OLSON

64. Norman O. Brown, *Love's Body* (New York: Random House, 1966), p. 161.

65. Freud, *Standard Edition*, 18: 28.

66. Ibid., 17: 139.

67. Sandra Gilbert and Susan Gubar, *The Madwoman in the Attic: The Woman Writer and the Nineteenth-Century Literary Imagination* (New Haven: Yale University Press, 1979), p. 6.

68. Friedrich Nietzsche, *The Birth of Tragedy and The Case of Wagner*, trans. Walter Kaufmann (New York: Random House, 1967), p. 59.

69. Pearce, *The Continuity of American Poetry*, p. 79.

70. Edwin H. Miller, *Walt Whitman's Poetry*, p. 95.

71. James E. Miller, *Critical Guide to Leaves of Grass*, pp. 23, 24.

72. Gelpi, *Tenth Muse*, p. 204.

73. Irwin, *American Hieroglyphics*, p. 109.

74. H. J. Rose, *A Handbook of Greek Mythology* (London: Methuen & Co., 1964), p. 154.

75. Cited in ibid., p. 255.

76. Richard Chase, "One's Self I Sing," from *Walt Whitman Reconsidered* (New York: William Sloane Associates, 1955), rpt. in *Whitman's "Song of Myself"—Origin, Growth, Meaning*, ed. James E. Miller, Jr. (New York: Dodd, Mead & Co., 1964), p. 164.

77. Malcolm Cowley, "Introduction" to *Walt Whitman's Leaves of Grass: The First (1855) Edition*, ed. Malcolm Cowley (1959; rpt. New York: Penguin Books, 1976), p. xxvii.

78. Carl Gustav Jung, *The Portable Jung*, ed. Joseph Campbell (New York: Viking Press, 1971), pp. 85, 83.

79. Ibid., pp. 84–86.

80. Ibid., p. 88.

81. Carl Gustav Jung, *Two Essays on Analytical Psychology*, trans. R. F. C. Hull, vol. 7 of *Collected Works* (New York: Meridian Books, 1956), p. 83.

82. Friedrich Nietzsche, *Selected Letters of Friedrich Nietzsche*, ed. and trans. Christopher Middleton (Chicago: University of Chicago Press, 1969), pp. 345–46.

83. Gelpi, *Tenth Muse*, p. 203.

84. James E. Miller, *Critical Guide to Leaves of Grass*, p. 23.

85. Gelpi, *Tenth Muse*, p. 204.

86. James E. Miller, *Critical Guide to Leaves of Grass*, p. 29.

87. Cowley, "Introduction" to *Walt Whitman's Leaves of Grass*, p. xxviii.

88. Ibid., p. xiv.

89. Bové, *Destructive Poetics*, p. 149.

90. Ibid., p. 60.

91. Roger Asselineau, *The Evolution of Walt Whitman: The Creation of a Personality*, 2 vols. (Cambridge, Mass.: Harvard University Press, 1960), 1: 71, 16.

92. Paul Tillich, *Love, Power, and Justice: Ontological Analyses and Ethical Applications* (New York: Oxford University Press, 1954), p. 40.

93. See Bové, *Destructive Poetics*, p. 147: "He is the possibility for dis-covery and dis-closure. He is the means for opening up the future and demonstrating the nature of man's being as potentiality."

94. Ralph Waldo Emerson, letter of July 21, 1855, to Walt Whitman. The text of this letter does not appear in *The Letters of Ralph Waldo Emerson*, ed. Ralph L. Rusk, 6 vols. (New York: Columbia University Press, 1939). It was printed in the *New-York Daily Tribune*, Oct. 10, 1855; rpt. *The Shock of Recognition*, ed. Edmund Wilson (New York: The Modern Library, 1955), pp. 247–48.

CHAPTER 5

1. Margaret Vanderhaar Allen, *The Achievement of Margaret Fuller* (University Park, Pa.: Pennsylvania State University Press, 1979), p. 38.

2. Quoted by Harry R. Warfel, "Margaret Fuller and Ralph Waldo Emerson," in *Critical Essays on Margaret Fuller*, ed. Joel Myerson (Boston: G. K. Hall, 1980), p. 173.

3. Allen, *The Achievement of Margaret Fuller*, pp. 38–39.

4. See Ann Douglas, *The Feminization of American Culture* (New York: Avon Books, 1977).

5. Barbara J. Berg, *The Remembered Gate: Origins of American Feminism* (New York: Oxford University Press, 1978), p. 67.

6. Ibid., p. 68.

7. This and the following quotation are from Eric Cheyfitz, *The Trans-Parent: Sexual Politics in the Language of Emerson* (Baltimore: Johns Hopkins University Press, 1981), p. 41.

8. Ibid., p. 61.

9. Ibid., pp. 70, 72.

10. Susan Griffin, *Woman and Nature: The Roaring Inside Her* (New York: Harper & Row, 1978), p. 1.

11. Annette Kolodny, *The Lay of the Land: Metaphor as Experience and History in American Life and Letters* (Chapel Hill, N.C.: University of North Carolina Press, 1975), p. 28.

12. Mary Daly, *Beyond God the Father: Toward a Philosophy of Women's Liberation* (Boston: Beacon Press, 1973), pp. 4, 49.

13. Ibid., p. 47.

14. This and the following quotation are from Berg, *The Remembered Gate*, p. 84.

15. Ibid., p. 85.

16. Douglas, *The Feminization of American Culture*, p. 315.

17. Quoted by Paula Blanchard, *Margaret Fuller: From Transcendentalism to Revolution* (New York: Delacorte Press, 1978), p. 1.

18. The phrase "Margaret-ghost" is from Henry James's tale "William Wetmore Story and His Friends," excerpted in Myerson, ed., *Critical Essays on Margaret Fuller*, pp. 131–32.

19. Allen, *The Achievement of Margaret Fuller*, p. 14.

20. Joel Myerson, "Introduction" to *Critical Essays on Margaret Fuller*, p. viii.

21. Quoted by Marie Olesen Urbanski, *Margaret Fuller's Woman in the Nineteenth Century: A Literary Study of Form and Content, of Sources and Influence*, Contributions in Women's Studies 13 (Westport, Conn.: Greenwood Press, 1980), p. 38.

22. Bell Gale Chevigny, "Growing Out of New England: The Emergence of Margaret Fuller's Radicalism," *Women's Studies* 5 (1977): 68.

23. Ibid., pp. 81, 87.

24. Bell Gale Chevigny, "Daughters Writing: Toward a Theory of Women's Biography," *Feminist Studies* 9 (1983): 97.

25. Susan Friedman, "Psyche Reborn: Tradition, Re-Vision and the Goddess as Mother-Symbol in H. D.'s Epic Poetry," *Women's Studies* 6 (1979): 149, 152.

26. Bell Gale Chevigny, *The Woman and the Myth: Margaret Fuller's Life and Writings* (Old Westbury, N.Y.: The Feminist Press, 1978), p. 77.

27. Quoted by Chevigny, "Growing Out of New England," p. 77.

28. Ibid., p. 81.

29. Blanchard, *Margaret Fuller*, p. 171.

30. Quoted in ibid., p. 172.

31. Quoted in ibid., p. 173.

32. Urbanski, *Margaret Fuller's Woman in the Nineteenth Century*, p. 119.

33. M. Esther Harding, *Women's Mysteries: Ancient and Modern* (New York: Longmans, Green & Co., 1935), p. 39.

34. Ibid., p. 76.

35. Ibid., pp. 78–79.

36. Ibid., p. 79.

37. Quoted by Blanchard, *Margaret Fuller*, p. 173.

38. Berg, *The Remembered Gate*, p. 86.

39. Julia Ward Howe, quoted by Robert D. Richardson, Jr., "Margaret Fuller and Myth," *Prospects* 4 (1979): 172.

40. Richardson, "Margaret Fuller and Myth," p. 172.

41. Ibid., p. 176.

42. Daly, *Beyond God the Father*, p. 4.

43. Michael Grant, *Myths of the Greeks and Romans* (New York: New American Library, 1962), p. 369.

44. Thomas Taylor, *The Hymns of Orpheus* (1787), rpt. in *Thomas Taylor the Platonist: Selected Writings*, ed. Kathleen Raine and George Mills Harper (Princeton, N.J.: Princeton University Press, Bollingen Series 88, 1969), p. 203.

45. Ibid., p. 220n.

46. *Plutarch's Morals: Translated from the Greek by Several Hands*, ed. William W. Goodwin, intro. R. W. Emerson, 5 vols. (Boston: Little, Brown & Co., 1878), 4: 121 (italics mine).

47. Thomas Taylor, trans., *The Metamorphosis, or Golden Ass, and Philosophical Works, of Apuleius* (London, 1822), p. 260n.

48. Ibid., p. 88n.

49. Ibid., pp. 90–91n.

50. This and the following quotation are from ibid., p. 91n.

51. *Plutarch's Morals*, 4: 80.

52. Ibid., 4: 120–21.

53. Urbanski, *Margaret Fuller's Woman in the Nineteenth Century*, p. 119.

54. Bernard Rosenthal, "*The Dial*, Transcendentalism and Margaret Fuller," *English Language Notes* 8 (1970): 35. Quoted by Urbanski, *Margaret Fuller's Woman in the Nineteenth Century*, p. 120.

55. Erich Neumann, *The Great Mother: An Analysis of an Archetype*, trans. Ralph Manheim (Princeton, N.J.: Princeton University Press, Bollingen Series 47, 1963), pp. 307–8.

56. Nor Hall, *The Moon and the Virgin: Reflections on the Archetypal Feminine* (New York: Harper & Row, 1980), p. 85.

57. Ibid., p. 26.

58. See Chevigny, "Daughters Writing," and Annette Kolodny, "Margaret Fuller: Recovering our Mother's Garden," *The Land Before Her: Fantasy and Experience of the American Frontiers* (Chapel Hill, N.C.: University of North Carolina Press, 1984).

59. Chevigny, "Growing Out of New England," p. 69.

60. Chevigny, "Daughters Writing," p. 88.

61. Neumann, *The Great Mother*, p. 331.

62. Ibid., p. 307.

63. Ibid., p. 319.

64. Annis Pratt, *Archetypal Patterns in Woman's Fiction* (Bloomington: Indiana University Press, 1981), p. 171.

65. Hall, *The Moon and the Virgin*, p. 18.

66. Carroll Smith-Rosenberg, "The Female World of Love and Ritual: Relations Between Women in Nineteenth-Century America," *Signs* 1 (1975): 9.

67. Elaine Showalter, "Feminist Criticism in the Wilderness," *Critical Inquiry* 8 (1981): 199. Showalter borrows the term "muted group" from Edwin Ardener.

68. Ibid., p. 200.

69. David M. Robinson, "Margaret Fuller and the Transcendental Ethos: *Woman in the Nineteenth Century*," *PMLA* 97 (1982): 84.

70. Ibid., p. 95.

71. Ibid., p. 93.

72. Charles F. Briggs, review of *Woman in the Nineteenth Century* (*Broadway Journal*, March 1845), rpt. in Myerson, ed., *Critical Essays on Margaret Fuller*, p. 9.

73. Ibid., p. 10.

74. Orestes A. Brownson, "Miss Fuller and Reformers," in *Brownson's Quarterly Review* 7 (April 1845), rpt. in Myerson, ed., *Critical Essays on Margaret Fuller*, p. 22.

75. Daly, *Beyond God the Father*, p. 13.
76. Hélène Cixous, "The Laugh of the Medusa," trans. Keith and Paula Cohen, *Signs* 1, no. 4 (1976): 880.
77. Daly, *Beyond God the Father*, p. 50.
78. Chevigny, "Growing Out of New England," p. 88.
79. Griffin, *Woman and Nature*, pp. xv–xvi.
80. Urbanski, *Margaret Fuller's Woman in the Nineteenth Century*, p. 136.
81. Ibid., p. 140.
82. Mary Jacobus, "The Question of Language: Men of Maxims and *The Mill on the Floss*," *Critical Inquiry* 8 (1981): 211.
83. See Friedrich Schlegel, *Aphorisms from the Lyceum* and *Selected Ideas*, in *Dialogue on Poetry and Literary Aphorisms*, trans. Ernst Behler and Roman Struc (University Park, Pa.: Pennsylvania State University Press, 1968).
84. Robinson, "Margaret Fuller and the Transcendental Ethos," p. 86.
85. Richardson, "Margaret Fuller and Myth," p. 172.
86. Quoted by Neumann, *The Great Mother*, p. 6.
87. This and the following quotation are from Henri F. Ellenberger, *The Discovery of the Unconscious: The History and Evolution of Dynamic Psychiatry* (New York: Basic Books, 1970), p. 204.
88. Robinson, "Margaret Fuller and the Transcendental Ethos," p. 93.
89. Chevigny, "Growing Out of New England," p. 95.
90. Briggs, review of *Woman in the Nineteenth Century*, p. 11.
91. Neumann, *The Great Mother*, p. 308.

CHAPTER 6

1. Philip F. Gura, *The Wisdom of Words: Language, Theology, and Literature in the New England Renaissance* (Middletown, Conn.: Wesleyan University Press, 1981), p. 105.
2. Philip F. Gura, "Language and Meaning: An American Tradition," *American Literature* 53 (1981): 16.
3. Evan Carton, *The Rhetoric of American Romance: Dialectic and Identity in Emerson, Dickinson, Poe, and Hawthorne* (Baltimore: Johns Hopkins University Press, 1985), pp. 25–26.
4. Gura, "Language and Meaning," pp. 19, 20.
5. Ibid., p. 14.
6. Ibid., p. 11; Gura, *The Wisdom of Words*, p. 168.
7. For an excellent discussion of James Marsh's popularization in America of Coleridge's theories of language, see Gura, *The Wisdom of Words*, pp. 35–51.
8. Samuel Taylor Coleridge, *The Statesman's Manual*, rpt. in *English Romantic Writers*, ed. David Perkins (New York: Harcourt, Brace & World, 1967), p. 503.
9. Jacques Derrida, *Writing and Difference*, trans. Alan Bass (Chicago: University of Chicago Press, 1978), p. 279.
10. Gura, "Language and Meaning," p. 3.

11. Ibid., p. 14.

12. Friedrich Nietzsche, *The Birth of Tragedy and The Case of Wagner*, ed. and trans. Walter Kaufmann (New York: Random House, 1967), p. 41.

13. Ibid., p. 43.

14. Ibid., pp. 66, 67.

15. Ibid., p. 68.

16. Robert D. Richardson, Jr., *Myth and Literature in the American Renaissance* (Bloomington: Indiana University Press, 1978), p. 56.

17. G. W. F. Hegel, *The Phenomenology of Mind*, trans. J. B. Baillie (New York: Harper & Row, 1967), p. 72.

18. Ibid., p. 71.

19. Ibid., p. 73.

20. Joel Porte, *Representative Man: Ralph Waldo Emerson in His Time* (New York: Oxford University Press, 1979), pp. 259ff.

21. Sigmund Freud, *The Future of an Illusion* in *The Standard Edition of the Complete Psychological Works*, ed. James Strachey, 24 vols. (London: Hogarth Press, 1953–74), 21: 43.

22. Ibid., 19: 56.

23. Ludwig Binswanger, *Being-in-the-World: Selected Papers of Ludwig Binswanger*, trans. Jacob Needleman (New York: Basic Books, 1963), p. 160.

24. It is fruitful to compare Emerson's vision of presence with that of Edmund Husserl, as characterized by Jacques Derrida in *Speech and Phenomena and Other Essays on Husserl's Theory of Signs*, trans. Newton Garver (Evanston: Northwestern University Press, 1973), p. 43: "The certitude of inner existence, Husserl thinks, has no need to be signified. It is immediately present to itself. It is living consciousness."

25. John T. Irwin, *American Hieroglyphics: The Symbol of the Egyptian Hieroglyphics in the American Renaissance* (New Haven: Yale University Press, 1980), p. 13; Michael Davitt Bell, *The Development of American Romance: The Sacrifice of Relation* (Chicago: University of Chicago Press, 1980), p. 125.

26. Bell, *The Development of American Romance*, p. 108: "Arabesque 'purity,' it is clear, consists primarily in the ability *not* to call submerged impulses and meanings to the surface."

27. Jacques Derrida, "Freud and the Scene of Writing," quoted by John Carlos Rowe, *Through the Custom-House: Nineteenth-Century American Fiction and Modern Theory* (Baltimore: Johns Hopkins University Press, 1982), p. 108.

28. For a discussion of the "veil" and unveiling, see Jacques Derrida, *Spurs: Nietzsche's Styles*, trans. Barbara Harlow (Chicago: University of Chicago Press, 1979), p. 59, where Derrida argues that truth depends upon veiling. The second phrase is from Gregory S. Jay, "Poe: Writing and the Unconscious," *Bucknell Review* 28 (1983): 146.

29. John Irwin argues in *American Hieroglyphics* (p. 13) that Emerson sees the outer shape as a decipherable "emblem."

30. Irwin's *American Hieroglyphics* provides the classic discussion of the cipher and the hieroglyph in Poe's writing.

31. Paul Tillich discusses the "phenomenology of power-relations" in *Love, Power, and Justice: Ontological Analyses and Ethical Applications* (New York: Oxford University Press, 1954), pp. 41–42: "The typical forms in which powers of being encounter each other are a fascinating subject of phenomenological descriptions. . . . One draws another power into oneself and is either strengthened or weakened by it. One throws the foreign power of being out or assimilates it completely. One transforms the resisting powers or one adapts oneself to them. One is absorbed by them and loses one's power of being, one grows together with them and increases their and one's own power of being." An important critical project, which remains to be written, would involve the systematic analysis of such power-relations, both in the psychological and social spheres.

32. For the classic discussion of this process, see Edmund Husserl, *Ideas: General Introduction to Pure Phenomenology*, trans. W. R. Boyce Gibson (New York: Collier, 1962), pp. 96–100.

33. Jacques Lacan, *The Language of the Self: The Function of Language in Psychoanalysis*, trans. Anthony Wilden (New York: Dell Pub. Co., 1968), p. 17.

34. Lacan provides an excellent discussion of the theatricality of self-reflection in his "Seminar on 'The Purloined Letter,'" trans. Jeffrey Mehlman, *Yale French Studies* 48 (1973): 41: "The narration, in fact, doubles the drama with a commentary without which no *mise en scene* would be possible. Let us say that the action would remain, properly speaking, invisible from the pit—aside from the fact that the dialogue would be expressly and by dramatic necessity devoid of whatever meaning it might have for an audience: —in other words, nothing of the drama could be grasped, neither seen nor heard, without, dare we say, the twilighting which the narration, in each scene, casts on the point of view that one of the actors had while performing it."

35. Sigmund Freud, *An Outline of Psychoanalysis*, in *Standard Edition*, 23:165, 173.

36. Erich Neumann provides a useful analysis of this progression into fascination in *The Great Mother: An Analysis of an Archetype*, trans. Ralph Manheim (Princeton, N.J.: Princeton University Press, Bollingen Series 47, 1963), p. 75: "Because the archetype fascinates consciousness and is dynamically very much superior to it, the ego consciousness, when it approaches the pole, is not only attracted by it but easily overwhelmed. The outcome is seizure by the archetype, disintegration of consciousness, and loss of the ego."

37. Freud, "The Uncanny," *Standard Edition*, 17:247–48.

38. Fyodor Dostoevsky, *Notes from Underground*, in *Existentialism from Dostoevsky to Sartre*, ed. Walter Kaufmann (New York: Meridian Books, 1956), p. 78.

39. Nietzsche discusses the necessary masquerade of consciousness in "On Truth and Lie in an Extra-Moral Sense," *The Portable Nietzsche*, trans. and ed. Walter Kaufmann (New York: Viking Press, 1968), p. 43.

40. Carl Gustav Jung, *The Archetypes and the Collective Unconscious*, vol. 9 of *The Collected Works of C. G. Jung*, trans. R. F. C. Hull, 20 vols. (Princeton, N.J.: Princeton University Press, 1957–79), par. 513.

41. Freud, *Standard Edition*, 21: 61.

42. Rowe, *Through the Custom-House*, p. 154.

43. Madeline B. Stern, *Heads and Headlines: The Phrenological Fowlers* (Norman: University of Oklahoma Press, 1971), pp. 42–44.

44. Sharon Cameron, *The Corporeal Self: Allegories of the Body in Melville and Hawthorne* (Baltimore: Johns Hopkins University Press, 1981), p. 79.

45. Perry Miller, *Nature's Nation* (Cambridge, Mass.: Harvard University Press, 1967), p. 250.

46. Barbara J. Berg, *The Remembered Gate: Origins of American Feminism* (New York: Oxford University Press, 1978), p. 179.

47. Eric J. Sundquist, *Home As Found: Authority and Genealogy in Nineteenth-Century American Literature* (Baltimore: Johns Hopkins University Press, 1979), p. 100.

48. Edgar A. Dryden, *Nathaniel Hawthorne: The Poetics of Enchantment* (Ithaca, N.Y.: Cornell University Press, 1977), pp. 70, 74.

49. Merton M. Sealts, Jr., "Melville and Emerson's Rainbow," *ESQ* 26, no. 2 (1980): 63.

50. Michael S. Kearns, "Phantoms of the Mind: Melville's Critique of Idealistic Psychology," *ESQ* 30, no. 1 (1984): 41. The next two quotations are from pp. 42, 43.

51. Richard Chase, *The American Novel and Its Tradition* (Garden City, N.Y.: Doubleday & Co., 1957), p. 105.

52. Lionel Trilling, *Sincerity and Authenticity* (Cambridge, Mass.: Harvard University Press, 1971), p. 1.

53. William James, *The Writings of William James: A Comprehensive Edition*, ed. John J. McDermott (New York: Modern Library, 1967), p. 9.

54. Bell, *The Development of American Romance*, p. 130.

55. Newton Arvin, *Herman Melville* (New York: William Sloane Associates, 1950), p. 222.

56. Henry A. Murray, "Introduction" to *Pierre, or The Ambiguities*, ed. H. A. Murray (New York: Hendricks House, 1949), pp. liii–liv.

57. Ibid., p. lxiv.

58. Isabel's equation of divinity with "impulse" is discussed by H. Bruce Franklin, *The Wake of the Gods: Melville's Mythology* (Stanford: Stanford University Press, 1963), p. 116.

59. Michael Paul Rogin, *Subversive Genealogy: The Politics and Art of Herman Melville* (Berkeley: University of California Press, 1985), p. 171.

60. Edgar A. Dryden, "The Entangled Text: Melville's *Pierre* and the Problem of Reading," *Boundary* 2, 7:3 (1979): 160.

61. Murray, "Introduction" to *Pierre*, p. xxxvii.

62. Charles Feidelson, Jr., *Symbolism and American Literature* (Chicago: University of Chicago Press, 1953), p. 187.

63. Samuel Taylor Coleridge, *Aids to Reflection* in *The Complete Works of Samuel Taylor Coleridge*, ed. W. G. T. Shedd, 7 vols. (New York: Harper & Bros., 1884), 1: 154, 242, 241.

64. Michel Foucault, "What Is an Author?" in *Language, Counter-Memory, Practice: Selected Essays and Interviews*, ed. Donald F. Bouchard (Ithaca, N.Y.: Cornell University Press, 1977), pp. 116, 121.

65. Ibid., p. 162.

CHAPTER 7

1. These phrases, used in another context, are from Lionel Trilling, *Sincerity and Authenticity* (Cambridge, Mass.: Harvard University Press, 1971), p. 119.

2. Hans Robert Jauss, *Aesthetic Experience and Literary Hermeneutics*, trans. Michael Shaw (Minneapolis: University of Minnesota Press, 1982), p. 168.

3. Carl Gustav Jung, *The Portable Jung*, ed. Joseph Campbell (New York: Viking Press, 1971), p. 451.

4. Paul Ricoeur, *Freud and Philosophy: An Essay on Interpretation*, trans. Denis Savage (New Haven: Yale University Press, 1970), p. 459.

5. Gaston Bachelard, *The Poetics of Space*, trans. Maria Jolas (Boston: Beacon Press, 1969), p. xv.

6. Ibid., p. xi.

7. Ricoeur, *Freud and Philosophy*, pp. 420, 422.

8. Ibid., p. 420.

9. Ibid., pp. 422–23.

10. Jacques Lacan, "Of Structure as an Inmixing of an Otherness Prerequisite to Any Subject Whatever," in Richard Macksey and Eugenio Donato, eds., *The Structuralist Controversy: The Languages of Criticism and the Sciences of Man* (Baltimore: Johns Hopkins University Press, 1970), pp. 188, 189.

11. Ibid., p. 186.

12. Jacques Lacan, *Ecrits: A Selection*, trans. Alan Sheridan (New York: W. W. Norton & Co., 1971), p. 285.

13. Lacan, "Of Structure," p. 189.

14. Ibid., p. 190.

15. Ibid., p. 190.

16. Friedrich Nietzsche, "On Truth and Lie in an Extra-Moral Sense," in *The Portable Nietzsche*, ed. Walter Kaufmann (New York: Viking Press, 1954), p. 44.

17. Northrop Frye, *Fables of Identity: Studies in Poetic Mythology* (New York: Harcourt, Brace & World, 1963), p. 187.

18. Nietzsche, "On Truth and Lie," p. 43.

19. See M. M. Bakhtin, *The Dialogic Imagination: Four Essays*, trans. Caryl Emerson and Michael Holquist (Austin: University of Texas Press, 1981).

20. Walter Kaufmann, "Translator's Introduction" to Friedrich Nietzsche, *The Gay Science*, trans. Walter Kaufmann (New York: Random House, 1974), p. 12.

21. Ibid., pp. 9, 10.

22. Ibid., p. 11.

23. Quoted by Walter E. Houghton, *The Victorian Frame of Mind, 1830–1870* (New Haven: Yale University Press, 1957), p. 429.

24. Trilling, *Sincerity and Authenticity*, p. 2.

25. Friedrich Nietzsche, *On the Genealogy of Morals & Ecce Homo*, trans. Walter Kaufmann and R. J. Hollingdale (New York: Random House, 1967), p. 45.

26. Friedrich Nietzsche, *Twilight of the Idols*, in *The Portable Nietzsche*, pp. 495, 482–83.

27. Friedrich Nietzsche, *The Will to Power*, trans. Walter Kaufmann and R. J. Hollingdale (New York: Random House, 1968), p. 266.

28. Nietzsche, *The Gay Science*, p. 80.

29. Nietzsche, *Ecce Homo*, p. 283.

30. Ibid., p. 283; *Thus Spoke Zarathustra*, in *The Portable Nietzsche*, p. 204.

31. Sigmund Freud, *Dora: An Analysis of a Case of Hysteria*, intro. Philip Rieff (New York: Collier Books, 1963), p. 31; Anthony Wilden, "Translator's Notes" to Jacques Lacan, *The Language of the Self: The Function of Language in Psychoanalysis*, trans. Anthony Wilden (New York: Dell Pub. Co., 1968), p. 98n.

32. Friedrich Nietzsche, *Beyond Good and Evil*, trans. Walter Kaufmann (New York: Random House, 1966), p. 11; Nietzsche, *The Will to Power*, p. 207.

33. Nietzsche, *The Gay Science*, p. 302.

34. Nietzsche, *Beyond Good and Evil*, p. 160.

35. Nietzsche, *On the Genealogy of Morals*, p. 20.

36. Ibid., p. 20.

37. Nietzsche, *Ecce Homo*, p. 225.

38. For a general discussion of the Calvinist components of the Gothic imagination, see Joel Porte, "In the Hands of an Angry God: Religious Terror in Gothic Fiction," in G. R. Thompson, ed., *The Gothic Imagination: Essays in Dark Romanticism* (Pullman: Washington State University Press, 1974).

39. Kenneth Burke, *Language as Symbolic Action: Essays on Life, Literature, and Method* (Berkeley: University of California Press, 1966), p. 188. The following quotation is from the same source.

40. Jacques Derrida, *Speech and Phenomena and Other Essays on Husserl's Theory of Signs*, trans. Newton Garver (Evanston, Ill.: Northwestern University Press, 1973), p. xxxiii.

41. Ibid., p. 35.

Index

I wish to express my gratitude to Elizabeth Wyatt for her help in preparing this index.

Index

211

den, 122, 123; on Greece, 122–23; on
Rome, 122–23, 127–28; on Eden, 123; on
amaranth, 124; sexualization of Transcendentalism, 126; contemporary reactions to, 126–27; idea of woman, 126–
27, 130, 131; on female separatism, 127;
on female submissiveness, 127; on Cassandra, 128; on electricity, 128; on prostitution, 128; on woman as slave, 128; on
Miranda, 128, 129–30, 131; on Muse, 128,
132; use of dialogue, 129; on female genius, 130; on Iduna, 133; on religion,
133; works: "autobiographical romance,"
122, 124, 125; "Bettine Brentano and Her
Friend Gunderode," 122, 125, 126; "Conversations on Mythology," 106, 111, 114,
115, 117, 119, 120, 121; "Dialogue," 129;
"Festus," 129; "The Great Lawsuit," 105,
129; "Leila," 121–22, 123, 124, 126; "The
Magnolia of Lake Pontchartrain," 109–
11, 123, 129; "Marie van Oosterwich,"
129; *Memoirs of Margaret Fuller Ossoli,*
104, 107; *Woman in the Nineteenth Century,* 12, 101, 105, 111, 112, 115, 116, 118, 121,
125, 126, 128–30, 131, 132, 133; "Yuca
Filamentosa," 109, 111, 112–13, 116

Gadamer, Hans-Georg, 25–26
Gap, 55, 144, 150, 169, 180; as lack, 10; in
Emerson's writing, 37; in Thoreau's
writing, 59
Gelpi, Albert, 67, 74, 90
Gennep, Arnold van, 75
Gibson, Walker, 5, 7
Gilbert, Sandra, 86
God: internalization of, 14, 15, 21, 23, 25,
29, 31, 35, 105, 168; the Father, 103, 127.
See also Goddess
Goddess, 105, 111, 114, 116, 121, 123, 133
Goethe, Johann Wolfgang von, 125; and
Whitman, 89, 91; *Wilhelm Meister,* 131
Golden Ass, The, 115–16, 118, 119. *See also*
Apuleius
Gothic (Gothicism), 146, 149, 161, 163, 182,
206 (n. 38)
Grace, preparation for, 28
Griffin, Susan, 103, 129
Griselda, 100
Gubar, Susan, 86
Gura, Philip, 135, 136

H. D. (Hilda Doolittle), 106
Habit: Thoreau's view of, 62; Whitman's
view of, 75
Habitation, 59, 192 (n. 8)
Hall, Nor, 121, 123
Harding, Esther, 111, 112
Hartman, Geoffrey, 28
Hawthorne, Nathaniel, 43, 68, 98, 104,
109, 135, 138, 147, 163, 172, 174, 176, 177;
personality as mask in, 2, 43; deflates
Emersonian self-reliance, 7; hermeneutic suspicion of, 9; deflates imperialistic
rhetoric, 10; personal unconscious in,
39; social relation in, 43, 48, 151–59 passim; and Emerson, 151–52, 153; socializes
Transcendentalist psyche, 152; portrayal
of victimization, 152–53, 156–58; masks
in, 153; and Nietzsche, 153; portrayal of
repression, 153, 156; return of the repressed in, 153, 157–58; portrayal of fault
lines, 153, 158; and stain, 153–54, 159; repression of substantive being in, 154;
masculinity in, 154, 156, 158; repression
of the feminine in, 154–55, 156; repression of the body in, 155, 157; on the Father and patriarchy, 156; uncanniness of
the repressed in, 156–58; failure of transparency in, 157; analysis of stereotypes
in, 158; works: "Allegories of the
Heart," 46; "The Birth-mark," 154, 155,
156–57; *The Blithedale Romance,* 104, 155,
158, 183; "The Gentle Boy," 154; "The
Great Carbuncle," 109; *The House of the
Seven Gables,* 154; "Rappaccini's Daughter," 154, 155, 156–57; *The Scarlet Letter,*
139, 154, 157–58; "Young Goodman
Brown," 152
Hegel, Georg Wilhelm Friedrich, 43; on
substantive fullness of life, 68, 138;
works: *Phenomenology of the Spirit,* 35
Heidegger, Martin, 32, 46, 58, 84, 98; on
readiness-to-hand, 38, 47; on "fore-
sight," 47
Hermeneutic: of faith, 5–6, 8, 135; of suspicion, 8–9; circle, 18; process, 25;
awareness in Thoreau, 47; theory, 172,
185
Heroism, 92–93
Hester Prynne, 157–58
Heterosexuality, 109

Index

Self-analysis, 27
Self-consciousness, 1, 28, 29, 50
Self-division. *See* Alienation
Self-faith, 59, 61
Self-fragmentation, 92–93
Self-reliance, 56, 61, 67, 82, 97, 101, 153, 171, 179; and Whitman, 76, 82, 93, 97; and Fuller, 101, 111, 114, 116, 126, 127, 129–30; Melville's view of, 159, 165; limitations of, 160, 165; decentering of, 170, 176; critique of, 176
Sexual politics, 102, 126, 156
Showalter, Elaine, 125
Sincerity, 172, 179. *See also* Mask
Smith, Henry Nash, 4
Smith-Rosenberg, Carroll, 125
Social relation, 151–59 passim, 164, 182, 184
Spiritual authority, 5, 17, 18
Stage (of consciousness), 10, 11–12, 50, 185, 203 (n. 34); of self-reflection, 145. *See also* Field; Phenomenology
Stereotype(s), 104; fallen Eve as, 103; female, 103, 104; Hawthorne's analysis of, 158
Stewart, Dugald, 159
Strangeness, 34, 48. *See also* Uncanny
Sturgis, Caroline, 108, 113, 114, 124
Sublimation, 86, 92, 124, 140, 160, 164, 165
Sublime, 85, 93
Sundquist, Eric, 156
Swedenborg, Emanuel, 16, 24, 101, 131; and Emerson, 101; and Fuller, 114
Symbol, 17, 37, 112; Emerson's use of, 17, 37, 41, 139; of divine unconscious, 26; of libido, 82

Taylor, Thomas, 116–17, 118, 119, 131
Terminology: psychological, of Emerson, 14, 20; and Daseinsanalysis, 46; Freudian, 54–55; of religion, 96; of Transcendentalist psychologies, 134–37; Nietzsche's view of, 179. *See also* Language
Texas martyrs, 92
Thoreau, Henry David, 69, 109, 134, 174, 175, 184; and hermeneutic faith, 6; and symbolic action, 40; and the wild, 40; view of time, 40–41, 51–52, 54, 56; and Emerson, 40–44, 51; on the body, 43;

and Marx, 43–45; on decentering, 44; on corruption of the senses, 44–45; and process of existence, 45; reader of, 45, 49, 54, 57, 65; on bloom, 46, 62; on dwelling, 47; on the unconscious, 47; on prospect, 47, 50; and reality as imaginative construction, 47, 50; view of world (*Lebenswelt*), 47, 60; on the profane, 48; on strangeness, 48; on wonder, 48, 60; emblems of regeneration in, 49, 50, 51, 54; psychological mythmaking of, 49, 59, 65, 66; on being "beside ourselves," 50; on self-consciousness, 50; and Wordsworth, 51; and existential geography, 51, 52, 53; extension of being in, 51, 60; and space, 51–52; on the fresh, 52; and correspondence, 53; scenes of interior distance in, 53; scenes of presence in, 53–54, 59, 64; on the body's presence, 54; and organicism, 57, 61; scenes of prospect in, 57–58; and deconstruction, 59; gap of writing in, 59; model of attention in, 59–60, 62, 63; and dawn, 61; on going abroad (extra-vagrance), 62, 63; on Golden Age, 63, 64; on rebirth, 63–64; on innocence, 64; on transfigured being, 64; use of Oriental philosophy, 64; and Whitman, 69, 95; works: *Cape Cod*, 51; "Life without Principle," 28, 62; "A Natural History of Massachusetts," 41, 51; *Walden*, 6, 12, 46–47, 48, 50, 53–68 passim, 95, 109; *A Week on the Concord and Merrimack Rivers*, 52, 53
Tillich, Paul, 98–99
Time: Emerson's view of, 24, 54; Emerson's and Thoreau's views of, compared, 40–41, 54, 56; and Thoreau, 51–52, 56; gaps, in Poe's stories, 144
Transcendentalism, 1, 5, 9, 11, 12, 14, 18, 101, 106, 126, 178, 184, 188 (n. 33); Melville's critique of, 140, 159, 170, 181; Poe's demystification of, 142, 146; demystification of, 146, 168, 172, 178, 183; Hawthorne's socialization of, 152, 158–59; blindness to social factors of, 182, 184
Transcendental signified, 23, 24